OXIDATION AND REDUCTION

Reagents in Organic Synthesis

Dr. Nandkishor Chandan

D.Phil. (Ph.D.) Oxford University, England
(NET-JRF-CSIR, SET, NET-ICAR, GATE)
Associate Professor, Vice-Principal
Head, Department of Chemistry
Siddharth College, Fort, Mumbai (M.S.).INDIA

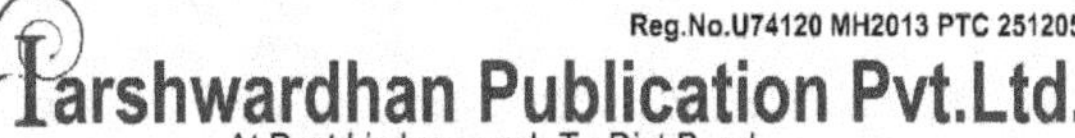

Reg.No.U74120 MH2013 PTC 251205

Harshwardhan Publication Pvt.Ltd.
At.Post.Limbaganesh,Tq.Dist.Beed
Pin-431126 (Maharashtra) Cell:07588057695,09850203295
harshwardhanpubli@gmail.com, vidyawarta@gmail.com

All Types Educational & Reference Book Publisher & Distributors   www.vidyawarta.com

OXIDATION AND REDUCTION
Reagents in Organic Synthesis

© **Dr. Nandkishor Chandan**

❖ **Publisher :**

Harshwardhan Publication Pvt.Ltd.
Limbaganesh, Dist. Beed (Maharashtra)
Pin-431126, vidyawarta@gmail.com

❖ **Printed by :**

Harshwardhan Publication Pvt.Ltd.
Limbaganesh, Dist. Beed, Pin-431126
www.vidyawarta.com

❖ **Page Design & Cover :**
Shaikh Jahuroddin,Parli-V

❖ **Edition: 14 Oct. 2018**

ISBN   978-93-87990-41-8

❖ **Price : 299/ –**

This book is dedicated to
"All My Respected Teachers"
who taught me at different levels

Acknowledgment

I am very much thankful to my Guru Dr. (Mrs.) Sushama Ambadekar, Associate Professor at Institute of Science, Mumbai who always inspired and encouraged me to write books on my subject of specialisation. I also extended my sincere thanks to all my teachers who taught me at different levels and make me able to write my first book on Organic chemistry......sincere thanks and oblige to Dr. B. G. Khobragade sir, Dr. Narwade sir, Dr. K. N. Wadodkar sir,   Dr. A. R. Raut sir, Prof. Wankhade sir, Dr. V. G. Thakarey sir, Dr. Subhash Bhadange sir, Dr. Anand Aswar sir, Dr. Jamode sir, Dr. Ravi Jumle sir, Dr. Sanjay Kolhe, Dr. Wagh sir, Dr. Makode sir. I am very much gratified by my research supervisor Prof. Mark Moloney, Oxford University who always encouraged me to draw electron flow mechanisms, indeed in this book throughout for all the mechanisms I have drew in same style and it will be very easily to understand the mechanisms.

I express my sincere thanks to the publisher Harshwardhan Publication Pvt.Ltd for publishing this book and taking keen interest in it.

Finally, I owe a sense of gratitude to my wife Mrs. Venu Nandkishor Chandan, my son Ninad and daughter Angel for their pleasant cooperation and moral support during writing this book.

.... 

Dr. Nandkishor S. Chandan

Preface

This book entitled "OXIDATION AND REDUCTION REAGENTS IN ORGANIC SYNTHESIS" has been particularly addressed to the graduate and postgraduate students who have opted for the Organic Chemistry study course as per the UGC syllabus. This book is equally useful for those students who are preparing for the NET-JRF-CSIR, SET, SLET, GATE, NET-ICAR and other competitive examinations like MPSC and UPSC. This book includes two volumes which divided into four chapters as volume-I cover oxidation and volume-II covers reduction in which general methods of preparations, synthetic applications and mechanism is discussed in details with different sets of examples. The large numbers of problems with solutions have been included at the end of each reagent discussions and covering the questions asked in different universities and competitive examinations. The organic synthesis is one of the most important branch of chemical science which wide exploited in the architecture of organic molecules with high biological significance.

Dr Nandkishor Chandan,
D.Phil. (Ph.D.) Oxford University, England
(NET-JRF-CSIR, SET, NET-ARS-ICAR, GATE)
Associate Professor, Vice Principal,
HOD, Department of Chemistry
Siddharth College of ASC, Fort, Mumbai.
nandkishorc@gmail.com

About the Author

 **Dr. Nandkishor S. Chandan,** is Associate Professor, Vice Principal and Head Department of Chemistry, Siddharth College of Arts, Science and Commerce, Buddha Bhavan, Fort Mumbai, University of Mumbai. He obtained his D.Phill. (Ph.D.) degree from University of Oxford, England (St. Peter's College) in the year 2011 under the guidance of Prof. Mark Moloney at Chemistry Research Laboratory (CRL), Oxford on the topic *"Novel Methodology for Synthesis of Trisubstituted Pyrrolidines; Application towards the Synthesis of Kaitocephalin"*. The complete study course Ph.D at Oxford University was sponsored by Government of India as National Overseas Scholarship (NOS) through the Ministry of Social Justice and Empowerment. He has published many research papers in international and national journals in the area synthetic chemistry and developed many methodologies to get the five member heterocycles. He has attended many international conferences and represented his research work and he is also member of Royal Society of Chemistry (Associate Member) AMRSC and the Indian Science Congress Association. He has also worked as Junior Research Fellow under the scholarship NET-JRF-CSIR awarded at Department of Organic Chemistry Technology (OCT), National Chemical Laboratory (NCL) in the year 2002. The author while studying M.Sc. in Organic Chemistry at Government Institute of Science and Humanities, Amravati passed exams NET-JRF-CSIR, SET, GATE, NET-ARS-CSIR and stood 5th merit in M.Sc at SGB University Amravati. Dr. N. S. Chandan has participated and delivered invited lectures at various national symposia and workshops for NET/SET exam. Dr Chandan is actively involved in post-graduate teaching in Mumbai University different institutes and colleges as well as in the different universities. As a social responsibility Dr. Chandan is a founder chairman of NGO called YES (Youth Empower and Social) Foundation through he sponsors scholarships to the economically backward students and arranged many motivational speeches, career guidance workshops, medical heath check up camps and parents awareness camps at different districts of Maharashtra.

Dr. Nandkishor S. Chandan

Contents
Volume-I OXIDATION
❖ Oxidation:

I. Dehydrogenation:
- a) Dehydrogenation of C-C bonds including aromatization of six membered rings using;
- 1) Metal Pt or Pd or Ni and organic reagents
- 2) DDQ
- 3) Chloranil.

II. Oxidation of alcohols to aldehydes and ketones
- a) Chromium based reagents such as
- 1) $K_2Cr_2O_7/H_2SO_4$ (Jones reagent) 2) CrO_3-pyridine (Collin's reagent) 3) PCC (Corey's reagent) and
- 4) PDC (Cornforth reagent).
- b) Hypervalent Iodine reagents
- 1) IBX 2) Dess-Martin periodinane.
- c) DMSO based reagents
- 1) Swern oxidation
- 2) Corey-Kim oxidation - Advantages over Swern oxidation and limitations Swern oxidation.
- 3) Pfitzner-Moffatt oxidation-(DCC/DMSO) and
- 4) Oppenauer oxidation.

III. Oxidation involving C-C bonds cleavage:
- a) Cleavage of Glycols using 1) HIO_4, 2) $Pb(OAC)_4$.
- b) Cycloalkanones using 1) CrO_3.
- c) Carbon-carbon double bond using
- 1) Ozone (O_3), 2) $KMnO_4$, 3) OsO_4, 4) I_2/CH_3COOAg dry condition, 5) I_2/CH_3COOAg wet condition 6) $OsO_4/NaIO_4$ or $KMnO_4/NaIO_4$ 7) CrO_3.
- d) Oxidation of aromatic rings using
- 1) $RuO_4/NaIO_4$, 2) V_2O_5

IV. Oxidation involving replacement of hydrogen by oxygen:

a) Oxidation of CH_2 to CO by using

1) SeO_2 2) Alkyl Nitrite

b) Oxidation of arylmethanes by using

1) CrO_2Cl_2 (Etard oxidation).

c) Oxidation of aldehydes and ketones: with

1) H_2O_2 (Dakin reaction) and with

2) Peroxy acid (Baeyer-Villiger oxidation)

Volume-II REDUCTION

❖**Reduction:**

I. Reduction of carbonyl group CO to methylene group -CH_2- in aldehydes and ketones.

1) Zn/HCl (Clemmensen reduction)

2) Wolff-Kishner reduction

3) Huang-Minlon modification.

II. Metal hydride reduction

a) Boron based reagents

1) $NaBH_4$ 2) $NaCNBH_3$

3) B_2H_6/BH_3 (diborane) 4) 9-BBN

5) $Na(OAc)_3BH$.

b) Aluminium based reagents

1) $LiAlH_4$ 2) DIBAL-H 3) Red-Al

4) L and K-selectrides.

III. Non-metal based agents including organic reducing agents

1) NH_2NH_2 (diimide reduction)

2) Dihydropyridine (Hantzsch Synthesis)

IV. Dissolving metal reductions

1) Zn, Li, Na, and Mg under neutral and acidic conditions,

2) Li/Na-liquid NH_3 mediated reduction (Birch reduction) of aromatic compounds and acetylenes.

Chapter 1

Oxidation

Oxidation of organic molecules involves a gain in oxygen or loss of hydrogen or loss of electrons. Oxidation of a "C" atom in an organic compound involves one or more of the following changes;

a) An increase in the multiple bond order of the Carbon

$$-H_2C-CH_2- \xrightarrow{-2H} -HC=CH- \xrightarrow{-2H} -C\equiv C-$$

Alkane　　　　　　　　Alkene　　　　　　　　Alkyne

b) Addition of Oxygen

Aldehyde　　　　　　　　Carboxylic acid

c) Removal of Hydrogen

$$R\text{—}OH \xrightarrow{-2H} R\text{—}CHO$$

1° Alcohol   Aldehyde

d) Removal of electron

Phenoxide   Phenoxy radical

Oxidation and Reduction are complementary to each other in the process of chemical reactions, in which the compounds undergoes oxidation with the help of certain oxidising reagent itself get reduced to complete the process. The complete chemical reaction refers as the Redox reaction, where both chemical processes occur simultaneously as oxidation and reduction.

I. Dehydrogenation (Aromatization)

a) Dehydrogenation of C-C bonds including aromatization of six membered rings using following metals

1) Oxidation by Pt or Pd or Ni metal

Dehydrogenation is a chemical reaction that involves the removal of hydrogen from an organic molecule and it is exactly the reverse of hydrogenation reaction. The benzene derivatives are prepared by the process dehydrogenation of cyclohexane, cyclohexene or cyclohexadiene with very high temperature in presence of catalyst as metal Pt or Ni or Pd on charcoal as shown below examples.

1)   Pd or Pt or Ni / Charcol / $350^{\circ}C$ →   + $3H_2$

2)   Pd or Pt or Ni / Charcol / $300^{\circ}C$ →   + $2H_2$

3)   Pd or Pt or Ni / Charcol / $90^{\circ}C$ →   + H_2

Fig. Aromatization of six member ring

The same reaction can be carried out under mild conditions if a hydrogen accepter such as maleic acid is use which will remove hydrogen as it is formed in reaction. As the mechanism of catalytic dehydrogenation is a reverse of double bond hydrogenation but formation of an aromatic system driven the reaction towards dehydrogenation. Hence the cyclohexadiene dehydrogenation requires mild condition of temperature $90^{\circ C}$ as the aromatization gives stable product over the entropy change of the reaction. The same principle of aromatization is applicable to all six member rings as well as condensed aromatic compounds.

Perhydro mean fully hydrogenated compounds are readily dehydrogenated catalytically with Pd/C or Pt/C or Ni/ C but are affected by the presence of sulphur in the chemical reaction. The method of dehydrogenation has many applications in the elucidation of structure in terpenoid and steroid chemistry. The problem arises when compounds containing certain functional groups could also be dehydrogenated.

1) [cyclohexane with CH3] → Pd/C or Pt/C or Ni/C, 350°C → [toluene with CH3] + 3H$_2$

2) [octahydronaphthalene] → Pd/C or Pt/C or Ni/C, 350°C → [naphthalene] + 3H$_2$

3) [2-methylbiphenyl with CH3] → Pd/C → [fluorene] + H$_2$

4) [2,2'-dimethylbiphenyl with CH3 CH3] → Pd/C → [phenanthrene] + 2H$_2$

5) [decahydroquinoline, N-H] → Pd/C or Pt/C or Ni/C → [quinoline, N] + 3H$_2$

6) [methyl-substituted tetrahydrophenanthrene with H3C and CH3] → Pd/C or Pt/C or Ni/C → [dimethylphenanthrene with H3C and CH3] + 2H$_2$

7) [dihydroisoquinoline, N] → Pd/C or Pt/C or Ni/C → [isoquinoline, N] + H$_2$

8) [dihydropyridine, N-H] → Pd/C or Pt/C or Ni/C → [pyridine, N] + H$_2$

9) [tetrahydroquinoline, N-H] → Pd/C or Pt/C or Ni/C → [quinoline, N] + 2H$_2$

10)

Pd/C or Pt/C or Ni/C

$+$ $3H_2$

11)

Pd/C or Pt/C or Ni/C

$+$ $2H_2$

2) DDQ (2,3-Dichloro-5,6-dicyanobenzoquinone)

DDQ was first introduced for the dehydrogenation of hydroaromatic compounds such as tetralin and bibenzyl which gives naphthalene and stilbene respectively. It is high potential quinone skeleton with multifunctional as 2,3-dichloro-5,6-dicyanobenzoquinone (DDQ) is a powerful organic reagent for aromatization or dehydrogenation. The reagent is useful for the dehydrogenation of steroids and its scope has been extended to carbonyl compounds including ketones, lactones, alcohols and phenols as well. Reaction with DDQ may be carried out in the inhert solvents such as benzene, totuene, dioxane, THF or acetic acid. The DDQ decomposes in water but is stable in aqueous mineral acids. The driving force of the reaction includes the both substrate as well as reagent aromatization to $DDQH_2$. The $DDQH_2$ formed in the reaction is insoluble in solvent and can be removed easily by filtration. A number of side products can be formed with skeleton quinone as dienophile or α,β- unsaturated ketone it include Diels-Alder adduct or Michael adducts with substrate.

a) Dehydrogenation of ketones

DDQ

$-DDQH_2$

b) Benzylic Oxidation

Dehydrogenation by DDQ can only be possible if benzylic carbon and it's α-carbon has one hydrogen each as shown following examples.

1)

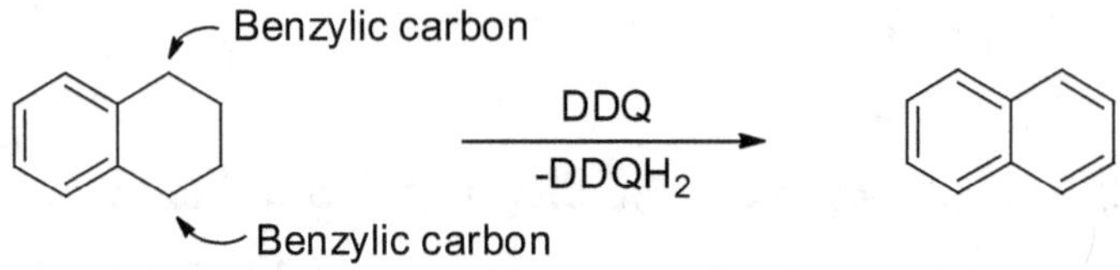

2)

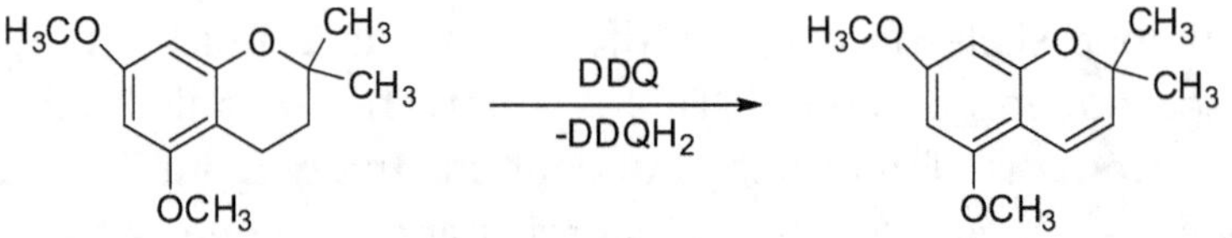

3)

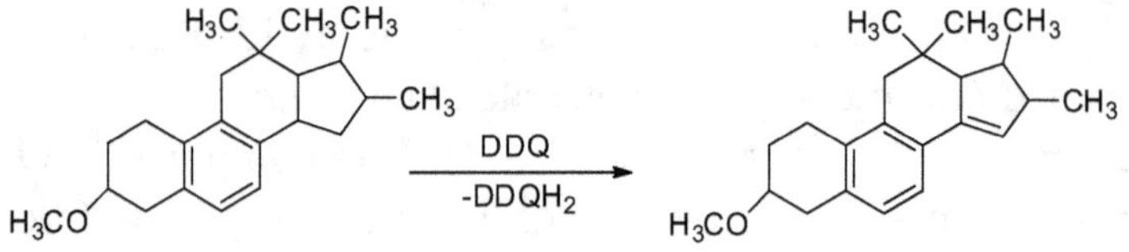

c) Aromatization

1)

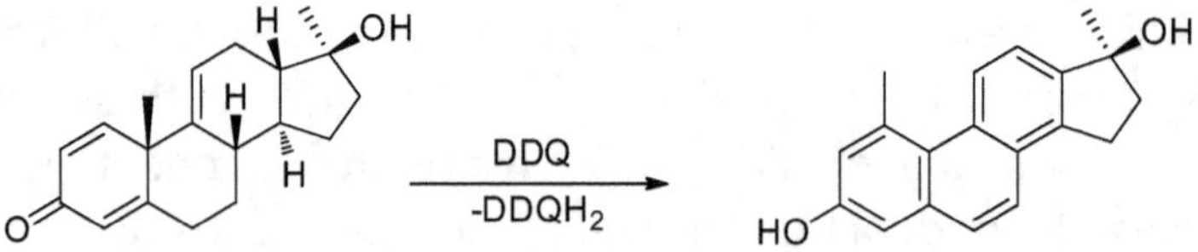

2)

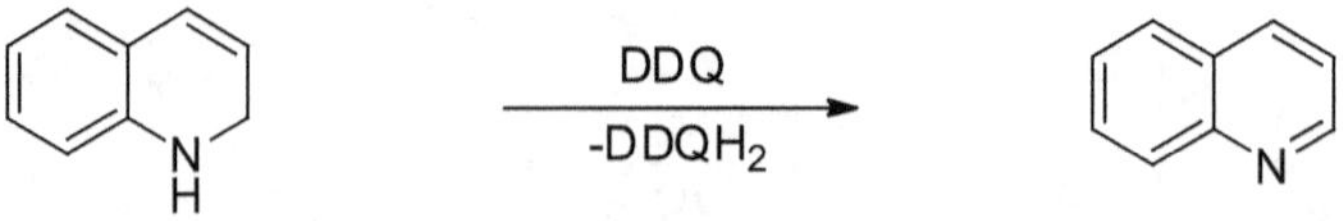

3)

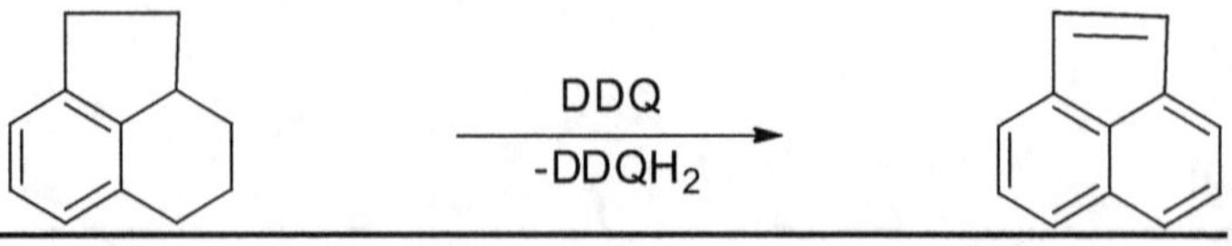

4)

$$\text{(dihydropyridine)} \xrightarrow[-\text{DDQH}_2]{\text{DDQ}} \text{(pyridine)}$$

d) Rearrangements of the alkyl group take place while the process of aromatization.

3)

$$\text{(1,1-dimethyltetralin)} \xrightarrow[-\text{DDQH}_2]{\text{DDQ}} \text{(2,3-dimethylnaphthalene)}$$

methyl group rearranged

e) Oxidative coupling

$$\xrightarrow[-\text{DDQH}_2]{\text{DDQ}}$$

f) Oxidation of Alcohols:

Saturated primary alcohols are not oxidised by DDQ but sterically hindered secondary saturated alcohols can oxidised by the DDQ as oxidising reagent hence this reagent is very useful in terpenoid chemistry.

1)

$$\xrightarrow[-\text{DDQH}_2]{\text{DDQ}}$$

hindered 2° alcohol

2)

DDQ
-DDQH$_2$

hindered 2° alcohol

3)

DDQ

No reaction Because less hinder 2° alcohol

4)

DDQ
-DDQH$_2$

hindered 2° alcohol

5)

DDQ

No reaction Because less hinder 2° alcohol

g) Allylic or Benzylic alcohols can readily undergo oxidation with DDQ.

1)

DDQ
-DDQH$_2$

2)

DDQ
-DDQH$_2$

Preparation of DDQ

1) KCN/HCl/EtOH

2) KClO$_4$/HCl

(reaction mechanism schemes for the oxidation of quinone to DDQ via KCN/HCl, keto-enol tautomerism, and successive KClO₄ oxidation steps)

Mechanism of Dehydrogenation

e.g.

(scheme: 1,4-dihydro aromatic compound with two H atoms converts to benzene via DDQ, losing DDQH₂)

Mechanism

(scheme: substrate + DDQ → carbocation intermediate + phenolate → benzene + DDQH₂)

Driving force results from the conversation of both the quinone derivative (DDQ) and the substrate as aromatic compounds. The mechanism involved the transfer of hydride ion from substrate to the quinone oxygen and subsequent abstraction of proton by phenolate ion. In the dehydrogenation process by DDQ the intermediate electron deficient carbocation formed and the same undergoes 1,2-shift of substituent results in rearranged aromatic products. For examples 1,1-dimethyltetralin readily undergo aromatization in presence of DDQ with 1,2-shift of methyl group.

a) Rearrangement of methyl group

e.g.

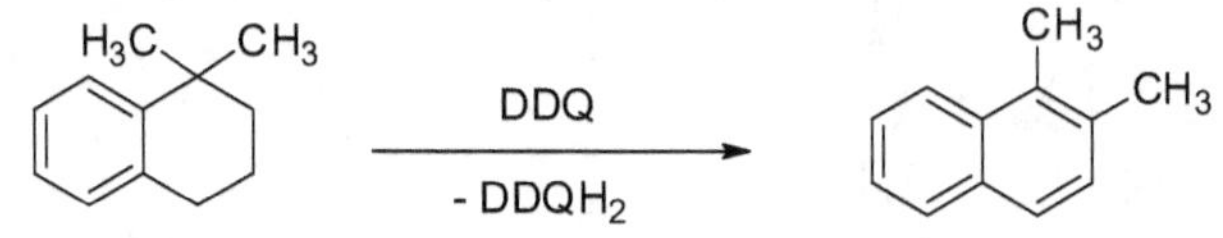
DDQ
- DDQH2

Mechanism

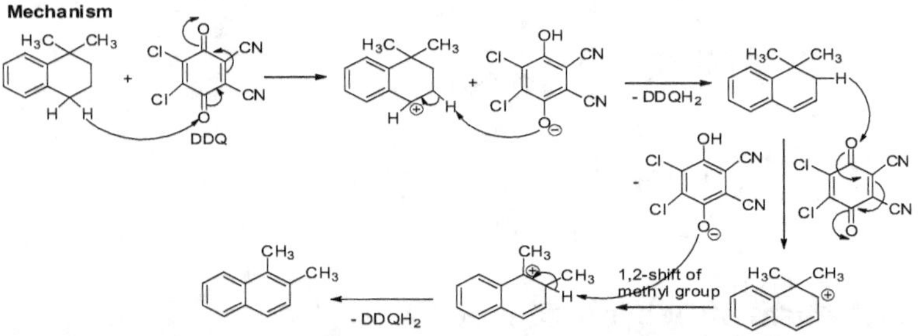
DDQ
- DDQH2
1,2-shift of methyl group
- DDQH2

Some examples of dehydrogenation by DDQ as below.

1)

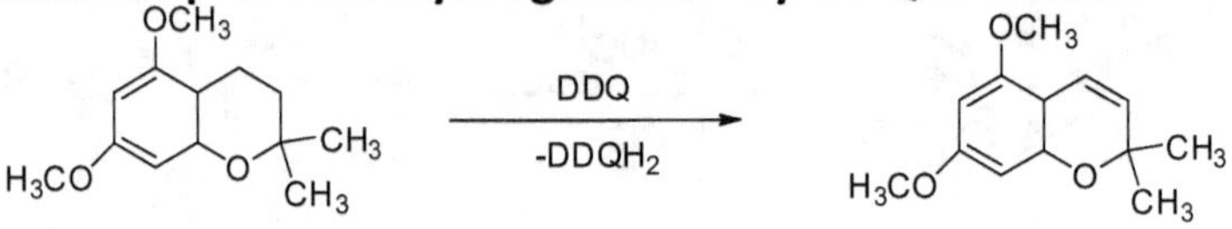
DDQ
-DDQH2

2)

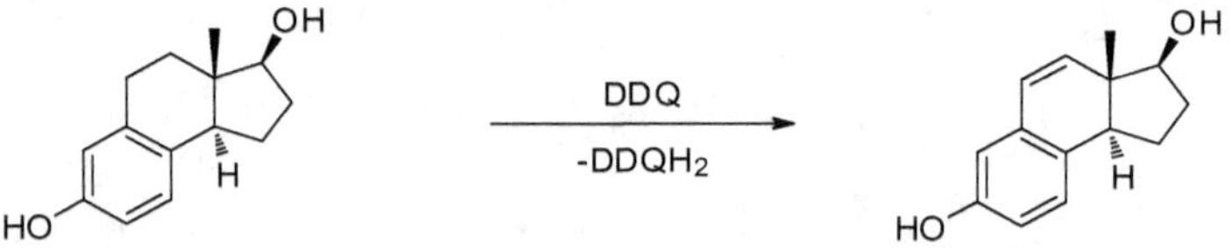
DDQ
-DDQH2

3)

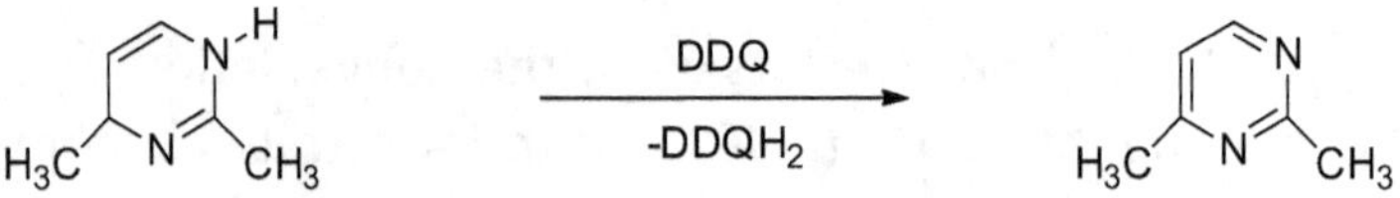
DDQ
-DDQH2

4)

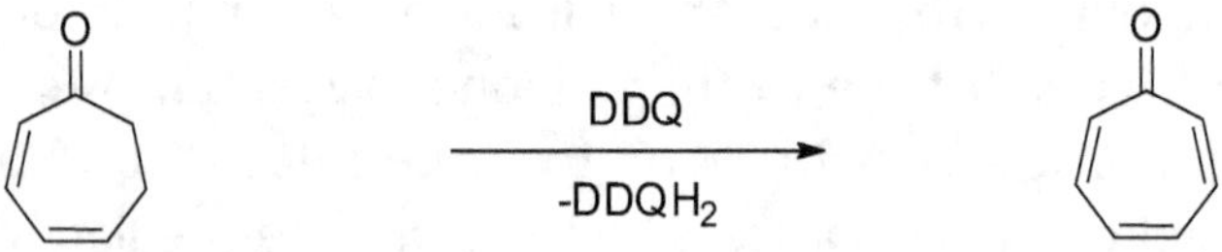
DDQ
-DDQH2

5)

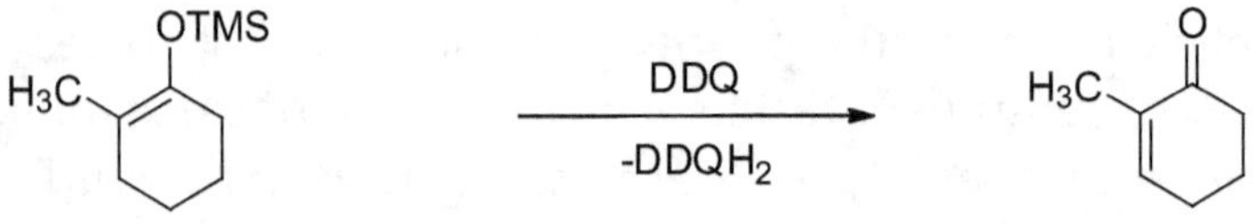
DDQ
-DDQH2

6)

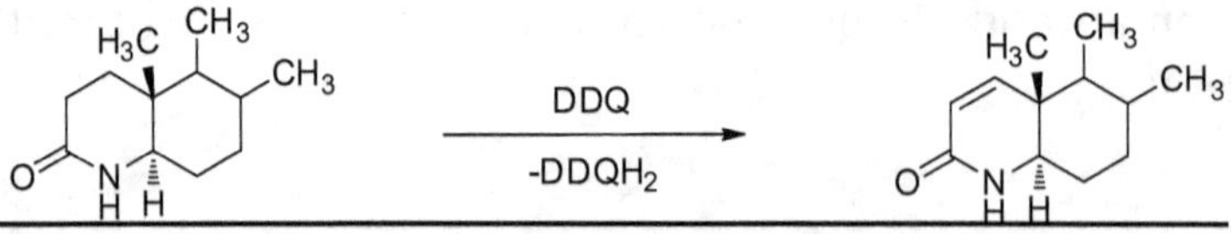
DDQ
-DDQH2

a) Phenolic cyclization substituted phenols.

Phenols undergo a wide variety of reaction with DDQ. The initial step is the formation of the phenoxyl radical and subsequent processes include coupling reaction or electron transfer to give a phenonium ion, which force the another molecule of same or quinone of DDQ to couple under mild condition.

Mechanism of coupling reaction

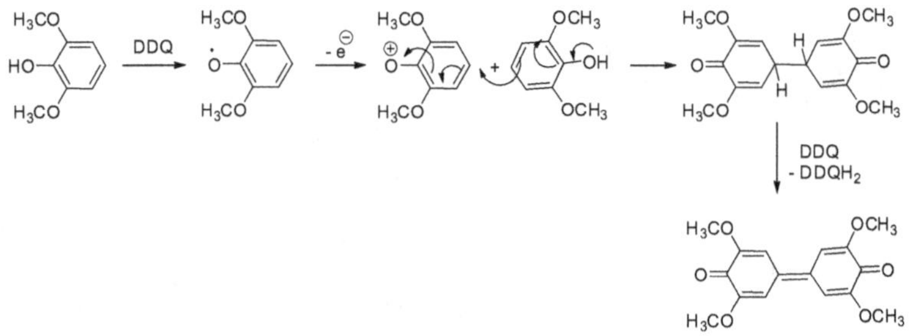

Mechanism of coupling reaction with DDQ

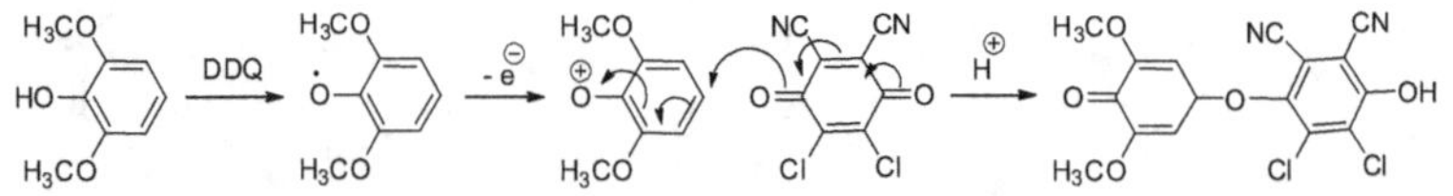

Precautions: DDQ is stable in a dry atmosphere but decomposes in the presence of water with the evolution of HCN gas, hence store under nitrogen in a sealed container. The Chloranil have similar applications and it is safe and easy to handle as compare to DDQ.

3) Chloranil (Tetrachloro-1,4-benzoquinone)

Chloranil is also a good dehydrogenating reagent. It is less powerful oxidizing reagent as compare to DDQ because Chloranil is having all four chlorides as substituents whereas in DDQ two cyano substituents make the reagent further electrons deficient. It has similar applications as partially unsaturated alicyclic rings are dehydrogenated by chloranil through hydride ion transfer. The driving of the chemical reaction i.e. dehydrogenation is similar to that of DDQ as aromatic product as well the by-product aromatic as $DDQH_2$.

Preparation of Chloranil: It is prepared by heating benzoquinone with potassium perchlorate ($KClO_4$) and HCl as in the following reaction.

e.g.

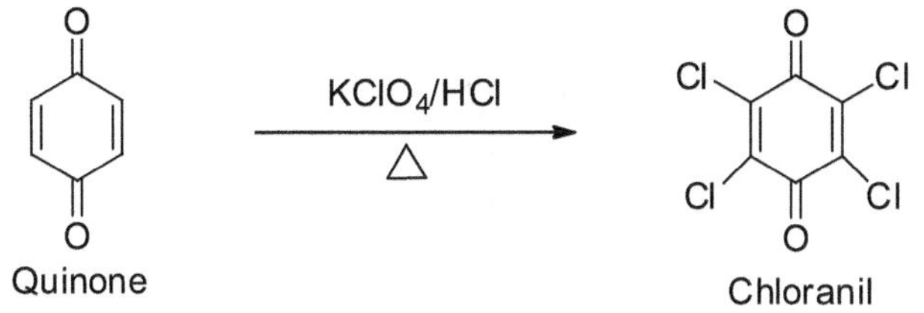

Mechanism

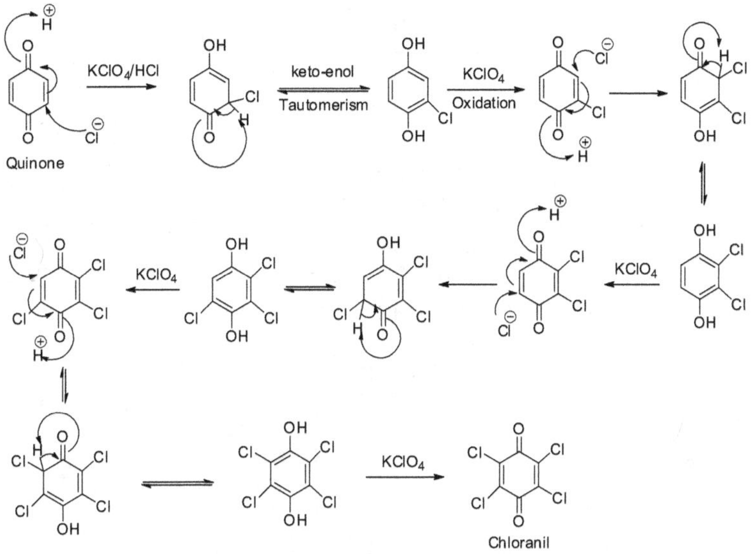

Chloranil is frequently used in the synthesis of *p*-terphenyl as shown in following example.

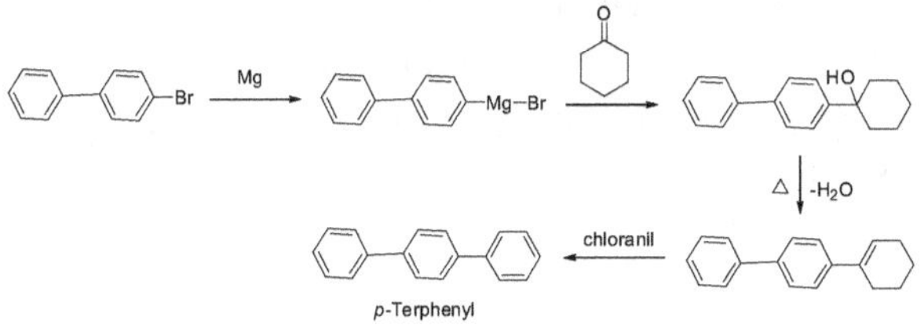

Dehydrogenation leads to the aromatization of dehydronaphthalenes to naphthalene as well the heterocyclic compound like dehydroquinolines to quinolines.

1)

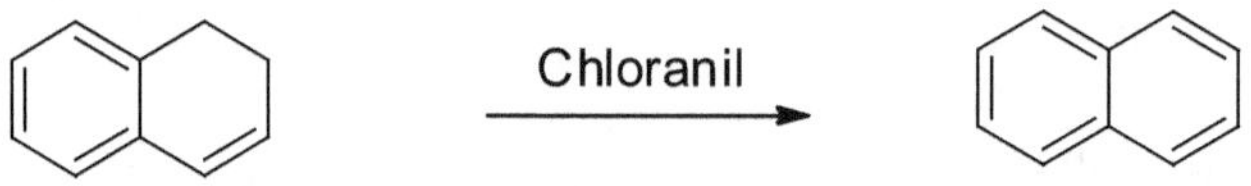

Chloranil

2)

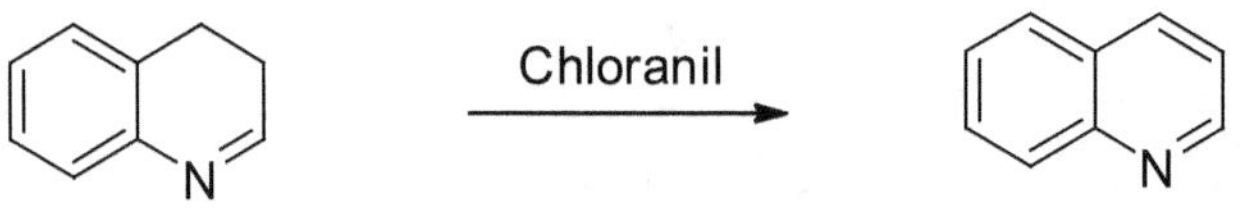

Chloranil

3)

Chloranil

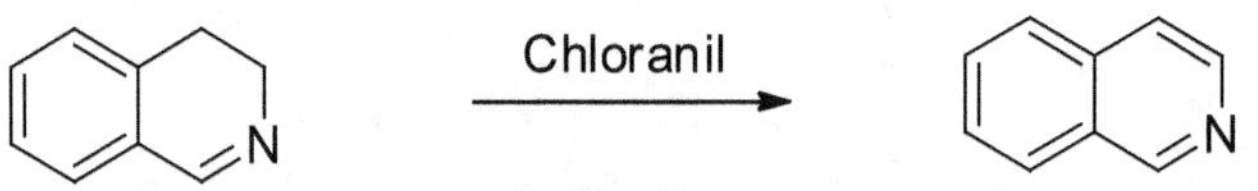

In case of cyclic α,β-unsaturated ketones dehydrogenation take place in homoannular ring.

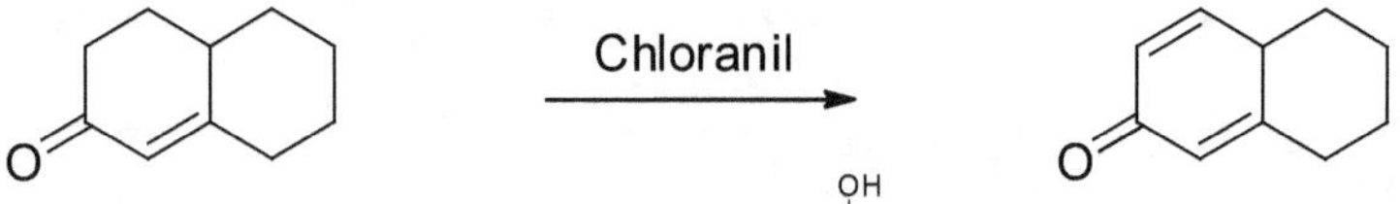

Chloranil

Mechanism

DDQ

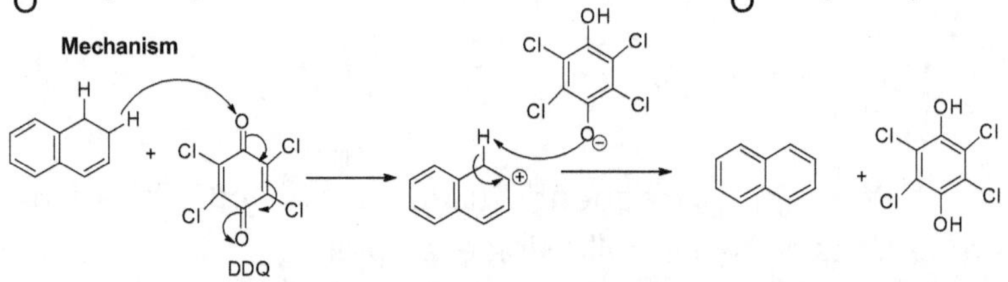

Quinone of the Chloranil is less reaction compares to the DDQ hence the product formed using Chloranil & DDQ varies as kinetically and thermodynamically controlled products respectively.

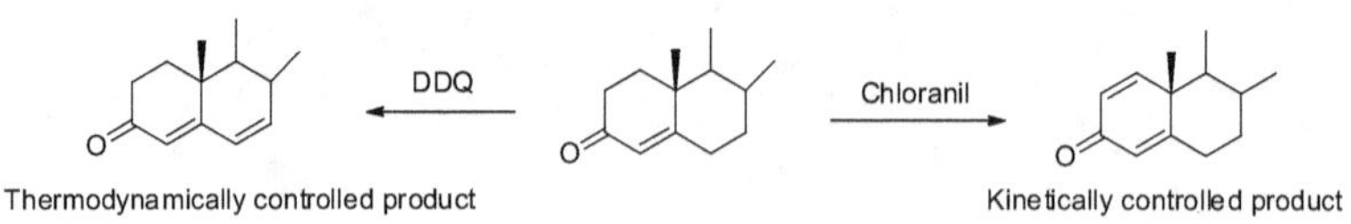

DDQ

Chloranil

Thermodynamically controlled product

Kinetically controlled product

Chloranil is stable in closed containers slowly decomposed by sunlight and stable in acidic media. When it decomposed it release fumes of HCl gas.

II) Oxidation of Alcohols to Aldehydes and Ketones

a) Chromium Base Reagents

Oxidation of primary alcohols gives aldehydes and further oxidation i.e. over-oxidation of aldehydes to gives carboxylic acids and oxidation of secondary alcohols gives ketones as below.

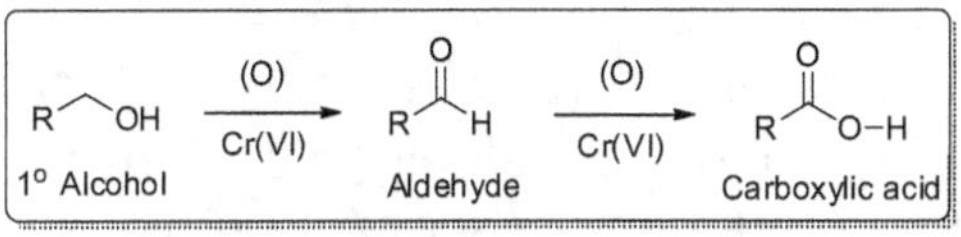

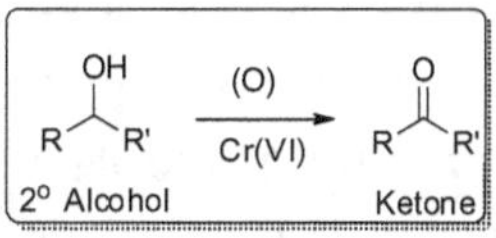

The common oxidising reagents are $K_2Cr_2O_7$ Or $Na_2Cr_2O_7$ and CrO_3 with Chromium metal oxidation state Cr(VI) changes to Cr(IV) oxidation state during the process of oxidation of alcohols to aldehydes as well as for over-oxidation to carboxylic acid.

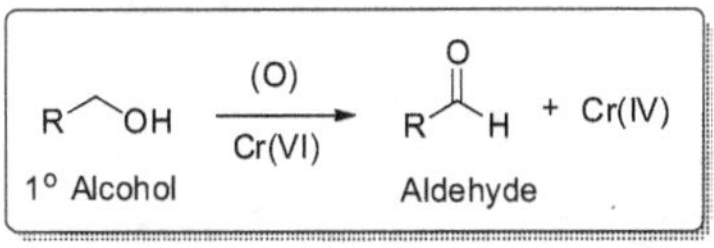

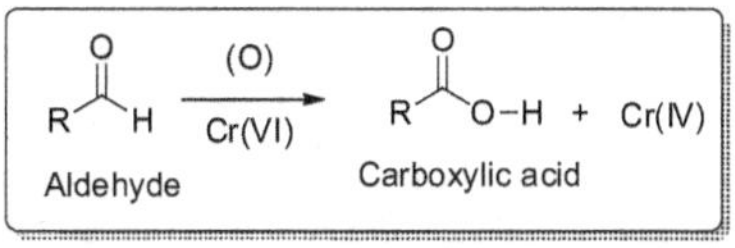

Chromate and Dichromate Reagent

We can prepare these Cr(VI) reagents by adding Potassium or Sodium dichromate ($K_2Cr_2O_7$ or $Na_2Cr_2O_7$) or chromium trioxide (CrO_3) to aqueous solution of H_2SO_4 or CH_3COOH. The chromate ion ($CrO4^{-2}$) forms from dichromate ($Cr_2O_7^{-2}$) by the loss of chromium trioxide (CrO_3) or that it forms from addition of H_2O to CrO_3 followed by deprotonation as below.

$$K_2Cr_2O_7 \text{ Or } Na_2Cr_2O_7 + aq.H_2SO_4 \rightleftharpoons H_2Cr_2O_7 \rightleftharpoons H_2CrO_4 + CrO_3$$

$$CrO_3 + H_2O \rightleftharpoons H_2CrO_4 \quad (CrO_4^{-2}) \text{ Chromate}$$

1) Jones Reagent ($K_2Cr_2O_7/H_2SO_4$)

Acyclic ketones are relatively stable to Cr(VI) i.e Chromate or Dichromate oxidation, hence acetone is frequently used as the solvent for the oxidation of alcohols. In these reactions a CrO_3 in H_2SO_4/H_2O or $K_2Cr_2O_7/H_2SO_4$ mixture is slowly added to an acetone solution of alcohol is called as Jones reagent (CrO_3 or $K_2Cr_2O_7$ in H_2SO_4/H_2O/Acetone) and the process is known as Jones oxidation. It is a relatively mild oxidising reagent for the oxidation of 1° or 2° alcohol to carboxylic acid or ketone. This reagent is very sensitive as it is useful for the oxidation of unsaturated alcohols which containing double or triple bonds as well allylic or benzylic group, the reactions are carried out at low temperature.

Examples of Jones Oxidation of 1^0 and 2^0 alcohols to carboxylic acids and ketones;

1)

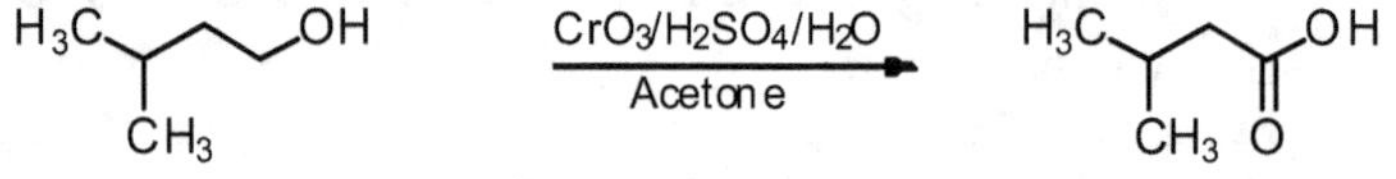

2)

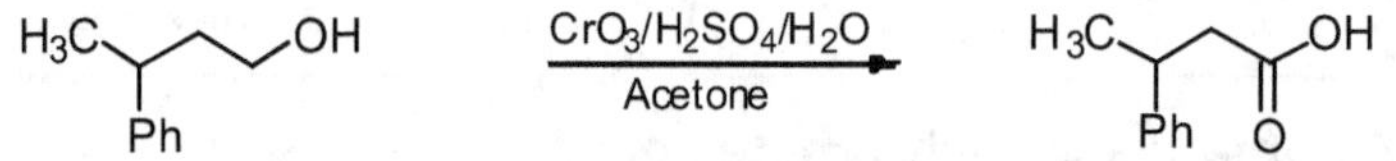

3)

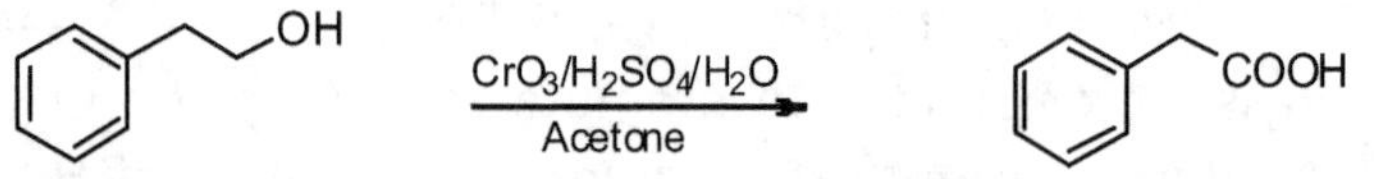

4)

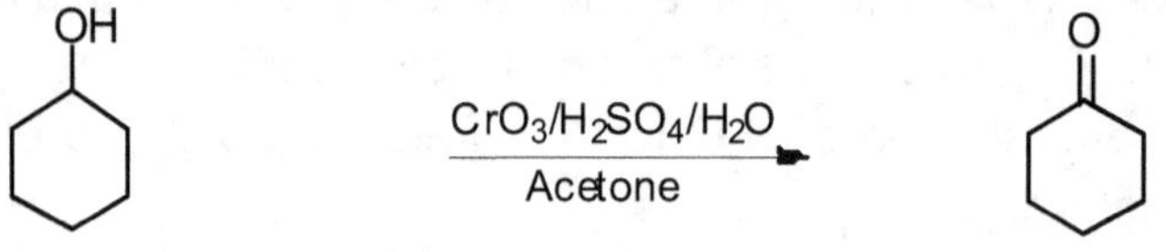

5)

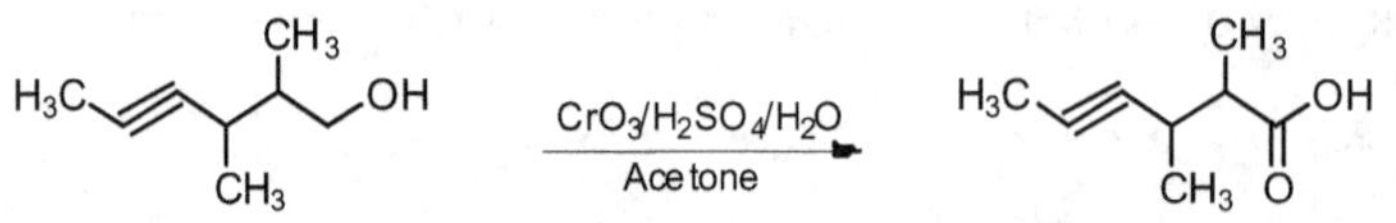

6)

$CrO_3/H_2SO_4/H_2O$ / Acetone

7)

$CrO_3/H_2SO_4/H_2O$ / Acetone

8)

$CrO_3/H_2SO_4/H_2O$ / Acetone

The oxidation of primary allylic and benzylic alcohols gives aldehydes because that do not form hydrates in significant amounts hence can be selective in oxidation with unmodified Jones Reagent to yield aldehydes.

1)

$CrO_3/H_2SO_4/H_2O$ / Acetone

2)

$CrO_3/H_2SO_4/H_2O$ / Acetone

Mechanism of Jones Oxidation

The mechanism begins with the reaction of CrO_3 with acid (H_2SO_4/H_2O) to form chromic acid Cr(VI) or dichromic acid Cr(VI) in more concentrated form of solution to the same solution alcohol is added slowly. In the process of alcohol oxidation chromic acid with oxidation state Cr(IV) get reduced to Cr(IV) and same lower oxidation state Cr(IV) subsequently reacts with Cr(VI) as reagent to yield two Cr(V) oxidation states. In the further process of oxidation Cr(V) species can oxidise alcohols in the same way and reduced to Cr(III). The progress of chemical reaction is easy to follow by colour change as Cr(VI) is orange and Cr(III) is green.

Formation of chromic acid

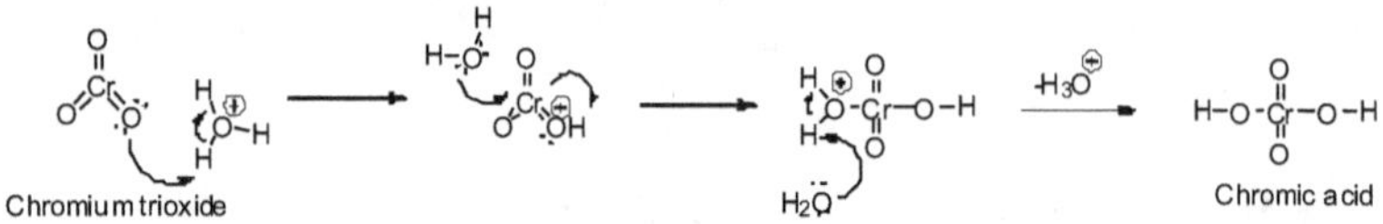

Chromium trioxide

H_2O

Chromic acid

Dehydration of Chromic acid

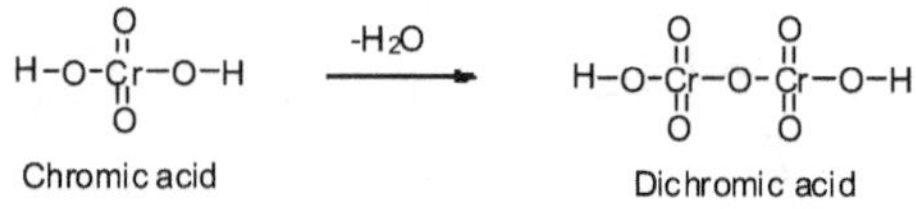

Chromic acid

$-H_2O$

Dichromic acid

Mechanism (Oxidation of Alcohols)

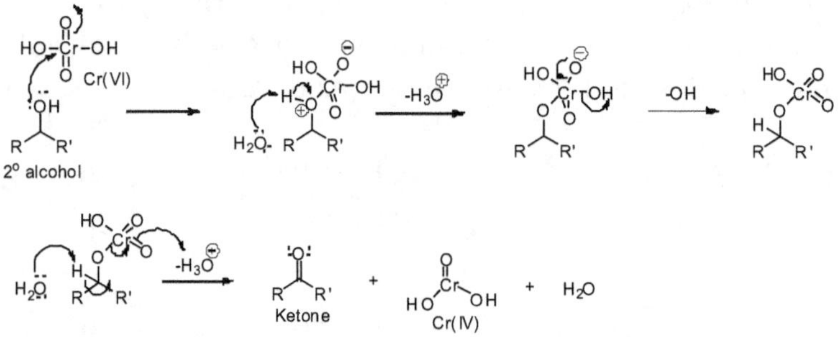

Cr(VI)

$2°$ alcohol

$-H_3O$

$-OH$

Ketone

Cr(IV)

$+\ H_2O$

2) Collin's Reagent (CrO$_3$-Pyridine)

Collin's reagent is the complex of Chromium trioxide CrO_3(VI) with anhydrous pyridine in a solvent as dichloromethane. It is selectively oxidize primary alcohols and secondary alcohols to aldehydes and ketones keeping many other functional groups within the molecule intact. The acid sensitive alcohols can be oxidized with Collin's reagent, unlike Jones Reagent. In Collin's oxidation process the anhydrous conditions avoid the over-oxidation of primary alcohols leads to aldehydes formation. Collin's reagent is difficult to prepare and dangerous as it is very hygroscopic and can inflame during preparation.

Preparation of Collin's Reagent

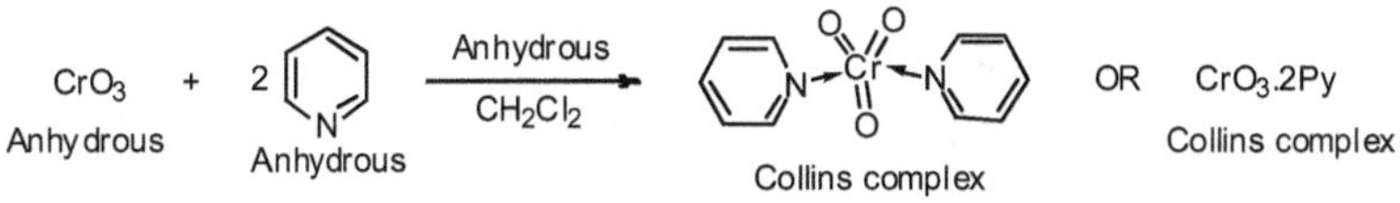
CrO3
Anhydrous
+ 2
N
Anhydrous
Anhydrous
CH2Cl2
Cr
N
N
Collins complex
OR CrO3.2Py
Collins complex

Examples of Collin's Oxidation of 1⁰ alcohol to aldehyde and 2⁰ alcohols to ketones.

1)
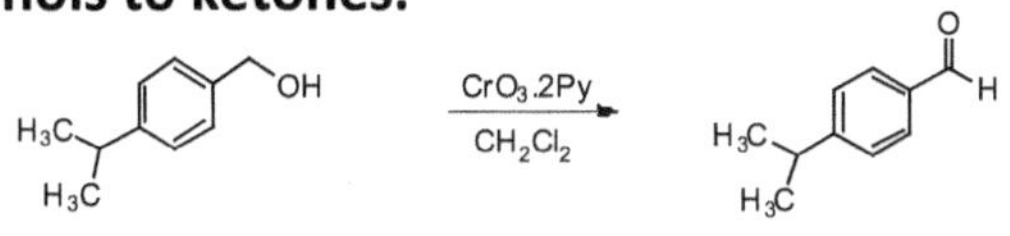
H3C
H3C
OH
CrO3.2Py
CH2Cl2
H
H3C
H3C

2)
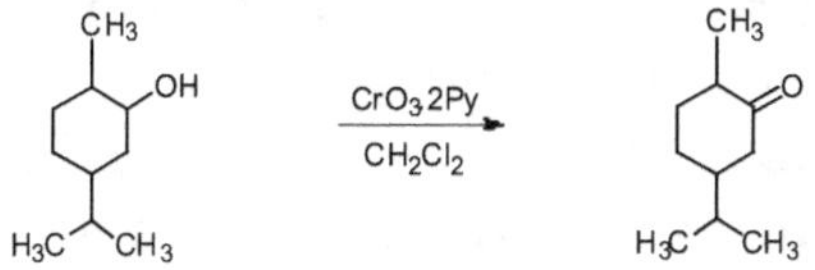
CH3
OH
H3C
CH3
CrO3.2Py
CH2Cl2
CH3
O
H3C
CH3

3)
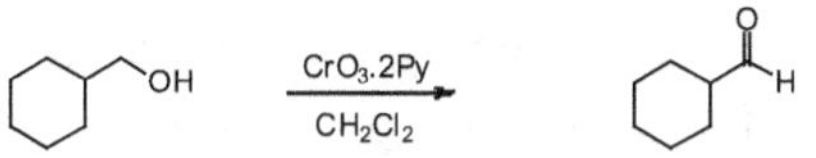
OH
CrO3.2Py
CH2Cl2
O
H

4)
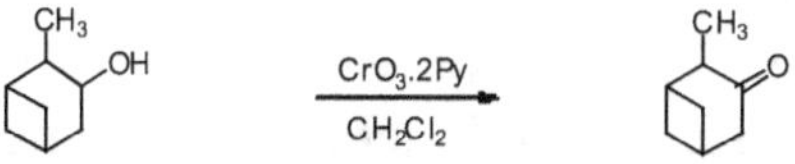
CH3
OH
CrO3.2Py
CH2Cl2
CH3
O

5)
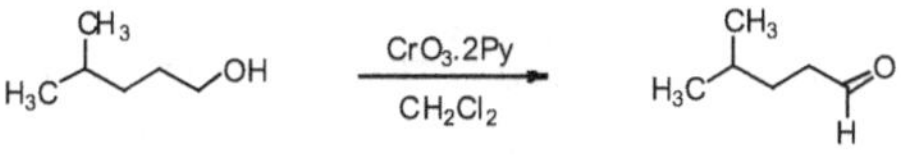
CH3
H3C
OH
CrO3.2Py
CH2Cl2
CH3
H3C
O
H

6)
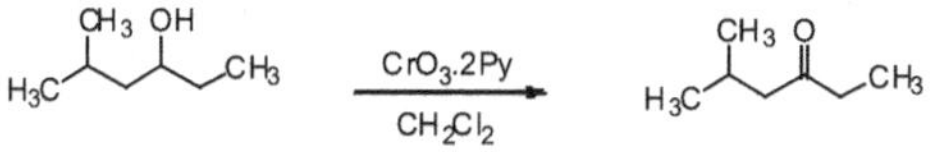
CH3 OH
H3C
CH3
CrO3.2Py
CH2Cl2
CH3 O
H3C
CH3

7)
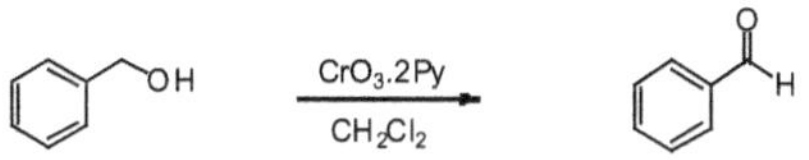
OH
CrO3.2Py
CH2Cl2
O
H

8)
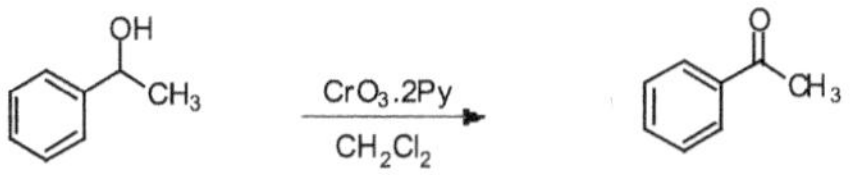
OH
CH3
CrO3.2Py
CH2Cl2
O
CH3

9)
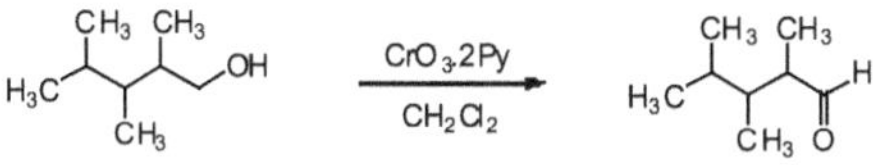
CH3 CH3
H3C
OH
CH3
CrO3.2Py
CH2Cl2
CH3 CH3
H3C
H
CH3 O

Mechanism of Collin's Oxidation

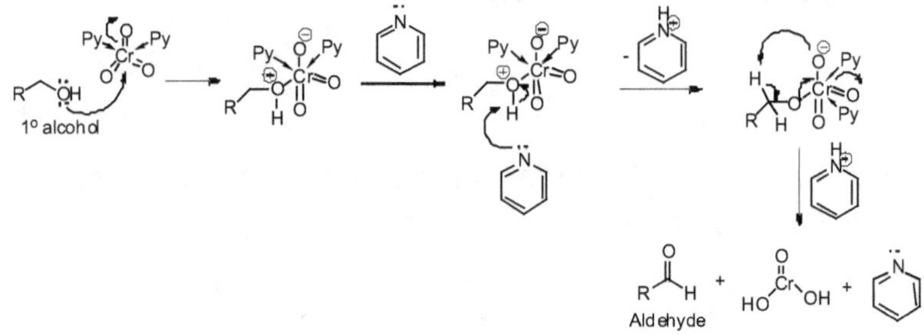

3) Corey's Reagent (Pyridinium Chlorochromate/PCC)

PCC is prepared by dissolving Chromium trioxide (CrO_3) in 6M aqueous HCl to get chromic acid followed by addition of pyridine to the same solution gives pyridinium chlorochromate (PCC) reagent as orange crystals. PCC is slightly acidic but can be buffered with sodium acetate (NaOAc). It is highly effective oxidising agent to oxidise primary and secondary alcohols into aldehydes and ketones respectively. It is less hygroscopic, stable, commercially available and can be stored for longer time on shelf. PCC is soluble in many organic solvents and particularly dichloromethane (CH_2Cl_2) at room temperature has been use in most cases oxidation. Whereas Dimethyl formate (DMF) supports the over-oxidation of primary alcohols into carboxylic acids.

Preparation

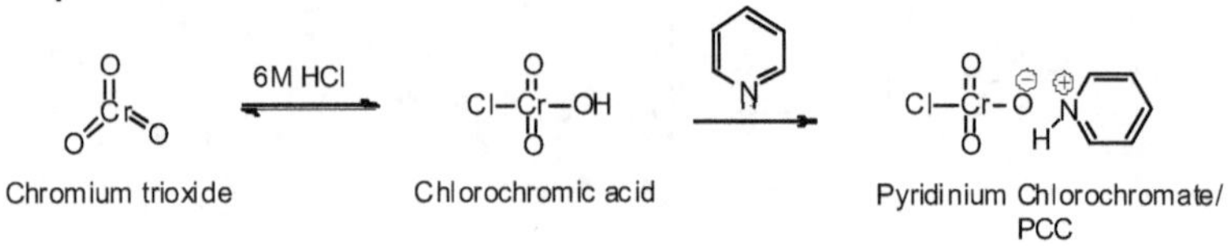

Examples of Corey's Oxidation (PCC)

i) Oxidation of primary and secondary alcohols into aldehydes and ketones.

1)

2)

3)

4)

5)

6)

7)

8)

9)

10)

ii) Oxidation of Organoboranes.

e.g.

$$\text{alkene} \xrightarrow[\text{2) PCC}]{\text{1) BH}_3/\text{THF}} \text{ketone}$$

Mechanism

1)

$$\text{cyclohexene} \xrightarrow[\text{2) PCC}]{\text{1) BH}_3/\text{THF}} \text{cyclohexanone}$$

2)

$$\text{1-methylcyclohexene} \xrightarrow[\text{2) PCC}]{\text{1) BH}_3/\text{THF}} \text{2-methylcyclohexanone}$$

iii) Deoximation.

1)

$$\text{acetone oxime} \xrightarrow[\text{CH}_2\text{Cl}_2]{\text{PCC}} \text{acetone}$$

2)

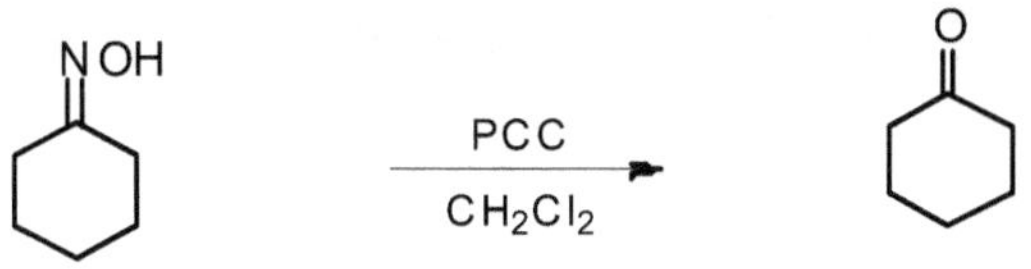

$$\text{(cyclohexanone oxime)} \xrightarrow[\text{CH}_2\text{Cl}_2]{\text{PCC}} \text{(cyclohexanone)}$$

3)

$$\text{(acetophenone oxime)} \xrightarrow[\text{CH}_2\text{Cl}_2]{\text{PCC}} \text{(acetophenone)}$$

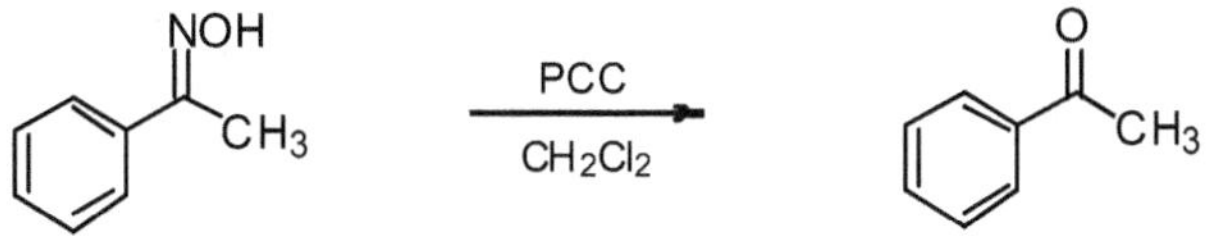

iv) Oxidation of tertiary allylic alcohols.

1)

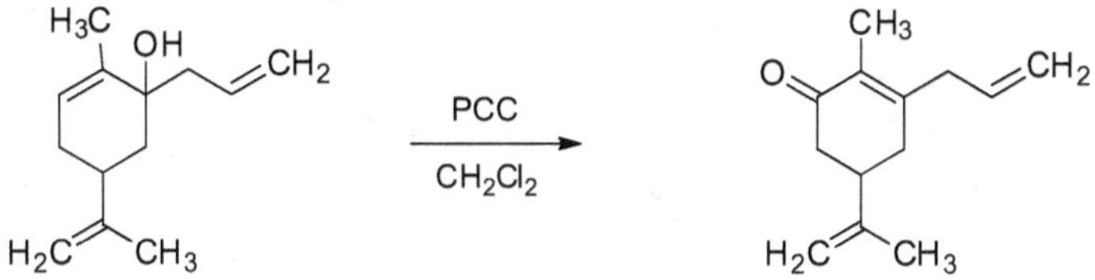

$$\xrightarrow[\text{CH}_2\text{Cl}_2]{\text{PCC}}$$

2)

$$\xrightarrow[\text{CH}_2\text{Cl}_2]{\text{PCC}}$$

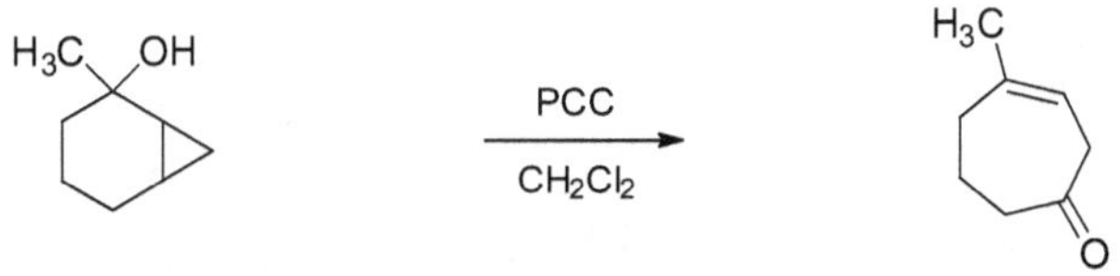

3)

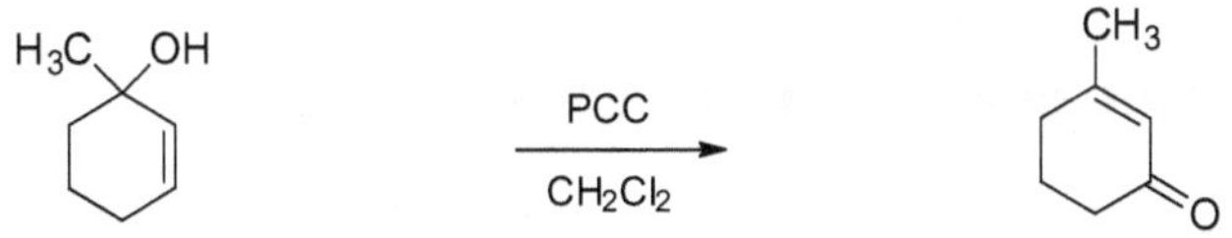

$$\xrightarrow[\text{CH}_2\text{Cl}_2]{\text{PCC}}$$

4)

$$\xrightarrow[\text{CH}_2\text{Cl}_2]{\text{PCC}}$$

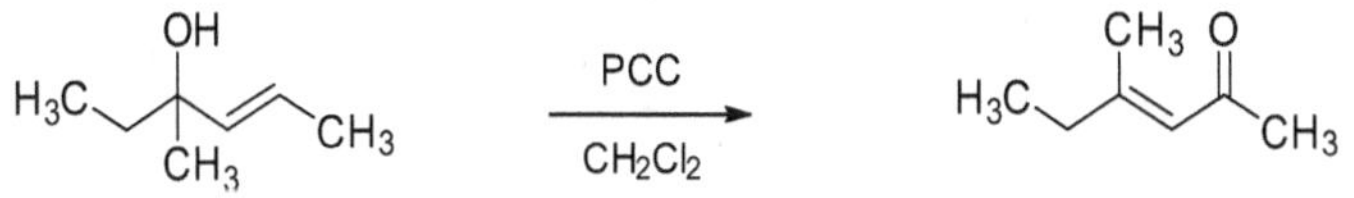

Mechanism

$$\xrightarrow{-\text{HCl}} \xrightarrow{3,3 \text{ shift}}$$

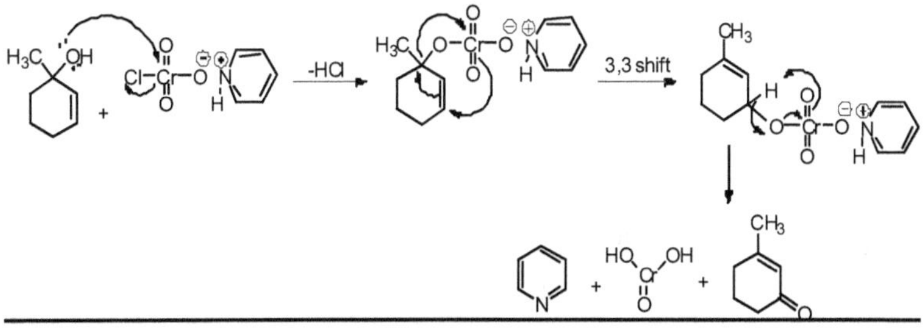

v) Oxidative Cationic Cyclization.

1)

PCC/CH$_2$Cl$_2$

Mechanism

1)

PCC/CH$_2$Cl$_2$ ENE reaction   PCC/CH$_2$Cl$_2$

2)

PCC / CH$_2$Cl$_2$ PCC / CH$_2$Cl$_2$

3)

PCC / CH$_2$Cl$_2$ PCC / CH$_2$Cl$_2$

vi) Oxidation of enol ethers to lactones.

1)

PCC / CH$_2$Cl$_2$

2)

PCC / CH$_2$Cl$_2$

Mechanism

vii) Oxidation of Furan Ring System.

1)

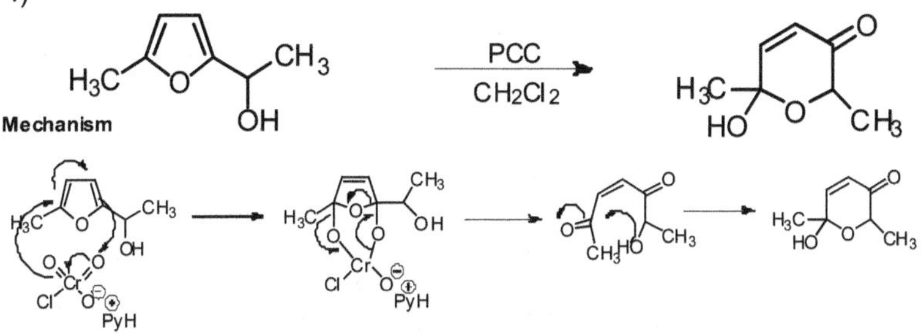

Mechanism

viii) Oxidation of active methylene group.

1)

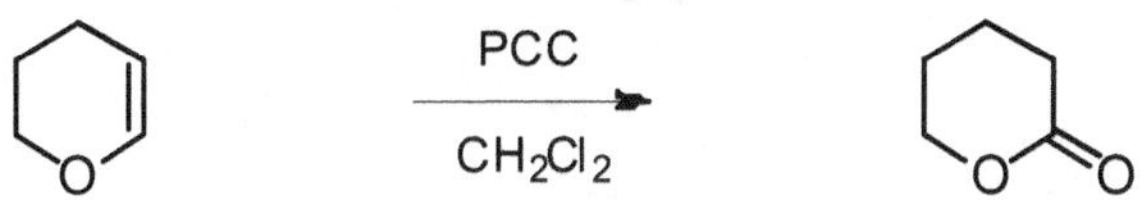

2)

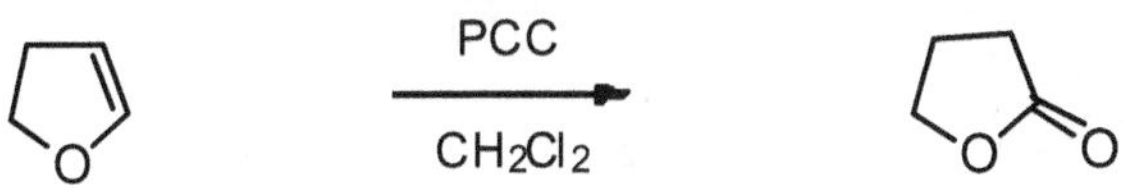

4) Cornforth Reagent (Pyridinium Dichromate/PDC)

PDC is prepared by adding up pyridine to a solution of Chromium trioxide in water, it is orange coloured pyridinium salt of dichromate. PDC is stable, less hygroscopic, stored longer time and commercially available. PDC have chemical properties are similar to that of PCC as it oxidises primary and secondary alcohols to aldehyde and ketones respectively. PDC is less acidic than PCC and hence it is more suitable for the oxidation of acid sensitive substrates.

Preparation of Pyridinium Dichromate (PDC)

Mechanism

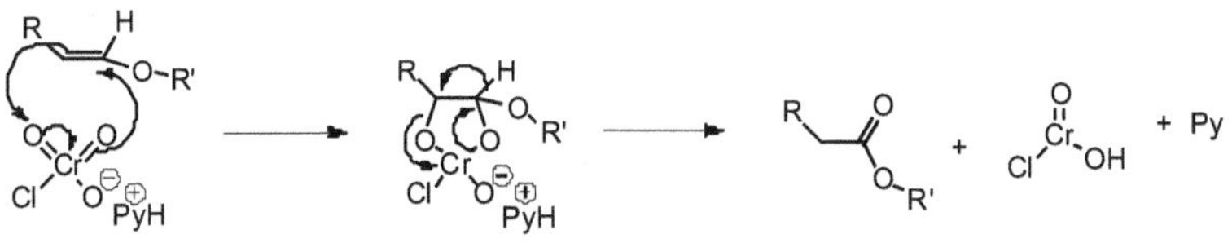

Examples of Pyridinium Dichromate (PDC) Oxidation

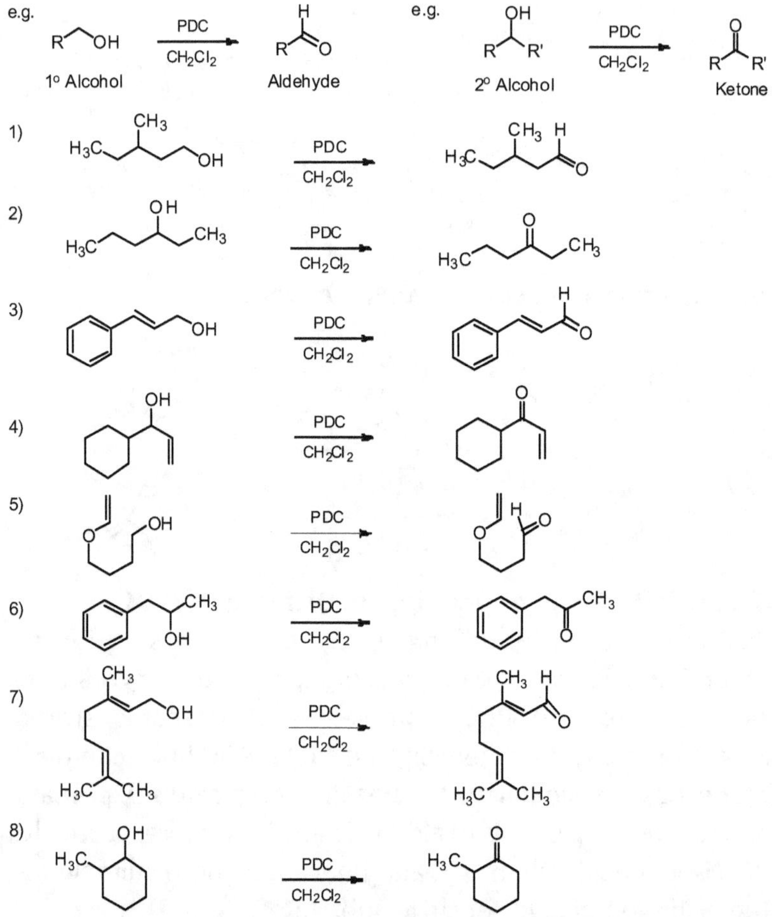

e.g.

$$R-CH_2OH \xrightarrow[CH_2Cl_2]{PDC} RCHO$$

1° Alcohol → Aldehyde

e.g.

$$R-CH(OH)-R' \xrightarrow[CH_2Cl_2]{PDC} R-CO-R'$$

2° Alcohol → Ketone

1) through 8) reaction examples with $\xrightarrow[CH_2Cl_2]{PDC}$

Compounds with primary and secondary alcohols can easy oxidised by using excess mole of PDC reagent in dichloromethane as solvent to aldehyde and ketone respectively.

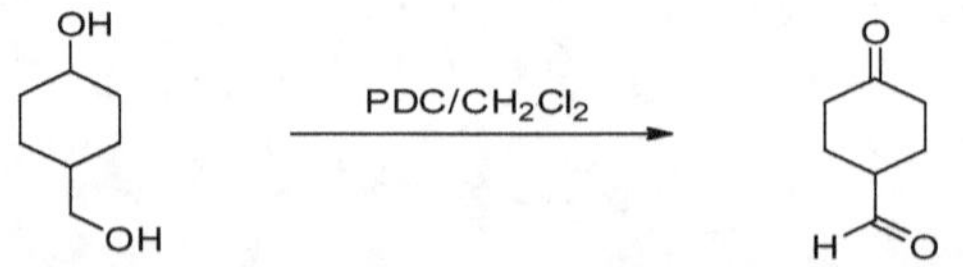

$$\xrightarrow{PDC/CH_2Cl_2}$$

Selective oxidation of primary alcohol to aldehyde keeping secondary alcohol unreacted by PDC in presence of Ruthenium dichlorotriphenyl phosphine ($RuCl_2P(ph_3)_3$) with solvent dichloromethane.

Effect of solvent on the process of oxidation by the PDC the non-conjugate alcohols are readily oxidised to carboxylic acid instead aldehyde by the oxidising reagent as PDC in DMF (Dimethyl formate) as solvent at room temperature.

Aldehyde   1° Alcohol   Carboxylic acid

b) Hypervalent Iodine reagents

Iodine most commonly found in monovalent oxidation state (-1) in many organic compounds because it is most polarizable and electropositive element of the 17th group of the periodic table. It also forms stable poly-coordinate & multivalent compounds as listed below scheme.   The first multivalent organic compound dichloroiodo benzene i.e. $phICl_2$ was prepared by German chemist C. Willgerodt in 1886. Although its oxidizing properties were known but past 20 years polyvalent iodine has been used in organic synthesis as good oxidizing reagents. There are many hypervalent iodine reagent has been discovered but most frequently used are as follows.

Scheme : List of hypervalent iodine reagents

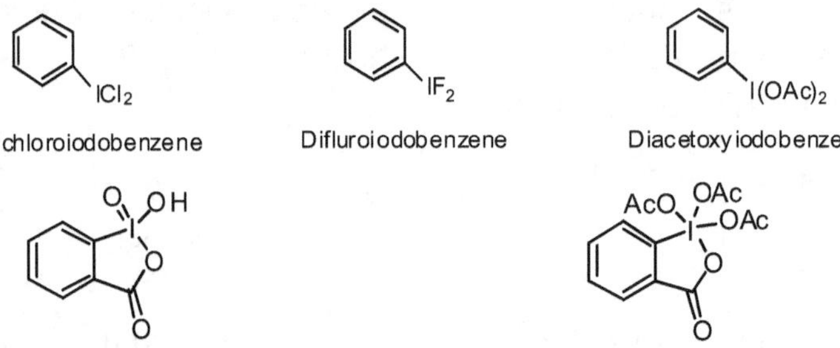

Dichloroiodobenzene (ICl_2)	Difluroiodobenzene (IF_2)	Diacetoxyiodobenzene ($I(OAc)_2$)

2-Iodoxybenzoic acid **(IBX)**   Dess Martin Periodinane **(DMP)**

Hypervalent iodine is a main group element that breaks the octet rule & has more than 8 electrons in its valence shell. Iodine most probable oxidation states are as iodine (I), Iodine (III), Iodine (V) & Iodine (VII).

1) IBX (2-Iodoxy benzoic acid)

IBX (2-Iodoxy benzoic acid) is an oxidizing reagent which specially oxidizes primary and secondary alcohols to aldehyde and ketone respectively. It is prepared by the oxidation of 2-iodobenzoic acid by potassium bromated ($KBrO_3$) or commercially available oxone as reagent. IBX is crystalline but highly explosive when it is dry.

Preparation of IBX reagent

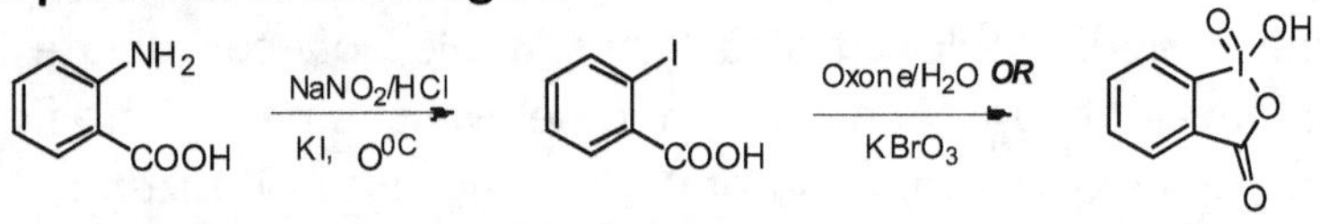

2-aminobenzoic acid → ($NaNO_2/HCl$, KI, 0^0C) → 2-Iodobenzoic acid → (Oxone/H_2O **OR** $KBrO_3$) → IBX

Examples of IBX oxidation

1) [phenethyl alcohol] → IBX → [phenylacetaldehyde]

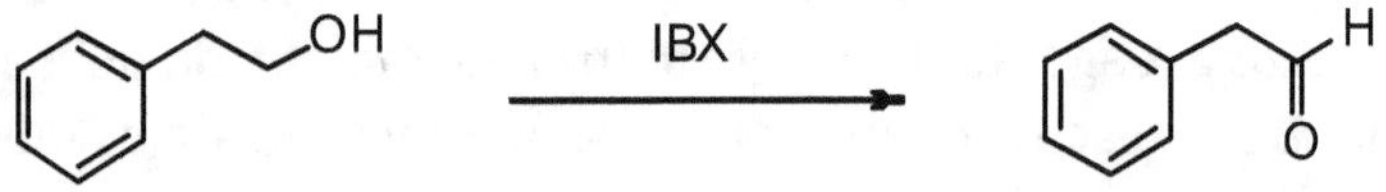

2) H_3C—CH=CH—CH_2OH → IBX → H_3C—CH=CH—CHO

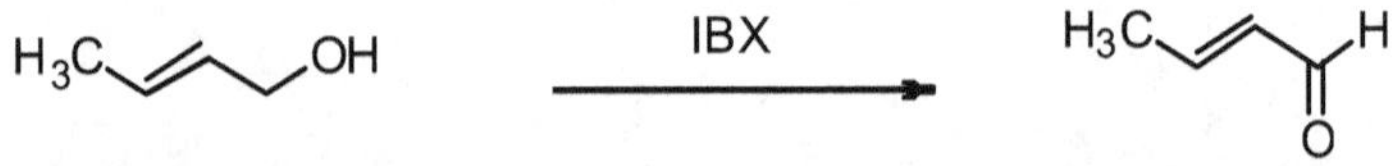

3) 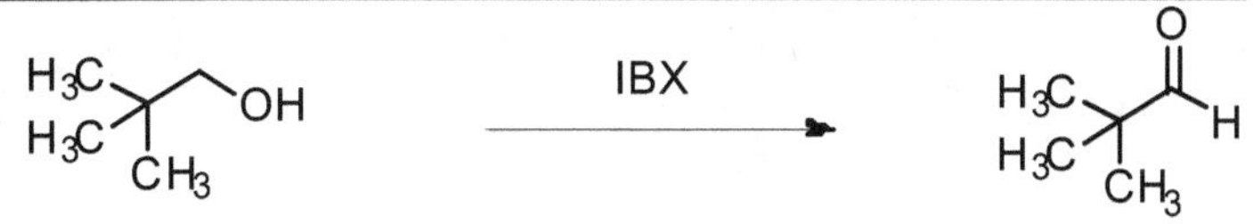

4) 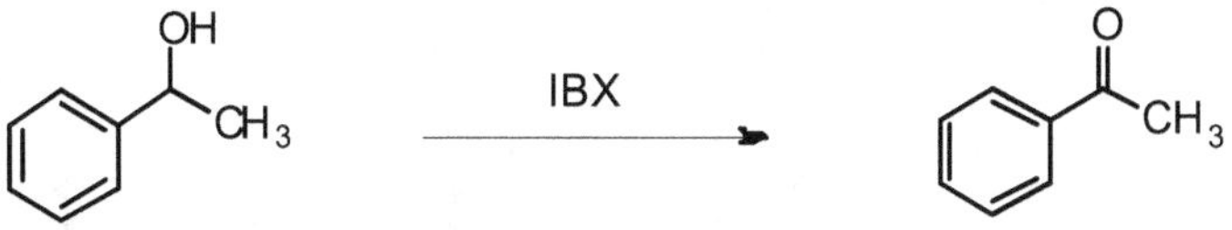

Mechanism of IBX Oxidation

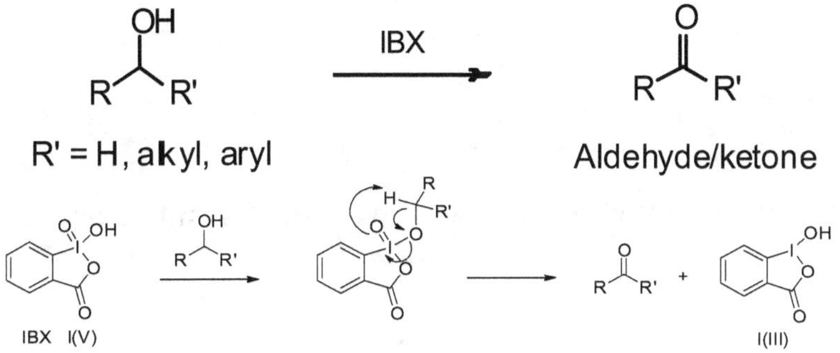

Oxidative cleavage through IBX.

IBX is a good reagent for the oxidative cleavage of vicinal diols (glycols) to aldehyde or ketone in the presence of DMSO as co-oxidant.

e.g.

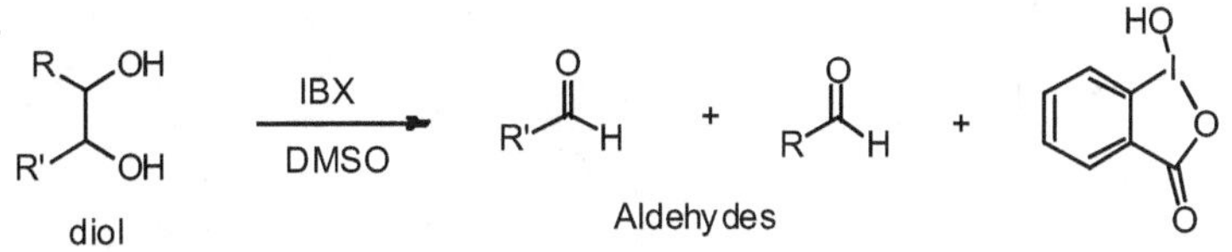

Examples of oxidative cleavage.

1) 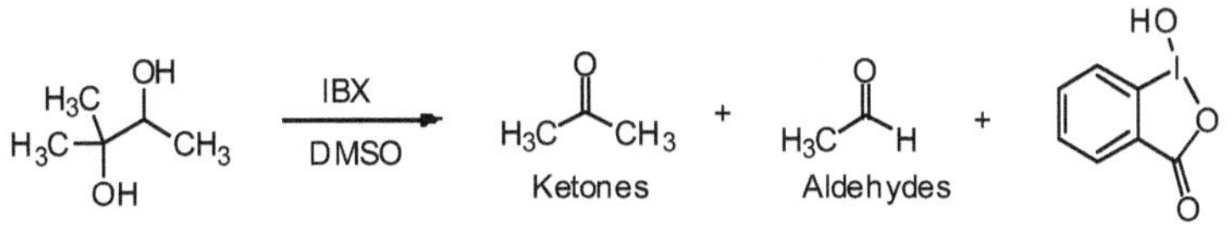

2) 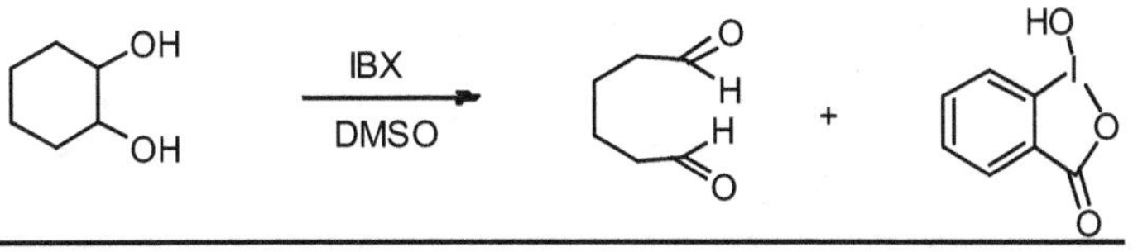

3)

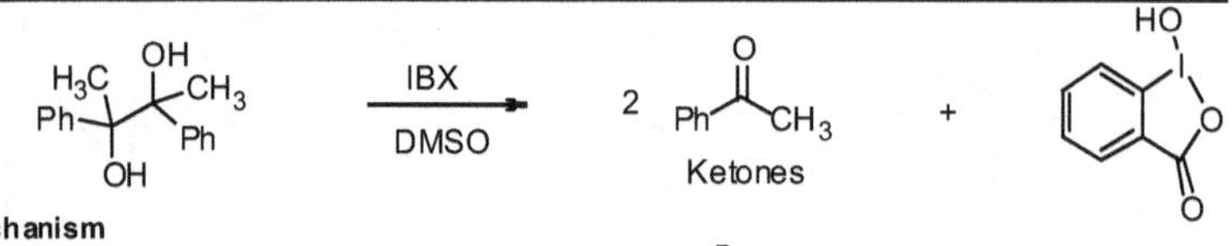

IBX / DMSO

2 Ph-CO-CH₃ (Ketones) + (2-iodoxybenzoic acid reduced form)

Mechanism

I(V) → DMSO → → (−S(CH₃)₂ / DMSO) →

→ +H₂O → → R'CHO + RCHO + I(III)

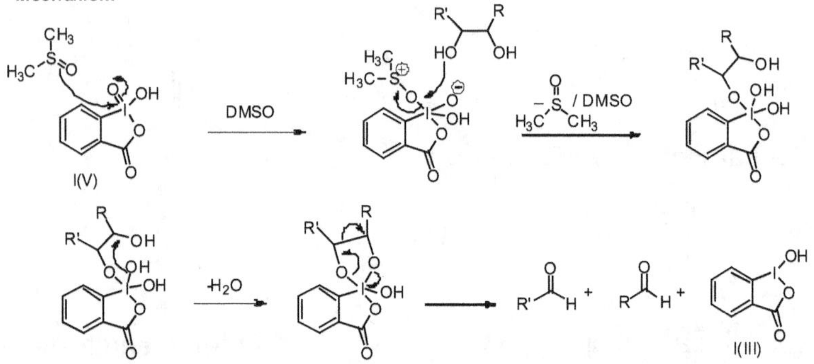

Oxidation of 1° and 2° alcohols to aldehydes and ketones

1)

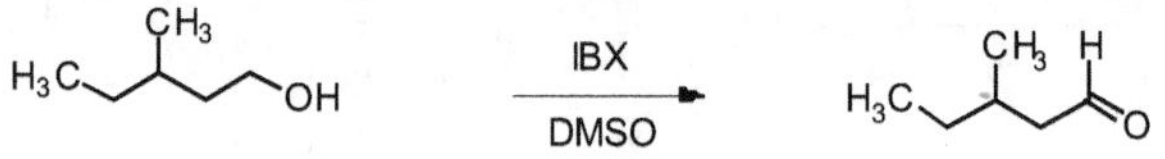

IBX / DMSO

2)

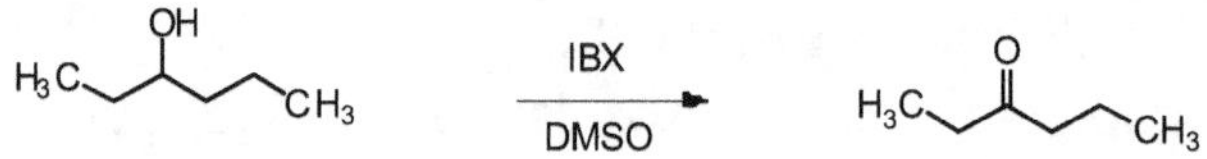

IBX / DMSO

3)

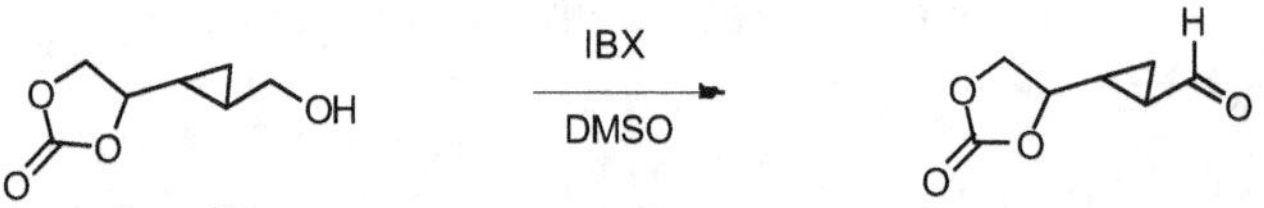

IBX / DMSO

4)

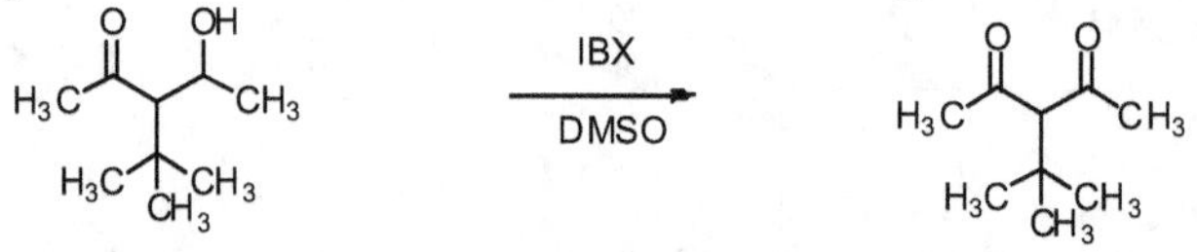

IBX / DMSO

5)

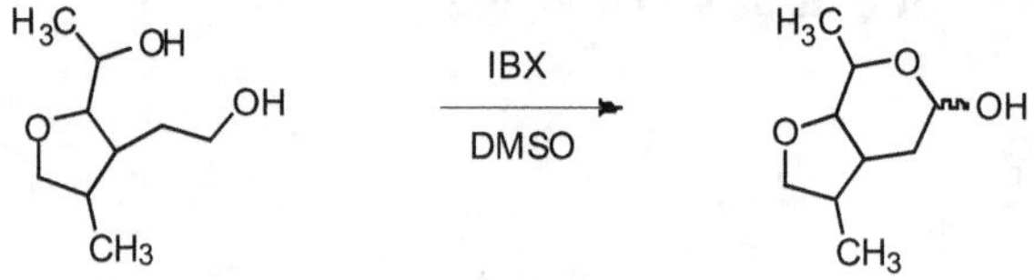

IBX / DMSO

6)

IBX / DMSO

Oxidation of diols which are separated by 4-5 carbon undergoes cyclisation as hemiacetal formation as shown below.

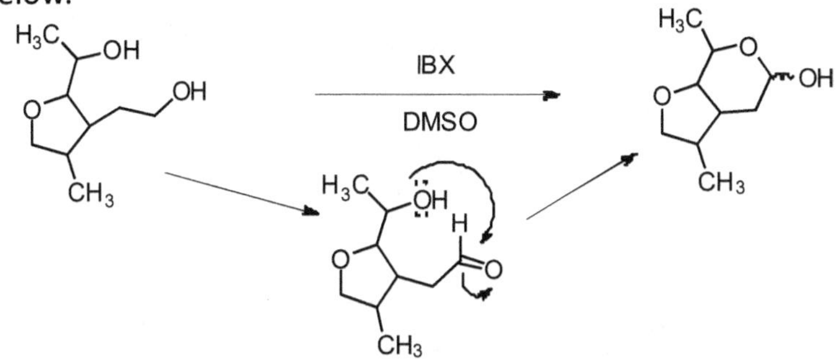

Selective Oxidation of Benzylic carbon.

The IBX is presence DMSO acts as useful oxidising reagent and it oxidizes benzylic carbon to carbonyl compounds as below.

1)

2)

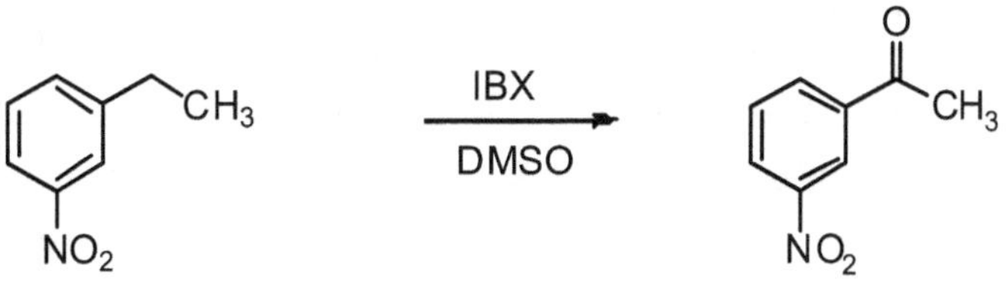

3)

Introduction of unsaturation through IBX oxidation as shown in the following examples.

1)

IBX / DMSO

2)

IBX / DMSO

3)

IBX / DMSO

4)

IBX / DMSO

Due to the hazardous condition and week solubility in organic solvent IBX has limitations in organic synthesis. Hence the better option in organic synthesis is available as DMP oxidation.

2) Dess–Martin Periodanane (DMP)

The Dess-Martin Periodanane (DMP) is a selective and very mild oxidizing reagent for the oxidation of primary and secondary alcohols to aldehydes or ketones respectively. It is the modified oxidizing reagent originated from IBX as acylated derivative using the same procedure.

Preparation of DMP

2-aminobenzoic acid   2-Iodobenzoic acid I(I)

IBX I(V)   DMP I(V)

It has several advantages over IBX include milder reaction conditions as room temperature, neutral *pH*, shorter reaction time, higher yield of the reaction, simplified workup, high chemoselectivity, tolerance of sensitive functional groups, long shelf life and good solubility in organic solvents. Some applications of DMP oxidation of 1° or 2° alcohols to aldehydes or ketones respectively as below.

1) Benzyl alcohol $\xrightarrow{\text{DMP}}$ Benzaldehyde

2) 1-Phenylethanol $\xrightarrow{\text{DMP}}$ Acetophenone

3) 2-(Tetrahydrofuran-2-yl)ethanol $\xrightarrow{\text{DMP}}$ 2-(Tetrahydrofuran-2-yl)acetaldehyde

4) 2-Cyclohexen-1-ol $\xrightarrow{\text{DMP}}$ 2-Cyclohexen-1-one

5) Ph–C≡C–CH$_2$OH $\xrightarrow{\text{DMP}}$ Ph–C≡C–CHO

6) 1,3-Diphenyl-1-propanol $\xrightarrow{\text{DMP}}$ 1,3-Diphenyl-1-propanone

7) 2-Phenylethanol $\xrightarrow{\text{DMP}}$ Phenylacetaldehyde

8) Cyclohexanol $\xrightarrow{\text{DMP}}$ Cyclohexanone

9) H$_3$C–CH=CH–CH$_2$–CH(OH)–CH$_3$ $\xrightarrow{\text{DMP}}$ H$_3$C–CH=CH–CH$_2$–CO–CH$_3$

10) 2-Acetoxy-3-cyclopentenol $\xrightarrow{\text{DMP}}$ 2-Acetoxy-3-cyclopentenone

11) Ph, OH, OH, Ph → DMP → Ph, OH, O, Ph

12) Ph, OH, OH, CH_3 → DMP → Ph, OH, O, CH_3

Mechanism

I(V) + R–CH(OH)–R' , –OAc → → R–CO–R' + I(III) + CH_3COOH

c) DMSO Base Reagents

Dimethyl sulfoxide (DMSO) based regents are very mild to do oxidation of alcohols to aldehydes or ketones without use of any heavy metals. There are many DMSO base reagents in organic synthesis as Kornblum oxidation, Barton modification, Moffatt–pfitzner oxidation, Torrsell mechanism, Parikh-Doering oxidation, Corey-Kim oxidation and Swern oxidation.

1) Swern Oxidation

Swern oxidation is a modern method normally preferred in organic synthesis. Where in 1^0 and 2^0 alcohols oxidises to aldehydes and ketones respectively using oxalyl chloride, DMSO and triethylamine as organic base at low temperature. The volatile by-products are dimethylsulfide (Me_2S), carbon monoxide (CO) and carbon dioxide (CO_2). Due to the unpleasant odors of Me_2S and CO is acutely toxic the reaction workup needs to be performed in a fume hood. The over oxidation of aldehyde to carboxylic acid will not occurred hence it is a selective oxidizing reagent for primary alcohols. e.g.

Examples of Swern Oxidation

The oxalyl chloride $(COCl)_2$ is a good effective electrophile reacts with alcohol at low temperature -78°C. There are two parts of the mechanism in first converting DMSO to dimethylsulfonium chloride by treating with oxalyl chloride and in second part dimethylsulfonium chloride reacting to the alcohol which undergo oxidation to have desired product as below.

Mechanism

part a

part b

The reaction temperature must be kept low to avoid side reactions because the oxalyl choride is a good dehydrating agent but temperature colder that -60^{oC} acts as a source of chloride in the reaction. In some reactions the use of triethylamine as the base can lead to epimerization at the carbon *alpha* to the newly formed carbonyl group. To avoid these side reaction bulky bases such as Lithium diisopropylethylamine (LDA) has been used.

2) Corey-Kim Oxidation (DMS/NCS/Et$_3$N)

Corey-Kim oxidation name after American chemist Nobel laureates Elias James Corey and Korean American chemist Choung Un Kim. It is a good oxidizing reagent for oxidation of 1° and 2° alcohols to aldehydes and ketones respectively by reacting dimethyl sulfide (DMS) with N-chlorosuccinimide (NCS) in presence of triethylamine as organic base. Corey-Kim oxidation reaction does require temperature above -25^{oC} whereas Swern oxidation requires very low temperature up -78^{0C} to avoid the by-products formation.

DMS-Dimethylsulfide, NCS- N-Chlorosuccinimide, Et$_3$N- Triethylamine

When Me$_2$S react with NCS results in the formation of an active DMSO species which further reacts with alcohol to give the oxidation product by proton abstraction using organic base Et$_3$N.

Mechanism

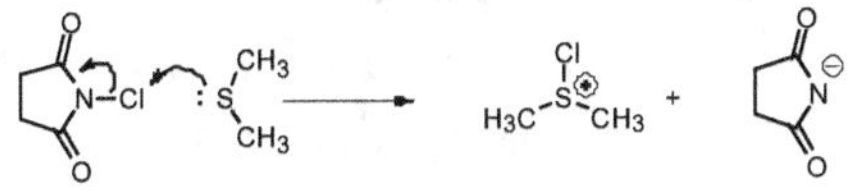

Following steps are similar to the swern oxidation

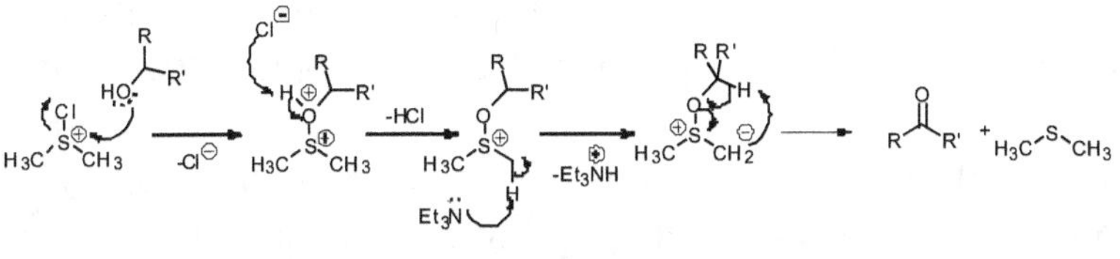

Examples of Corey Kim Oxidation

1)

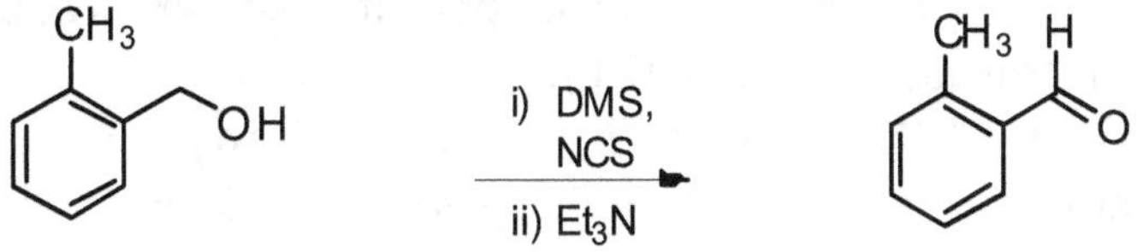

i) DMS, NCS
ii) Et$_3$N

2)

i) DMS, NCS
ii) Et$_3$N

3)

i) DMS, NCS
ii) Et$_3$N

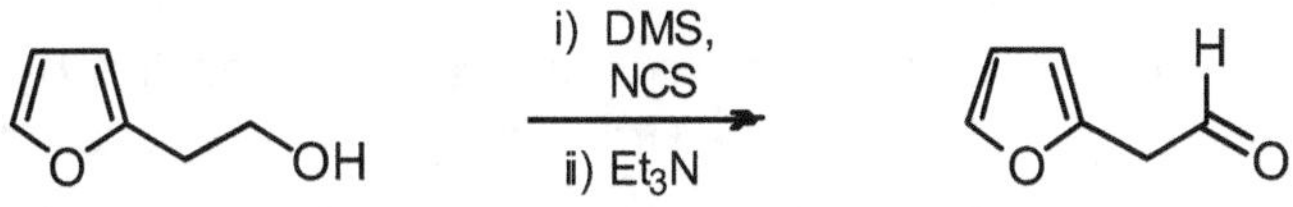

4)

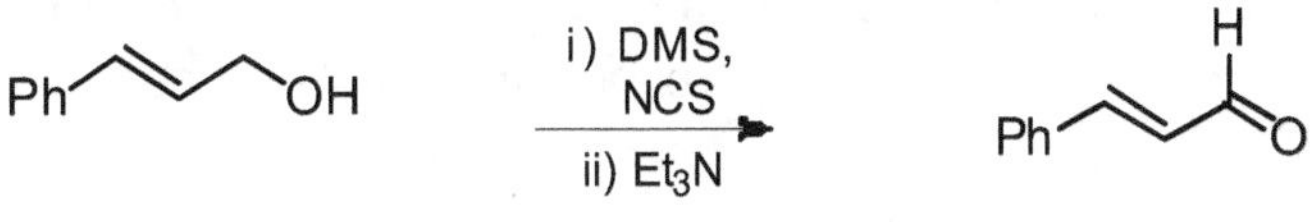

i) DMS, NCS
ii) Et$_3$N

5)

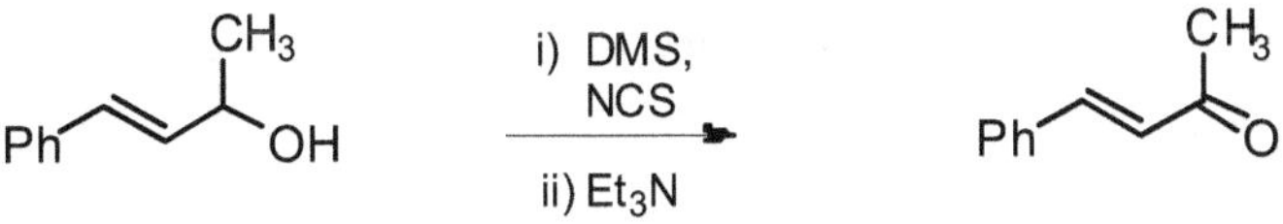

i) DMS, NCS
ii) Et$_3$N

6)

i) DMS, NCS
ii) Et$_3$N

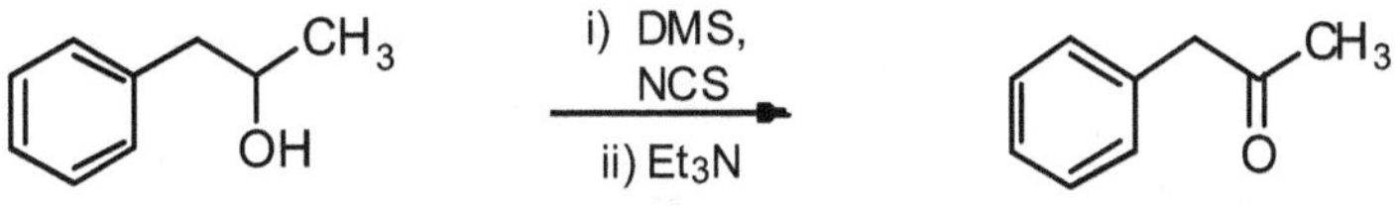

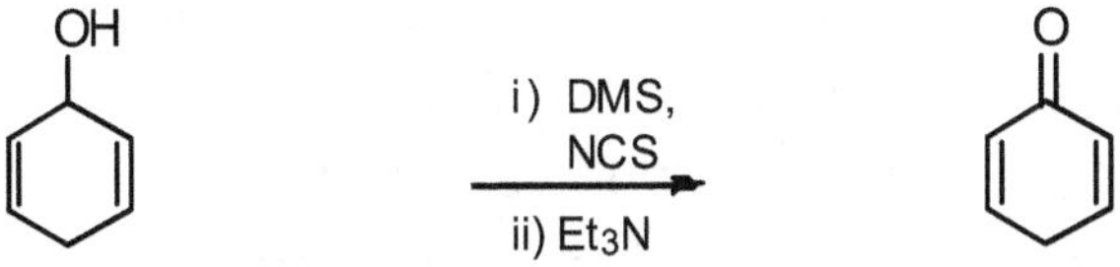

Advantages over Swern Oxidation.

1) Corey Kim Oxidation requires little higher temperature -25^{0C} than Swern oxidation -78^{0C}.

2) The reagent generated *in situ* "active DMSO" species which react with alcohol to have oxidised product where as in Swern oxidation oxalyl chloride as electrophile react with DMSO.

3) Use of oxalyl chloride is substituted with safe NCS in Corey-Kim oxidation and it's always a choice to use less noxious chemical safety point of view.

4) As like Swern oxidation, it does not produce any harmful gases (CO and CO_2).

5) As in part 'b' of the Swern oxidation the temperature of the reaction should be -78^{0C} to react the alcohol with dimethylchlorosulfonium ion to form alkoxysulfonium ion, where as in Corey-Kim oxidation in part 'b' the temperature condition is normal.

Limitations of Corey-Kim Oxidation

Corey-Kim oxidation has the issue of selectivity in case of substrates, as it is susceptible to chlorination by NCS (N-Chlorosuccinamide). The NCS/NBS are good reagent for allylic or benzylic chlorination/bromination under the Corey-Kim reaction conditions. The allylic and benzylic alcohols have a tendency to form the corresponding allyl and benzyl chloride or bromide unless the alcohol activation is very quickly followed by addition of triethylamine as organic base. If triethylamine avoid adding in reaction mixture the product affords will be the allyl or benzyl chloride in presence of other alcohols.

3) Pfitzner-Moffatt Oxidation (DMSO/DCC)

This reagent was first reported by J. Moffatt and his student K. Pfitzner in the year 1963 and reagent name is after their names. It is good oxidising reagent oxidises 1^{0} and 2^{0} alcohols to aldehydes and ketones respectively. The oxidant reagent is a combination of DMSO and DCC (Dicyclohexyl carbodiimide) at room temp. This oxidation was remarkable because it succeeded in sensitive substrates and no trace of over oxidation to carboxylic acid was detected in the oxidation of primary alcohols.

The active DMSO species of this reaction is bulkier than the Swern and Corey-Kim oxidation, hence its advantage of the fact that this reagent tends to be selective to steric influence and it is possible to oxidise less hindered hydroxyl groups selectively and this reaction can be carried out at room temperature. This reagent has some disadvantages including the removal of the cyclohexyl urea as by-product and the competitive reaction to methylthiomethyl ether formation.

e.g.

DMSO - Dimethylsulfoxide, DCC - Dicydohexylcarbodiimide

Mechanism

Examples of Pfitzner Moffatt Oxidation

1)

2) 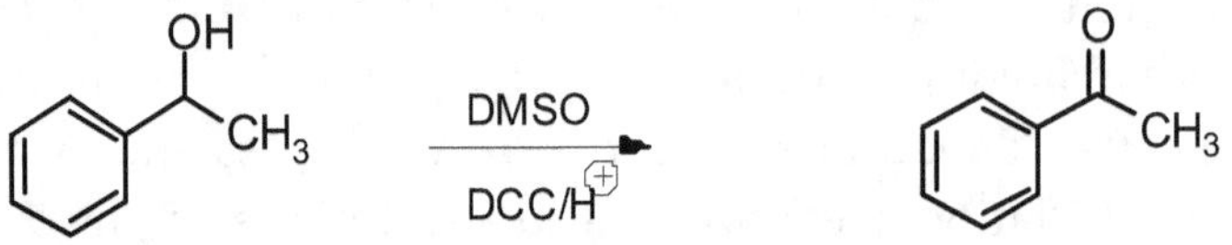 Ph–CH(OH)–CH₃ $\xrightarrow[\text{DCC/H}^{\oplus}]{\text{DMSO}}$ Ph–CO–CH₃

3) 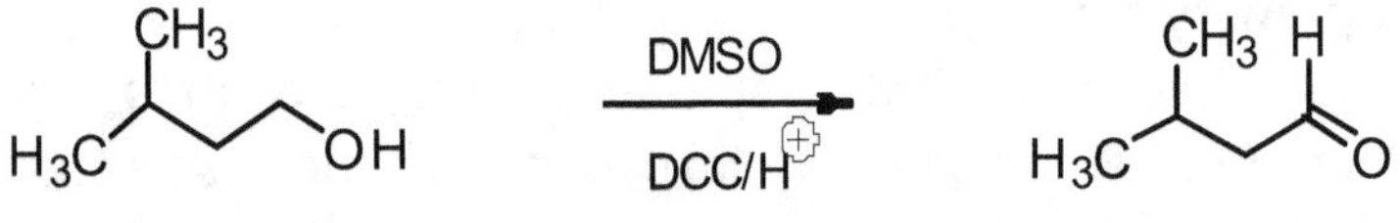 (CH₃)₂CH–CH₂–CH₂–OH $\xrightarrow[\text{DCC/H}^{\oplus}]{\text{DMSO}}$ (CH₃)₂CH–CH₂–CHO

4) 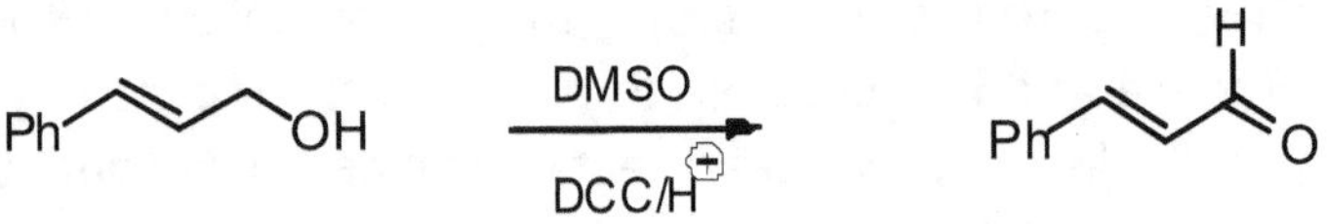 Ph–CH=CH–CH₂–OH $\xrightarrow[\text{DCC/H}^{\oplus}]{\text{DMSO}}$ Ph–CH=CH–CHO

5) 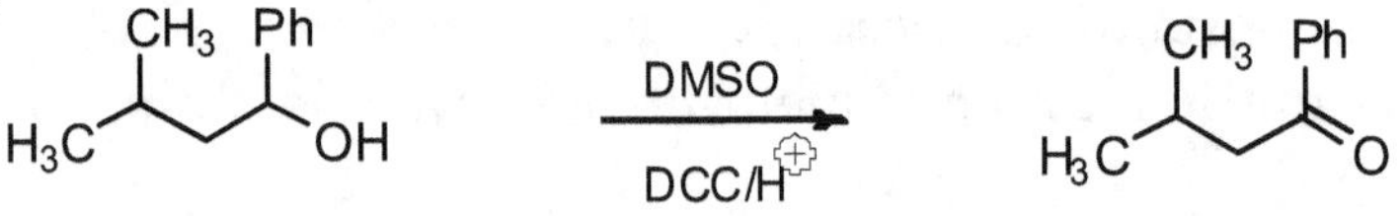 (CH₃)(H₃C)CH–CH₂–CH(Ph)–OH $\xrightarrow[\text{DCC/H}^{\oplus}]{\text{DMSO}}$ (CH₃)(H₃C)CH–CH₂–CO–Ph

6) 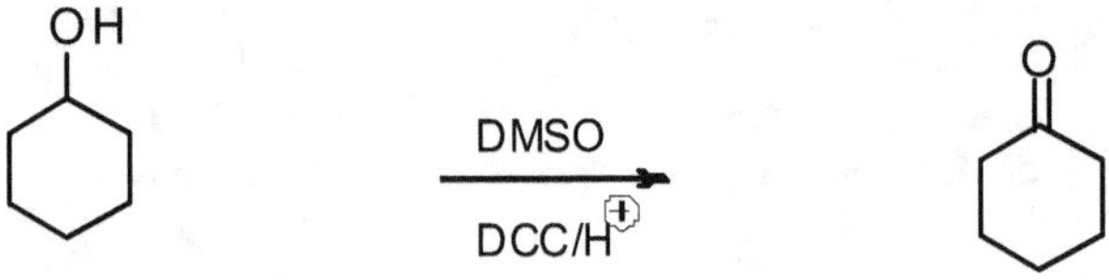 cyclohexanol $\xrightarrow[\text{DCC/H}^{\oplus}]{\text{DMSO}}$ cyclohexanone

4) Oppenauer Oxidation

Viktor Oppenauer has discovered first this type of oxidation of secondary alcohol to ketones in presence of aluminium isopropoxide and excess of acetone as solvent. This shifts the equilibrium towards the product side according to Le-Chatelier's principle. This reagent is highly selective for secondary alcohols and does not oxidises others sensitive functional groups such as amines, aldehyde, olefinic, acetylenic bonds and sulfides.

The primary alcohols are seldom oxidized by this method due to competing aldol condensation of aldehyde the products formed in the reaction and acid labile substrates are also oxidized by this reagent. This reagent has been largely used due to its relatively mild oxidising and non-toxic in nature as compare to other reagents. The Oppenauer oxidation is commonly used in various industrial processes such as the synthesis of steroids, hormones, alkaloids and terpenes etc. "This reaction is the opposite of the Meerwein-Ponndort-Verley reduction"

e.g.

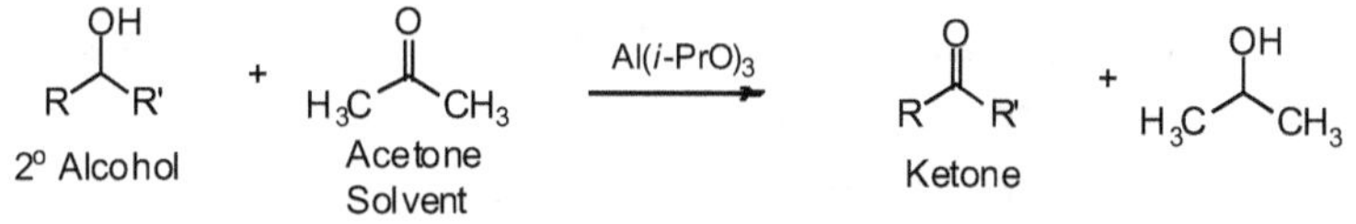

Al(i-PrO)$_3$-Aluminium isopropoxide

Mechanism

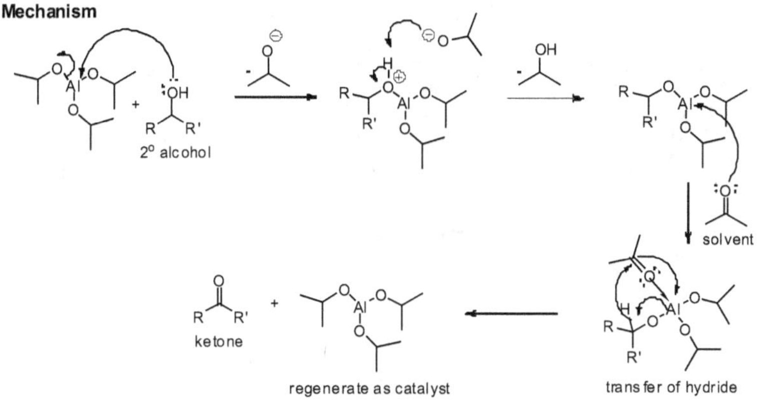

regenerate as catalyst

transfer of hydride

Examples of Oppenauer Oxidation

1)

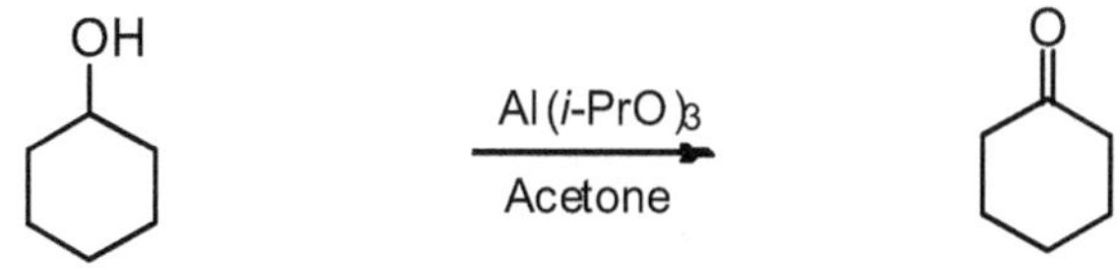

$$Al(i\text{-}PrO)_3 / Acetone$$

2)

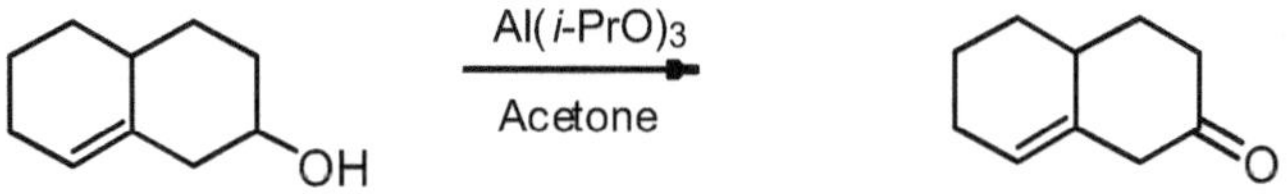

$$Al(i\text{-}PrO)_3 / Acetone$$

3)

$$Al(i\text{-}PrO)_3 / Acetone$$

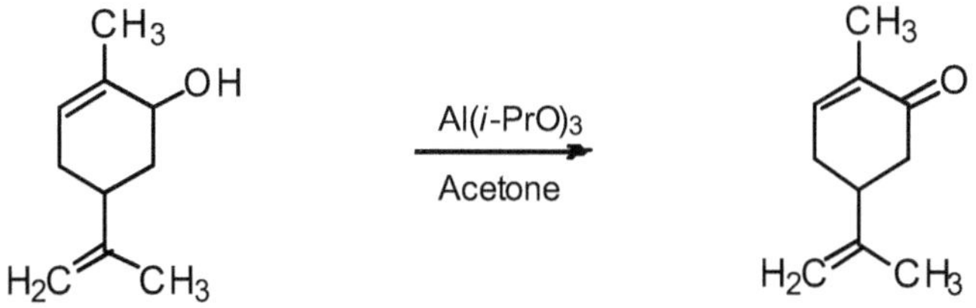

4)

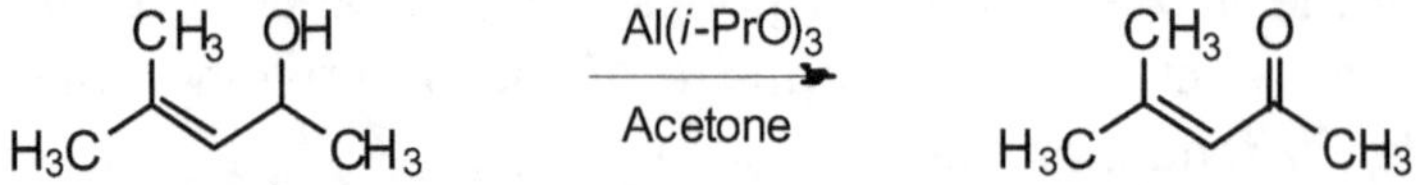

$$\text{(CH}_3\text{,OH substituted alkene)} \xrightarrow[\text{Acetone}]{\text{Al}(i\text{-PrO})_3} \text{(CH}_3\text{,O enone product)}$$

  The oxidation of 1° alcohol has limitations as the product formed as aldehyde undergoes condensation reaction with solvent acetone in the presence of Al(t-BuO)$_3$. However aldehyde can be prepared by this method if oxidant (hydride acceptor) is p-benzoquinone used.

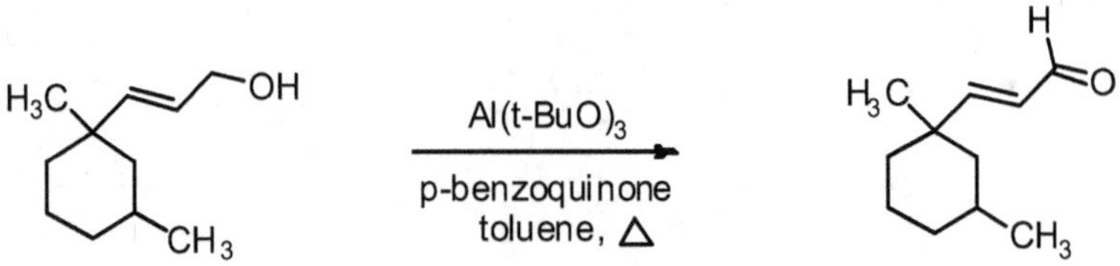

$$\text{(allylic alcohol)} \xrightarrow[\substack{p\text{-benzoquinone}\\ \text{toluene, }\triangle}]{\text{Al}(t\text{-BuO})_3} \text{(aldehyde)}$$

❏ ❏ ❏

Chapter 2

III) Oxidation Involving C-C bond cleavage

There are a variety of oxidizing reagents in which C-C, C=C or C≡C bonds undergo cleave to oxygenated products as mostly carbonyl compounds.

a) Oxidation/Cleavage of Glycols using HIO_4

1) HIO_4 (Periodic acid)

HIO_4 is the most common reagent used for vicinal diol (glycol) cleavage and this reaction is known as Malaprade oxidation as the reaction was first reported by Leon Malaprade in 1934. The products of oxidation reaction depend upon the substitution pattern of the diols as it may be either ketones, aldehydes or carboxylic acids. Glycol cleavage is an important reaction in the laboratory because it is useful for determining the structures of sugars. In the process of oxidation each vicinal diol group consumes one mole of the reagent for the breaking of carbon carbon bond.

❖ Periodic acid is the highest oxo-acid of Iodine, in which the Iodine exists in oxidation state VII. It exist in two forms *ortho* and *meta* periodic acid H_5IO_6 and HIO_4 respectively. Periodic acid was discovered by Heinrich Gustav Magnus and C.E. Ammermüller in 1833.❖

One bond Cleavage leads to two aldehyde formation

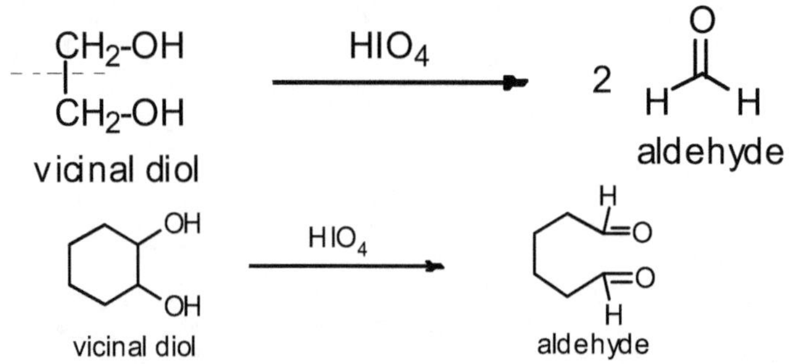

Two bonds Cleavage leads to ketone, aldehyde and Carboxylic acid formation

Two vicinal diol

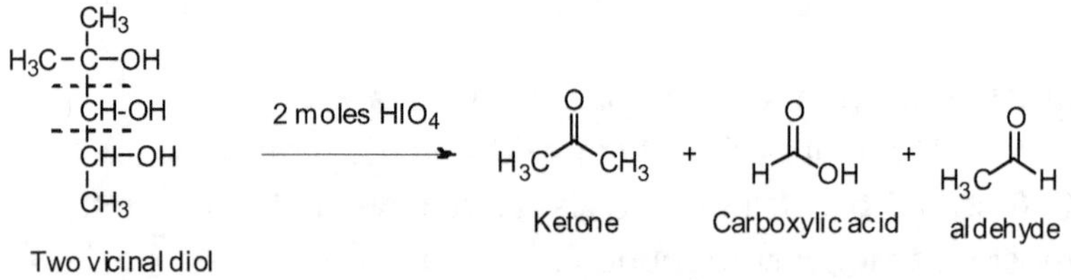

In the course of oxidation, if there is a cleavage of only one bond having hydroxyl group then the carbon having hydroxyl group converts into carbonyl group as aldehydes or ketones. Whereas cleavage of two bonds of the same carbon having hydroxyl group then one middle carbon having hydroxyl group oxidizes to the carboxylic acid.

four bonds Cleavage leads to two aldehyde and 3 Carboxylic acid formation

Four vicinal diol

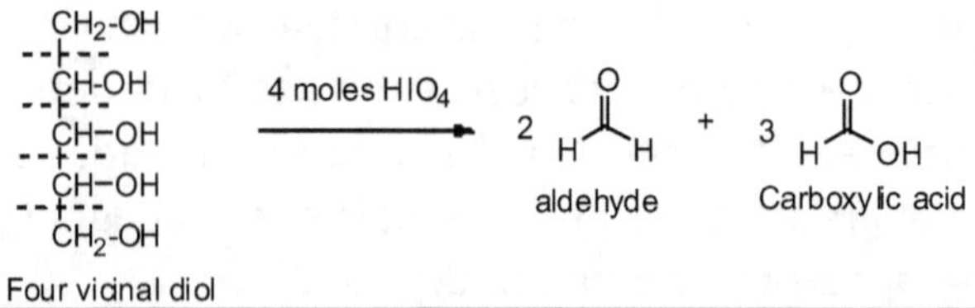

In the case of oxidation of α-hydroxy carbonyl compounds as aldehyde always oxidizes into carboxylic acid, whereas ketone carbonyl group oxidizes to CO_2 gas.

$$
\begin{array}{c}
CHO \\
| \\
CH\text{-}OH \\
| \\
CH\text{-}OH \\
| \\
CH_3
\end{array}
\xrightarrow{\text{2 moles } HIO_4}
2\ \underset{\text{Carboxylic acid}}{H\text{-}COOH}
\ +\
\underset{\text{aldehyde}}{H_3C\text{-}CHO}
$$

$$
\begin{array}{c}
CH_2\text{-}OH \\
| \\
C{=}O \\
| \\
CH\text{-}OH \\
| \\
CH_3
\end{array}
\xrightarrow{\text{2 moles } HIO_4}
\underset{\text{Carboxylic acid}}{HCHO}
\ +\
\underset{\text{aldehyde}}{H_3C\text{-}CHO}
\ +\ CO_2
$$

$$
\begin{array}{c}
CHO \\
H\text{—}OH \\
HO\text{—}H \\
H\text{—}OH \\
H\text{—}OH \\
CH_2OH
\end{array}
\qquad \xrightarrow{5\ HIO_4} \qquad
5\ HCOOH\ +\ HCHO
$$

D-Glucose

$$
\begin{array}{c}
CH_2OH \\
{=}O \\
HO\text{—}H \\
H\text{—}OH \\
H\text{—}OH \\
CH_2OH
\end{array}
\qquad \xrightarrow{5\ HIO_4} \qquad
3\ HCOOH\ +\ 2\ HCHO\ +\ CO_2
$$

D-Fructose

The amino group of α-amino alcohols behaves as hydroxyl group and gives same results as in the case of vicinal diols as shown in the below example.

$$
\begin{array}{c}
CH_2\text{-}OH \\
| \\
CH_2\text{-}NH_2
\end{array}
\qquad \xrightarrow{HIO_4} \qquad
2\ \underset{\text{aldehyde}}{H\text{-}CHO}
$$

Examples:- Cleavage of C-C bond of diols to gives aldehyde or Ketones:

1) HIO_4

2) HIO_4

3) HIO_4

4) HIO_4

5) HIO_4

6) HIO_4

7) HIO_4

8) HIO_4

H_5IO_6 (VII)

ortho periodic acid

HIO_4 (VII)

meta periodic acid

Orthoperiodic acid can be dehydrated to give metaperiodic acid by heating to 100^{0C}.

$$H_5IO_6 \rightleftharpoons HIO_4 \; + \; 2H_2O$$

ortho periodic acid   meta periodic acid

General example

Diol   + HIO_4 →   Ketone   +   Aldehyde

Mechanism

$$HIO_3 \; + \; \text{(Ketone)} \; + \; \text{(Aldehyde)}$$

Cleavage of C-C bond of dione to gives dicarboxylic acid by using HIO_4 in presence of alkali as shown in the following examples

e.g

$$\text{dione} \quad \xrightarrow{HIO_4/\overset{\ominus}{O}H} \quad 2 \; RCOOH$$

Mechanism

$$HIO_3 \; + \; 2 \; RCOOH$$

1)

2)

2) Pb(OAC)$_4$ (Lead Tetra-acetate)

Vicinal diols are cleaved under mild condition with Pb(OAc)$_4$) to give carbonyl compounds as aldehydes, ketones or carboxylic acid similar as that of oxidation by HIO$_4$. Oxidation of diols goes through a cyclic intermediate formation with change in oxidation state of Pb(IV) to Pb(II).

1)

2)

3)

4)

D-Glucose

$$5\,HCOOH \; + \; HCHO$$

5)

D-Fructose

$$3\,HCOOH \; + \; 2\,HCHO \; + \; CO_2$$

Mechanism of diol cleavage by Pb(OAc)$_4$

Reactivity of HIO$_4$ and Pb(OAc)$_4$

The two reagents HIO$_4$ (Periodic acid) and Pb(OAc)$_4$ (Lead tetra-acetate) are analogous in term of reactivity but geometrical diol are differ in reactivity as well as reaction conditions since HIO$_4$ is best used in water as solvent and Pb(OAc)$_4$ in organic solvents. Oxidation of *cis*-1,2-diols react more faster than *trans* isomers through cyclic intermediate hence HIO$_4$ could not oxidized below reaction.

Whereas Pb(OAc)$_4$ oxidized the same as it proceed through non cyclic intermediate for such compounds as.

trans

Mechanism

b) Oxidation of cycloalkanones using CrO_3

1) CrO_3 (Chromium trioxide)

Oxidation of cycloalkane i.e. cyclic ketone can bring about under vigorous condition using powerful oxidant as CrO_3, this lead usually to cleavage of the carbon chain adjacent to the carbonyl group to carboxylic acid. If the acidic condition used the Ketone converts to carboxylic acid through enol formation and in the basic condition of reaction goes through enolate formation. It is rarely used in organic synthesis.

1) cyclohexanone $\xrightarrow{CrO_3}$ COOH, COOH (adipic acid)

2) cyclopentanone $\xrightarrow{CrO_3}$ COOH, COOH

3) decalinone $\xrightarrow{CrO_3}$ COOH, COOH

4) cycloheptanone $\xrightarrow{CrO_3}$ COOH, COOH

Mechanism

Chromic acid

CrO_3/H_2O, over-oxidation

c) Oxidative cleavage of carbon-carbon double bonds.

Oxidative cleavage of carbon-carbon double leads to the destruction of both the ó and π bonds and the new bonds introduced between carbon and electronegative elements most commonly as oxygen. The oxidation of an alkene double bond take place with the help of using ozone O_3, $KMnO_4$, CrO_3

and Lemieux reagent (OsO_4 + $NaIO_4$) or ($KMnO_4$ + $NaIO_4$).

1) O_3 (Ozone)

Ozonolysis is the process where ozone (O_3) reacts as an electrophile with alkene double bond forming a primary ozonide which itself rearranged through cleave of C-C bond as a zwitterionic intermediate to an (isolable) ozonide.

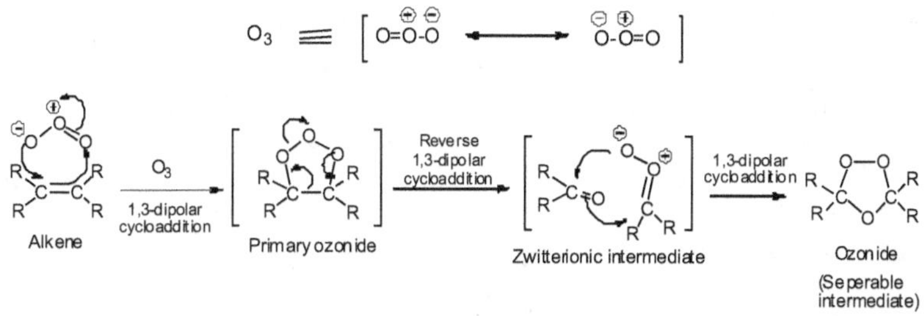

The ozonolysis reaction usually carried out by passing a stream of oxygen containing up to 10% of ozone (O_3) into a reaction solution at very low temperature -78^{0C}. This leads to the formation of ozonide which is dangerously explosive, hence immediately converts into product by reaction workup. It is of two type reaction workups as below.

i) Oxidative workup:- using H_2O_2 or H_2O.

ii) Reductive workup:- using Me_2S or Zn & AcOH.

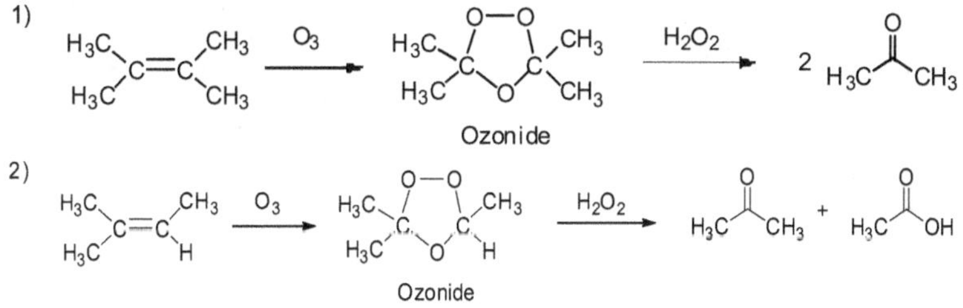

Oxidative workup of ozonide by H_2O_2 or H_2O leads normally to carboxylic acid or ketone and not aldehyde which undergo over-oxidation, where as in reductive workup by Me_2S, decomposed ozonide into aldehyde or ketone. The Zn/AcOH may further reduce the reducible groups; hence Me_2S is always preferred over Zn & AcOH.

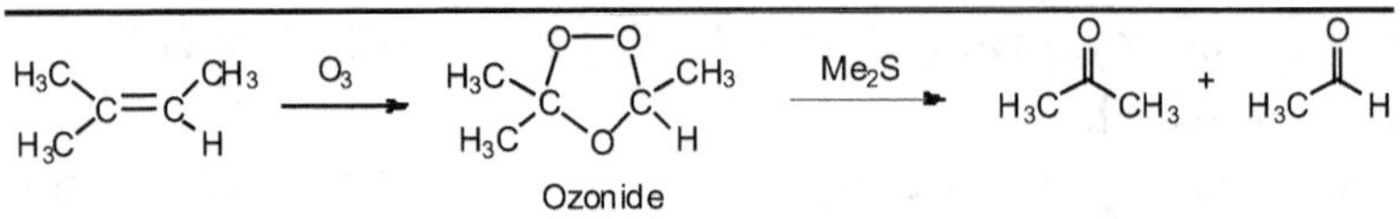

O3
Me2S
Ozonide

Mechanism (Oxidative)

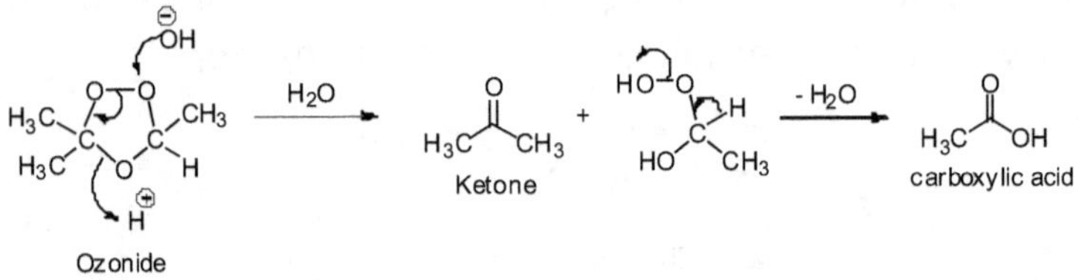

H2O
- H2O
Ketone
carboxylic acid
Ozonide

Mechanism (Reductive)

Ketone
aldehyde

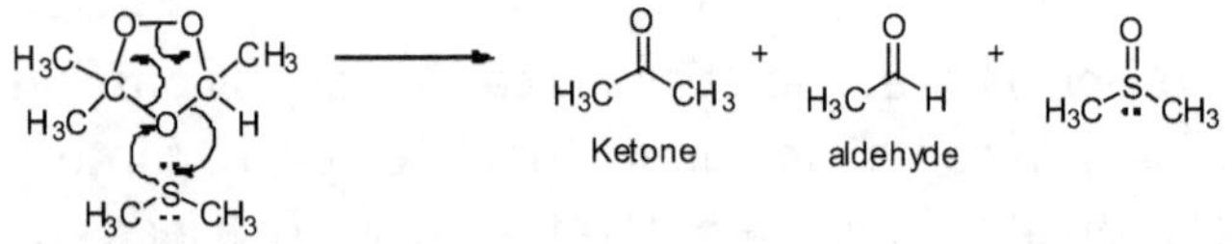

Complete Mechanism of Ozonolysis

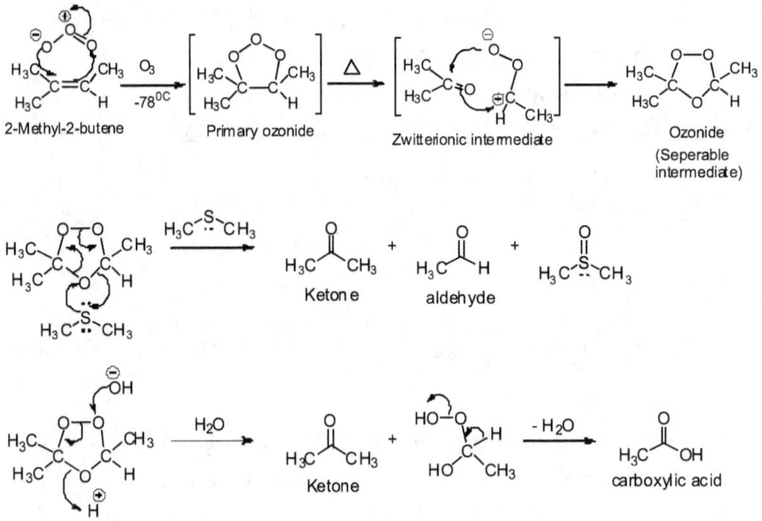

O3
-78⁰C
2-Methyl-2-butene
Primary ozonide
Zwitterionic intermediate
Ozonide
(Seperable intermediate)
Ketone
aldehyde
H2O
- H2O
Ketone
carboxylic acid

Examples of Ozonolysis

1)

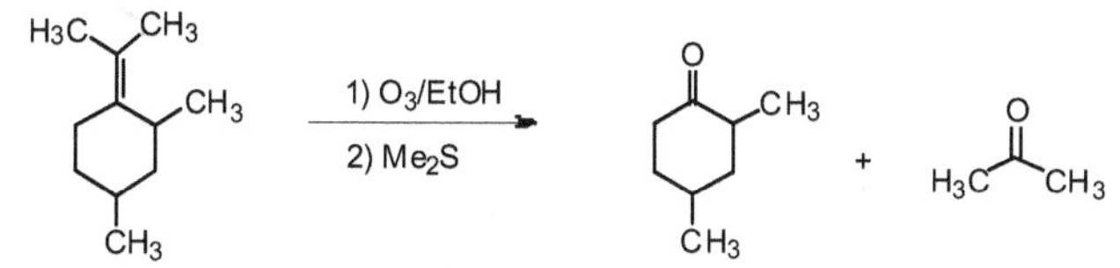

2)

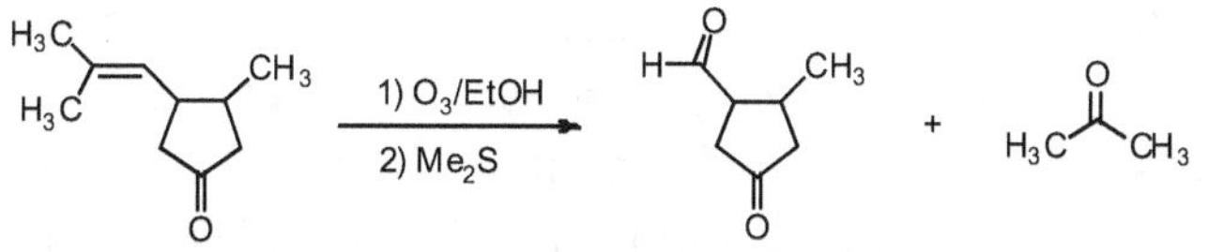

3)

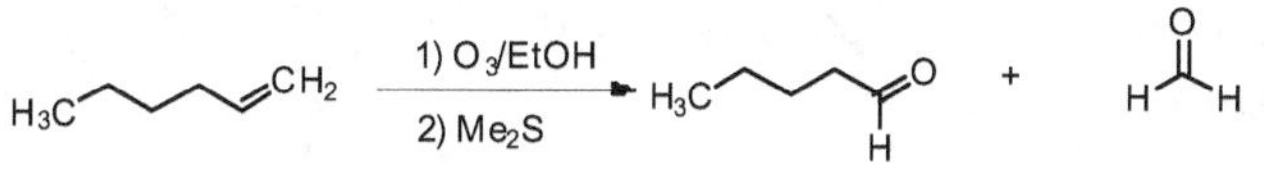

4)

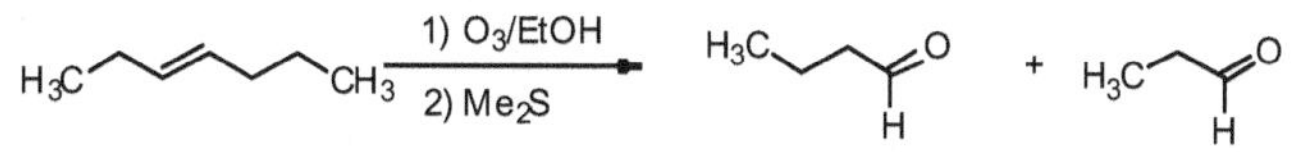

5)

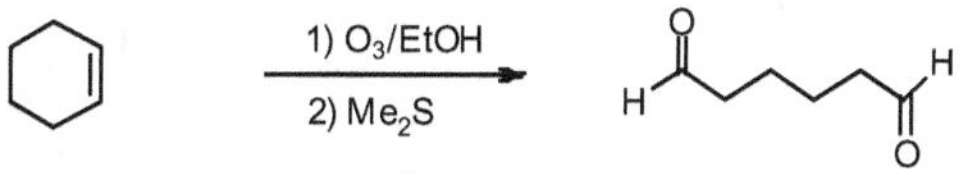

6)

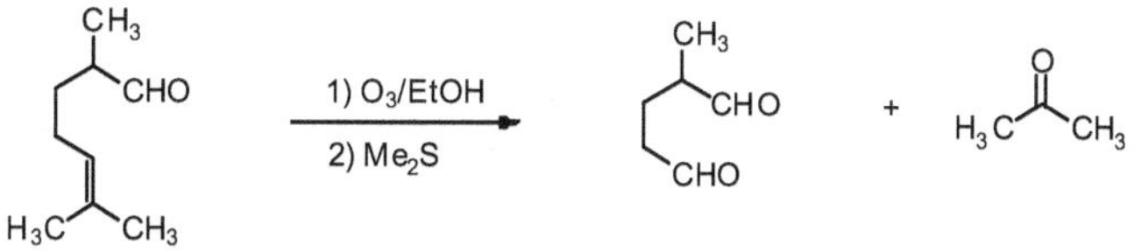

7)

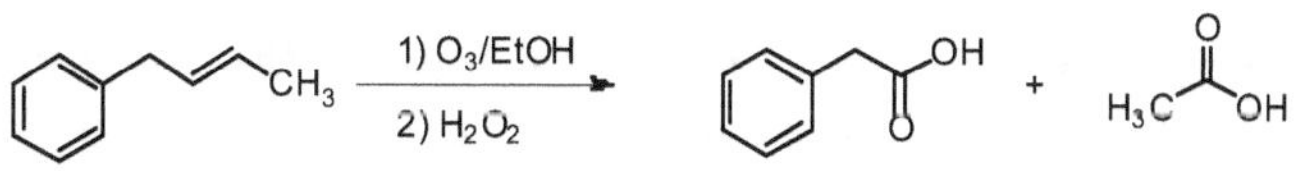

8)

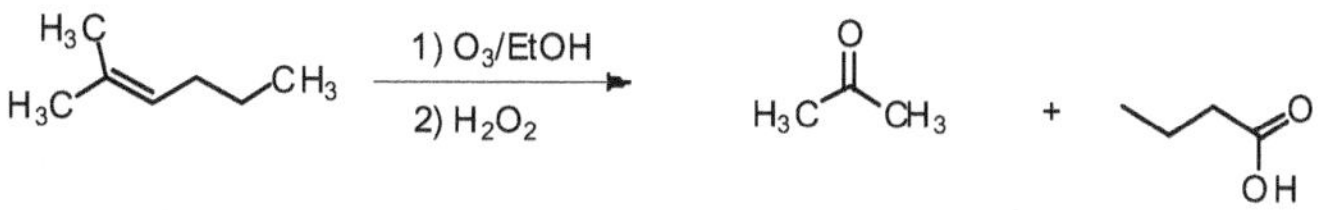

If LiAlH$_4$ as reducing reagent is used instead Me$_2$S in reductive workup furthers reduction give alcohols as the final products as shown in the following examples.

1)

(reaction: H₃C—CH=CH—CH₃ type alkene, 1) O₃ 2) LiAlH₄ → H₃C—CH₂—CH₂—OH + H₃C—CH₂—OH)

2)

(cyclohexene, 1) O₃ 2) LiAlH₄ → diol HO—(CH₂)₆—OH)

Alkynes are also oxidized by ozone but the rate of oxidation reactions is very slow, so selective oxidation of double bond in presence of acetylenic bond will be achieved. Reaction of acetylenic compound and ozone gives carboxylic acids as product with small quantity of α-dicabonyl compounds.

e.g.

$$H_3C-C{\equiv}C-CH_3 \xrightarrow{1)\ O_3} 2\ CH_3\text{-COOH}$$

Butyne

Mechanism

$$H_3C-C{\equiv}C-CH_3 \xrightarrow[-78\,^{0}C]{O_3} \left[\text{Primary ozonide} \right] \xrightarrow{\Delta} \left[\text{Zwitterionic intermediate} \right] \longrightarrow \left[\text{Ozonide} \right]$$

$$2\ CH_3\text{-CO-OH} \xleftarrow{H_2O/H^{\oplus}} H_3C-CO-O-CO-CH_3$$

The aromatic unsubstituted rings are also oxidized with the help of ozone, where the stabilization energy of aromatic ring requires vigorous reaction conditions. The reactions can result either in the cleavage of the ring or in the formation of quinones.

1)

(naphthalene $\xrightarrow{O_3}$ benzene-1,2-dicarboxylic acid with COOH, COOH)

2)

$$\text{(phenanthrene)} \xrightarrow{O_3} \text{(biphenyl-2,2'-dicarboxylic acid, COOH, COOH)}$$

Examples of Ozonolysis.

1)

$$\text{(cyclohexene)} \xrightarrow{O_3} \text{(ozonide)} \xrightarrow{H_2O_2} \text{(COOH, COOH)}$$

2)

$$\xrightarrow[Me_2S]{O_3} \xrightarrow{NaBH_4}$$

3)

$$\xrightarrow[H_2O_2]{O_3} \quad + \quad CH_3\text{-COOH}$$

2) KMnO$_4$ (Potassium permanganate)

KMnO$_4$ is use as oxidizing reagent to oxidized alkene to *cis*-diol and the process is called as *cis*-dihydroxylation. The reaction needs careful control to avoid over oxidation and the best results are obtained in alkaline solution at low temperature using water or aqueous soluble organic solvents as acetone, ethanol or *t*-BuOH. The poor solubility of substrate in aqueous solvent improves by adding phase transfer catalyst (PTC) as quarternary ammonium halide or a crown ethers.

The oxidation with KMnO$_4$ proceed through the formation of cyclic manganate esters as intermediate and which control the *syn* addition of two hydroxyl group. This oxidation reaction is stereospecific as shown in the following examples.

1)

$$\text{(cyclohexene)} \xrightarrow[\substack{KMnO_4 \\ Cold\ condition}]{Alkaline} \text{(cis-diol, OH, OH)}$$

cis-diol

2)

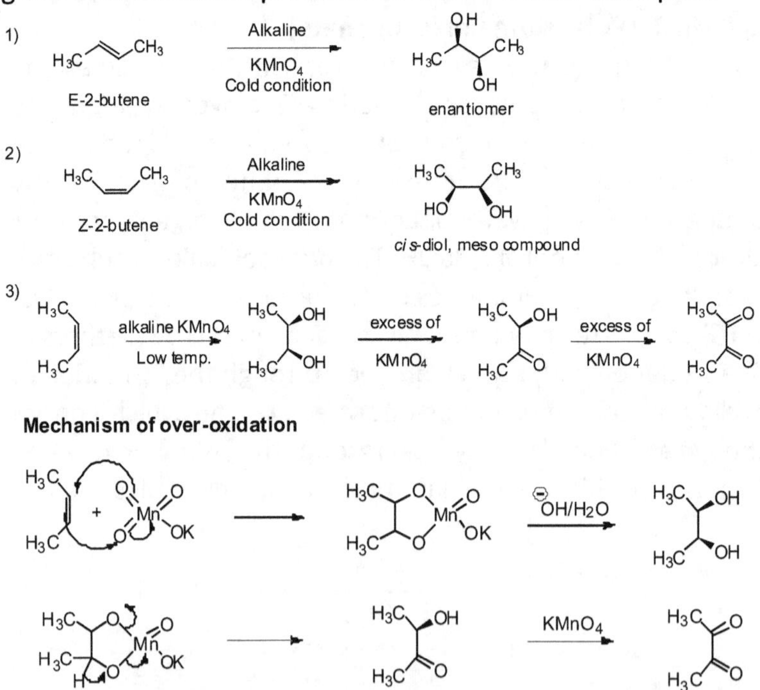

Z-2-butene → Alkaline KMnO₄ Cold condition → *cis*-diol

Mechanism

Mn (VII) → *Syn* Addition → Manganate ester → aq. NaOH → *Cis* Diol

Stereospecific reaction

When Z-2-butene react with alkaline KMnO$_4$ the stereospecifically manganate ester on hydrolysis gives *meso* optically inactive compounds, whereas E-2-butene gives optically active enantiomers and the excess of alkaline KMnO$_4$ gives over-oxidation products as shown below examples.

1) E-2-butene → Alkaline KMnO₄ Cold condition → enantiomer

2) Z-2-butene → Alkaline KMnO₄ Cold condition → *cis*-diol, meso compound

3) → alkaline KMnO₄ Low temp. → excess of KMnO₄ → excess of KMnO₄ →

Mechanism of over-oxidation

Although alkaline $KMnO_4$ gives *cis*-diol through dihydroxylation but use of acidic or neutral $KMnO_4$ changes the path of reaction as the possibility of over oxidation leads to the formation of others products as Ketones, α-hydroxy ketones or carboxylic acid as per the substituents pattern of alkene.

Alkaline condition

Oleic acid $\xrightarrow[\text{Cold condition}]{\text{Alkaline } KMnO_4}$ *cis*-diol

Neutral condition

Oleic acid $\xrightarrow{\text{Neutral } KMnO_4}$

By changing condition to hot acidified $KMnO_4$ the oxidation of alkene to diol which further oxidised to cleavage of carbon-carbon bond to final products are ketones, carboxylic acid or CO_2.

Acidic Condition

1) 3-heptene $\xrightarrow[\Delta]{KMnO_4/H^{\oplus}}$ $H_3C\text{-}COOH$ + $H_3C\text{-}COOH$

2) $\xrightarrow[\Delta]{KMnO_4/H^{\oplus}}$ $H_3C\text{-}CO\text{-}CH_3$ + $H_3C\text{-}COOH$

3) $\xrightarrow[\Delta]{KMnO_4/H^{\oplus}}$ $H_3C\text{-}CO\text{-}CH_3$ + CO_2 + H_2O

4) $\xrightarrow[\Delta]{KMnO_4/H^{\oplus}/H_2O}$ $2\ H_3C\text{-}COOH$

Mechanism for Acidic condition

Oxidation of alkene with $KMnO_4$ gives an alternative method for *cis*-dihydroxylation, avoiding the use of the toxic and expensive reagent as OsO_4 which having same application but less selective and therefore less satisfactory.

1)

Alkaline
$KMnO_4$

2)

$KMnO_4/H^{\oplus}$
or Neutral $KMnO_4$

3)

Alkaline
$KMnO_4$

4)

Alkaline
$KMnO_4$

❖ **Baeyer's Test:** This reaction is also referred as Baeyer's test for unsaturation of organic compounds. The purple color of $KMnO_4$ solution disappears and a cloudy brown color appears caused by the PPT of manganese (IV) oxide (MnO_2)❖

$$R_2C=CR_2 \xrightarrow[\text{NaOH, Cold}]{\text{KMnO}_4} \underset{\underset{\text{OH OH}}{|\quad|}}{R-\overset{R}{\underset{}{C}}-\overset{R}{\underset{}{C}}-R} + MnO_2$$

Diol

Use of PTC as trimethylbutylammonium chloride in the process of dihydroxylation of cyclooctene with alkaline $KMnO_4$ is water soluble and organic cyclooctene will form the two different layers will form, hence used of PTC would preferred as shown below example.

Cyclooctene $\xrightarrow[\text{BnMe}_3\overset{\oplus}{N}\ \overset{\ominus}{Cl}]{\text{KMnO}_4/\text{NaOH}/\text{H}_2\text{O}}$ Cis Diol

Examples of oxidation by KMnO$_4$.

1) $\xrightarrow[\text{Acetone}]{\text{KMnO}_4}$

2) $\xrightarrow[\text{Acetone}]{\text{KMnO}_4}$

3) Ph ... CH_3 $\xrightarrow[\text{Acetone}]{\text{KMnO}_4}$ Ph ... CH_3

4) $\xrightarrow{\text{KMnO}_4}$

5) $\xrightarrow{\text{KMnO}_4}$

6) $\xrightarrow{\text{KMnO}_4}$

3) OsO$_4$ (Osmium Tetroxide)

The most popular oxidising reagent as OsO$_4$ used for *cis*-dihydroxylation of double bond. This reagent can be used stoichiometrically although its expense and toxicity have led to the development of catalytic variants. The addition of an OsO$_4$ to alkene in ether causes the rapid precipitation of a cyclic osmate ester. The reaction is accelerated by tertiary amine and other bases such as pyridine which co-ordinates to the osmium metal. The osmates ester is then hydrolysed commonly with aqueous sodium sulphite to give a *cis*-vicinal diol. This reagent is classic example of a stereospecific oxidation as shown below.

e.g.

There has been considerable debate over the mechanism of the reaction, which has been postulated to proceed by a direct [3+2] cycloaddition or via [2+2] cycloaddition followed by rearrangement to give the intermediate as osmate.

Mechanism

Formation of cyclic osmate ester can be possible by two ways.

a) [3+2] cycloaddition

b) [2+2] cycloaddition

Osmium tetroxide (OsO_4) is expensive, so the conditions were developed that enable it to be used as a catalyst. It is found that 5% mole OsO_4 is sufficient to oxidise an alkene, if a stoichiometric amount of N-Methylmorpholine-N-Oxide (NMO) is used. The NMO in the reaction re-oxidises the Osmium (VI) to Osmium (VIII) *in situ*, thus very small amount of OsO_4 is needed for the oxidation.

OsO_4 is electrophilic reacts with the most electron rich double bond when more than one is present, so that it can be used for regioselective oxidation of double bonds.

It also attacks rigid cyclic systems from the less hindered side.

Oxidation of allylic alcohols with OsO_4 provides a route to 1,2,3-triols normally found in natural products. The reaction of allyl alcohols and allyl ether (Methoxy) with OsO_4 is highly stereospecific giving preferentially the isomer in which the original hydroxyl group or alkoxy group and newly introduced hydroxyl group are in *anti* (erythro) relationship.

The OsO_4 can also be used for the synthesis of vicinal hydroxylamines. The Reactions of alkene with chloramines-T in the presence of catalytic amount of OsO_4 affords the corresponding vicinal hydroxyl toluene-*p*-sulphonamide, which readily convert into the *cis*- hydroxylamine.

Some examples of dihydroxylation by OsO_4

1) Fumaric acid → enantiomers tartaric acid

2) Maleic acid → Meso tartaric acid

3) → enantiomers

4) I$_2$/CH$_3$COOAg/Dry Condition (Prevost Reagent)

The solution of Iodine (I_2) in dry solvent such as CCl_4 mixed with an equivalent amount of dry CH_3COOAg (Silver acetate) or dry PhCOOAg (Silver benzoate) is called as Prevost reagent. This reaction was developed by the French chemist Charles Prevost hence name after him as Prevost reagent. Under the anhydrous condition Prevost reagent converts alkenes into *trans*-1,2-diols, in the reaction course alkenes double bond reacts with Iodine in presence of dry CH_3COOAg (silver acetate) or PhCOOAg (Silver benzoate) to give the iodonium ion. The iodonium ion undergoes SN^2 type of displacement with acetate ion results into the formation of *trans*-iodoacetate which on further intramolecular SN^2 attack gives acetoxonium ion. Due to the dry condition another acetate ion attacked from the back side to have *trans*-diacetate derivatives which on alkaline hydrolysis (saponification) gives *trans*-1,2- diols.

e.g.

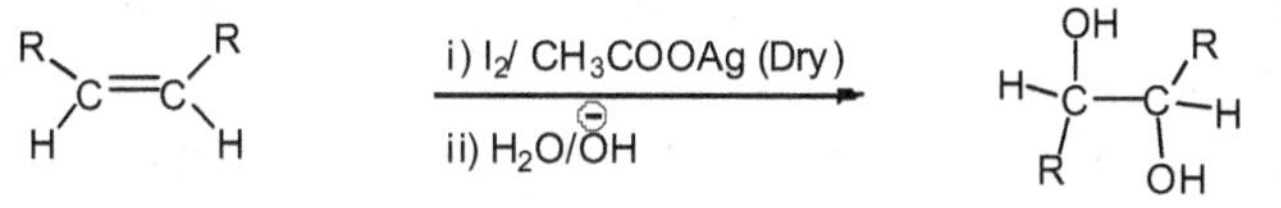

i) I_2/ CH_3COOAg (Dry)
ii) $H_2O/\overset{\ominus}{O}H$

1)

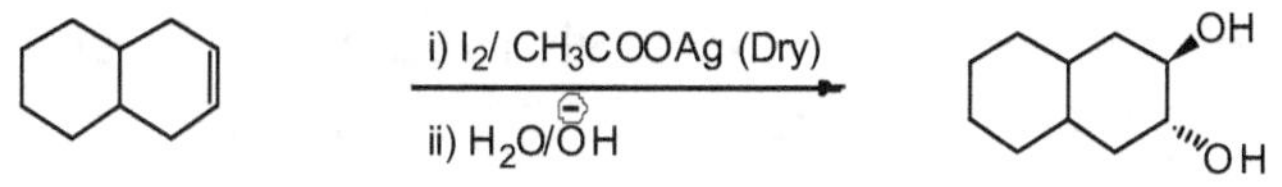

i) I_2/ CH_3COOAg (Dry)
ii) $H_2O/\overset{\ominus}{O}H$

2)

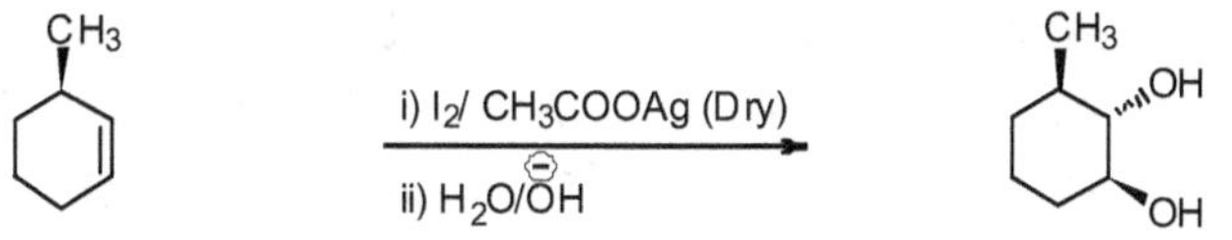

i) I_2/ CH_3COOAg (Dry)
ii) $H_2O/\overset{\ominus}{O}H$

3)

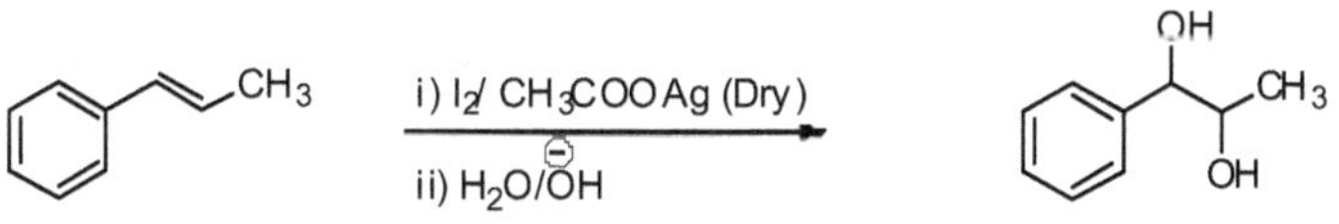

i) I_2/ CH_3COOAg (Dry)
ii) $H_2O/\overset{\ominus}{O}H$

4)

i) I_2/ CH_3COOAg (Dry)
ii) $H_2O/\overset{\ominus}{O}H$

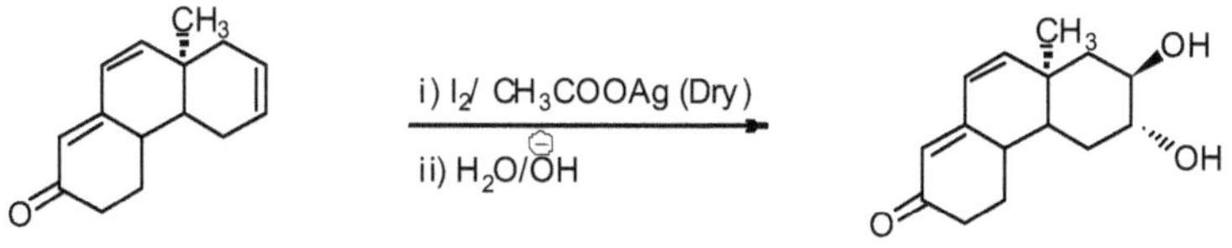

Mechanism (Prevost Reagent)

(scheme with intermediates: iodonium ion, *trans*-iodoacetate, Acetoxonium, Intramolecular SN² reaction, diacetyl derivative, *trans*-1,2-diol)

5) I_2/CH_3COOAg/Wet condition (Woodward Reagent)

The solution of Iodine (I_2) and equimolar CH_3COOAg (silver acetate) or $PhCOOAg$ (Silver benzoate) in moist acetic acid is called as Woodward reagent or Woodward *cis*-hydroxylation reaction. This reaction developed by chemist Robert Burn Woodward hence name after him as Woodward reagent. Under wet or moist condition Woodward reagent converts alkenes into *cis*-1,2-diols in the reaction course alkene double bond reacts with Iodine in presence of CH_3COOAg (silver acetate) or $PhCOOAg$ (Silver benzoate) give iodonium ion. The iodonium ion undergoes SN² displacement with acetate ion to give *trans*-iodoacetate which on further intramolecular SN² reaction with anchimeric assistance (Neighbouring group participation) of acetate group to give a cyclic acetoxonium ion. The same acetoxonium ion on acid hydrolysis give *cis*-hydroxyaceate which on saponification gives *cis*-1,2-diols.

1)

(reaction scheme: octahydronaphthalene with double bond, reagents i) I_2/ CH_3COOAg/CH_3COOH, ii) H_2O/$\overset{\ominus}{O}H$ iii) $H^{\oplus}$/H_2O, giving *cis*-diol product with two OH groups)

2)

(reaction scheme: $H_3C-(CH_2)_7$ and $(CH_2)_7COOH$ across a $C=C$ double bond, reagents i) I_2/ CH_3COOAg/CH_3COOH, ii) H_2O/$\overset{\ominus}{O}H$ iii) $H^{\oplus}$/H_2O, giving diol product with OH OH groups: $H_3C-(CH_2)_7$ and $(CH_2)_7COOH$)

3)

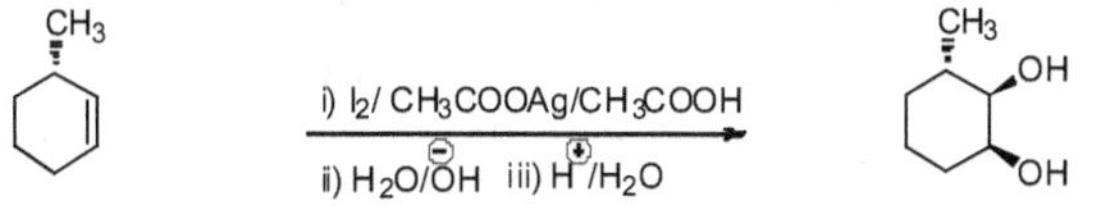

i) I$_2$/ CH$_3$COOAg/CH$_3$COOH

ii) H$_2$O/$\overset{\ominus}{O}$H   iii) H$\overset{\oplus}{}$/H$_2$O

4)

i) I$_2$/ CH$_3$COOAg/CH$_3$COOH

ii) H$_2$O/$\overset{\ominus}{O}$H   iii) H$\overset{\oplus}{}$/H$_2$O

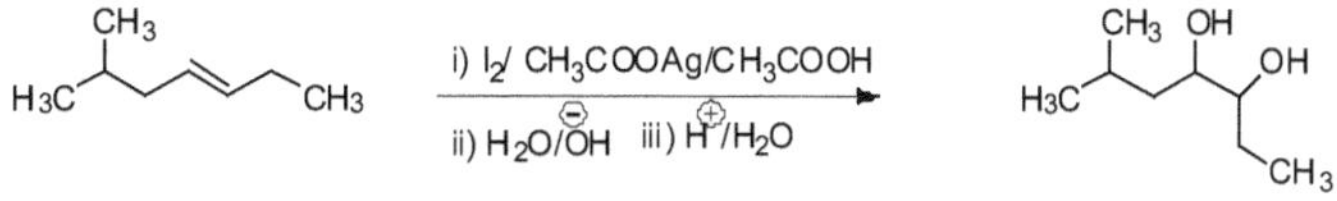

Mechanism (Woodward Reagent)

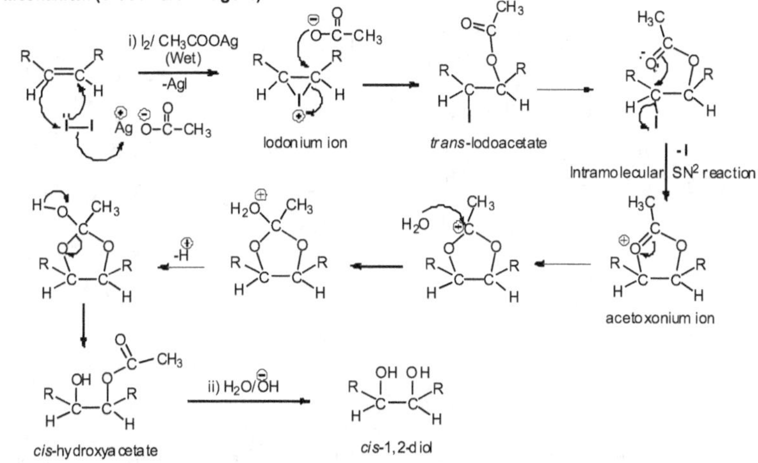

i) I$_2$/ CH$_3$COOAg (Wet) −AgI

Iodonium ion

trans-Iodoacetate

Intramolecular SN^2 reaction

acetoxonium ion

cis-hydroxyacetate

ii) H$_2$O/$\overset{\ominus}{O}$H

cis-1,2-diol

6) OsO$_4$/NaIO$_4$ or KMnO$_4$/NaIO$_4$ (The Lemieux Reagent)

Ozone (O$_3$) is unpleasant to handle and is not selective for alkenes oxidation e.g. secondary alcohols are oxidised to Ketones and tertiary C-H bonds to alcohols. Ozone (O$_3$) has therefore largely been displaced by the Lemieux reagent which consists of dilute aqueous solution NaIO$_4$ (Sodium periodate) with a catalytic amount of KMnO$_4$ or OsO$_4$ respectively. It is the reagents which do the cleavage of double bond of alkene in steps. In each case the double bond oxidised to *cis*-diol which is then cleaved by the NaIO$_4$ to give aldehydes or Ketones and the KMnO$_4$ over-oxidizes aldehydes to carboxylic acids. The low oxidation states of Mn or Os generated during the reactions are re-oxidized by the NaIO$_4$

to their original oxidation state, so that only catalytic amount of reagents are ($KMnO_4$ or OsO_4) required. The reactions are rapid at room temperature and selective for alkenes.

1)

H_3C—C(CH$_3$)=CH—CH_3 $\xrightarrow[NaIO_4]{KMnO_4}$ H_3C-CO-CH_3 + H_3C-CO-OH

2)

H_3C—C(CH$_3$)=CH—CH_3 $\xrightarrow[NaIO_4]{KMnO_4}$ H_3C-CO-CH_3 + H_3C-CO-H

Steps involved into the conversion.

1)

H_3C—C(CH$_3$)=CH—CH_3 $\xrightarrow{KMnO_4}$ (Ph OH diol) $\xrightarrow{NaIO_4}$ H_3C-CO-CH_3 + H_3C-CO-H $\xrightarrow{KMnO_4}$ H_3C-CO-OH

2)

H_3C—C(CH$_3$)=CH—CH_3 $\xrightarrow{OsO_4}$ (H_3C, OH, OH, CH$_3$ diol) $\xrightarrow{NaIO_4}$ H_3C-CO-CH_3 + H_3C-CO-H

No further oxidation of Aldehyde

3)

(CH$_3$ branched aldehyde) $\xrightarrow{KMnO_4}$ (CH$_3$ diol with CHO) $\xrightarrow{NaIO_4}$ H_3C-CO-CH_3 + (CH$_3$ aldehyde-ketone) $\xrightarrow{KMnO_4}$ (CH$_3$ diacid COOH, COOH)

Oxidation by $OsO_4/NaIO_4$ has the advantages over $KMnO_4/NaIO_4$ as it does not proceed beyond the aldehyde state. It produces the same results as ozonolysis followed by reductive cleavage of the ozonide as shown in the following example.

1)

(cyclohexene) $\xrightarrow{KMnO_4}$ (cyclohexane-1,2-diol, OH OH) $\xrightarrow{NaIO_4}$ (CHO CHO) $\xrightarrow{KMnO_4}$ (COOH COOH)

2)

(cyclohexene) $\xrightarrow{OsO_4}$ (cyclohexane-1,2-diol, OH OH) $\xrightarrow{NaIO_4}$ (CHO CHO)

3)

(cyclohexene) $\xrightarrow[Me_2S]{O_3}$ (CHO CHO)

4)

$$\text{cyclohexene} \xrightarrow[H_2O_2]{O_3} \text{(adipic acid: COOH, COOH)}$$

7) CrO_3 (Chromium (VI) Oxide)

The cleavage of C=C bonds with chromic acid is competitive with oxidation of allylic C-H bonds, when cyclohexene treated with CrO_3 gives the product cyclohexenone which further oxidizes to give adipic acid as the product.

e.g.

$$\text{Cyclohexene} \xrightarrow{CrO_3} \text{Cyclohexenone} \xrightarrow{CrO_3} \text{Adipic acid}$$

The use of a partially aqueous medium favours the cleavage process where as an anhydrous medium such as glacial acetic acid favours allylic oxidations. In addition cleavage is promoted by the presence of phenyl substituents, evidently because the first step involves the formations of a carbocation which is stabilized by adjacent aromatic rings.

stable carbocation

Examples of CrO_3 oxidation of olefinic compounds.

1)

$$\xrightarrow{CrO_3} \quad H_3C\text{-CO-}CH_3 \; + \; H_3C\text{-CO-}CH_3$$

2)

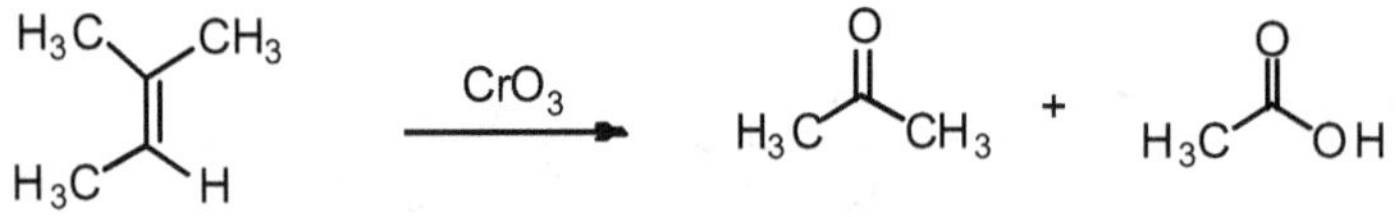

H_3C and CH_3 / H_3C and H alkene $\xrightarrow{CrO_3}$ H_3C-CO-CH_3 + H_3C-CO-OH

3)

(cyclohexylidene with CH_3) $\xrightarrow{CrO_3}$ (cyclohexanone) + H_3C-CO-OH

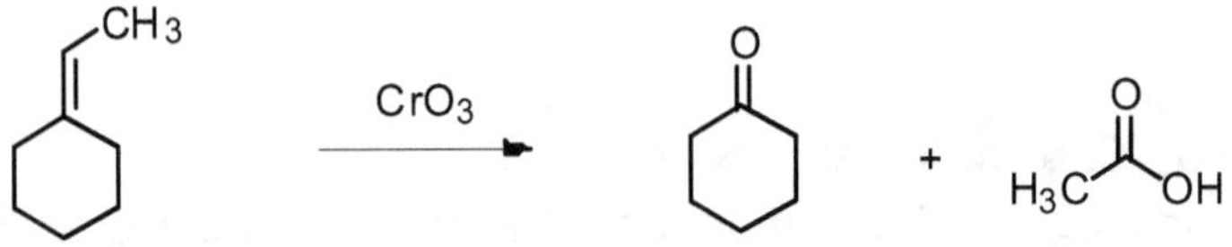

d) Oxidation of Aromatic Rings Using

1) $RuO_4/NaIO_4$

RuO_4 is another excellent oxidizing reagent for cleavage of carbon-carbon double bond as well the aromatic ring and variety of functional groups at room temperature. Since RuO_4 is costly, it is convenient to use catalytic amount of RuO_4 in the presence of $NaIO_4$, which re-oxidizes the reduced Ruthenium Ru (VI) to Ru (VIII) back to the active tetroxide *in situ* in solvent CCl_4 and CH_3CN. The carboxylic acids are normally produced from mono or 1,2-disubtituted alkene and aromatic ring cleaved to dicarboxylic acid if its fused and mono carboxylic when as separated by one bond. RuO_4 and $NaIO_4$ is good alternative to oxidative ozonolysis, $KMnO_4/NaIO_4$ as well $OsO_4/NaIO_4$ too.

1)

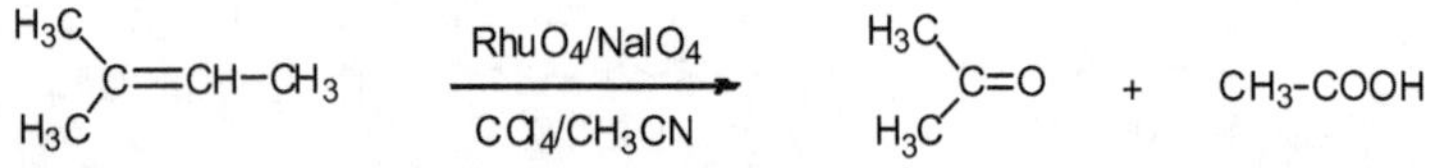

H_3C-C(H_3C)=CH-CH_3 $\xrightarrow[CCl_4/CH_3CN]{RuO_4/NaIO_4}$ H_3C-C(H_3C)=O + CH_3-COOH

2)

(cyclohexene) $\xrightarrow[CCl_4/CH_3CN]{RuO_4/NaIO_4}$ (chain with COOH, COOH)

3)

(naphthalene) $\xrightarrow[CCl_4/CH_3CN]{RuO_4/NaIO_4}$ (benzene ring with COOH, COOH)

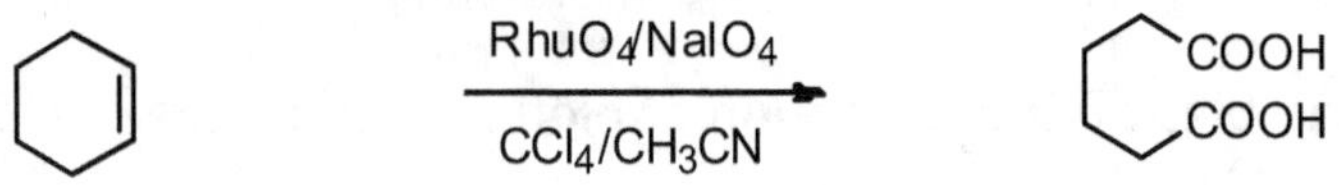

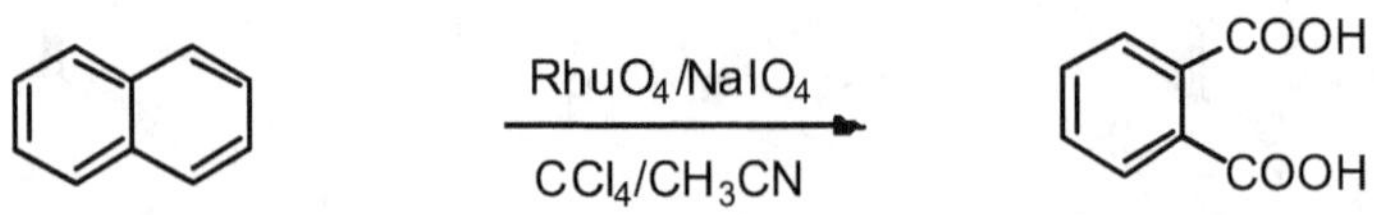

4)

$$\text{Cyclohexyl-benzene} \xrightarrow[\text{CCl}_4/\text{CH}_3\text{CN}]{\text{RhuO}_4/\text{NaIO}_4} \text{Cyclohexyl-COOH}$$

5)

$$\text{Quinoline} \xrightarrow[\text{CCl}_4/\text{CH}_3\text{CN}]{\text{RhuO}_4/\text{NaIO}_4} \text{pyridine-2,3-dicarboxylic acid}$$

6)

$$\text{Isoquinoline} \xrightarrow[\text{CCl}_4/\text{CH}_3\text{CN}]{\text{RhuO}_4/\text{NaIO}_4} \text{benzene-1,2-dicarboxylic acid}$$

Other functional groups such as alcohols e.g. primary alcohols oxidises to carboxylic acid and secondary alcohols oxidises to Ketones. Ethers in which at least one group in primary alkyl can be oxidizes to corresponding ester in high yield. Internal alkynes have been oxidized to -diketones and RuO_4 has number effect on ester and epoxide.

1)

$$\text{Ph}-\text{epoxide}-\text{CH}_2\text{OH} \xrightarrow[\text{CCl}_4/\text{CH}_3\text{CN}]{\text{RhuO}_4/\text{NaIO}_4} \text{Ph}-\text{epoxide}-\text{COOH}$$

2)

$$\text{4-hydroxycyclohexyl-COOCH}_2\text{-CH}_3 \xrightarrow[\text{CCl}_4/\text{CH}_3\text{CN}]{\text{RhuO}_4/\text{NaIO}_4} \text{4-oxocyclohexyl-COOCH}_2\text{CH}_3$$

3)

$$\text{epoxycyclohexyl-CH}_2\text{-CH}_2\text{-OH} \xrightarrow[\text{CCl}_4/\text{CH}_3\text{CN}]{\text{RhuO}_4/\text{NaIO}_4} \text{epoxycyclohexyl-CH}_2\text{-COOH}$$

4)

$$\text{H}_3\text{C-H}_2\text{C}-\text{C}\equiv\text{C}-\text{CH}_2\text{-CH}_3 \xrightarrow[\text{CCl}_4/\text{CH}_3\text{CN}]{\text{RhuO}_4/\text{NaIO}_4} \text{H}_3\text{C-H}_2\text{C}-\overset{\text{O}}{\overset{\|}{\text{C}}}-\overset{\text{O}}{\overset{\|}{\text{C}}}-\text{CH}_2\text{-CH}_3$$

5)

$$\text{(silyl ether tetrahydrofuran)} \xrightarrow[\text{CCl}_4/\text{CH}_3\text{CN}]{\text{RhuO}_4/\text{NaIO}_4} \text{(lactone)}$$

Preparation: RuO_4 is prepared by oxidation of $RuCl_3$ Ruthenium (III) Chloride with $NaIO_4$.

$$RuCl_3 \xrightarrow{\quad NaIO_4 \quad} RuO_4$$

Ru(III)   Ru(VIII)

Mechanism

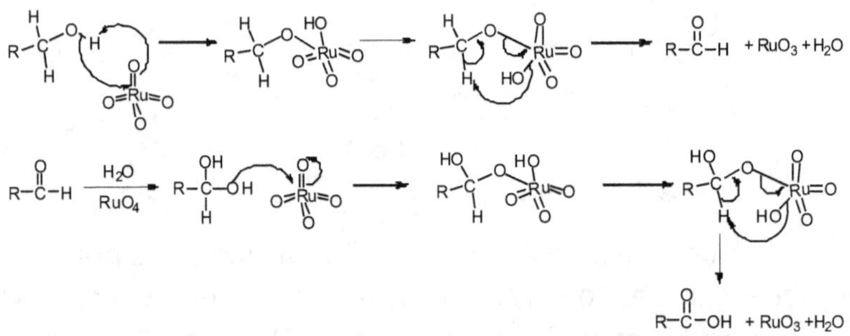

2) V_2O_5 **(Vanadium Pentoxide)**

Benzene ring is remarkably stable and is not affected by common oxidizing reagent hence in chemical reactions benzene is used as a solvent in the many organic reactions. But benzene and its fused derivatives undergoes aerial oxidation in the presence of V_2O_5 as shown in the following examples.

1)

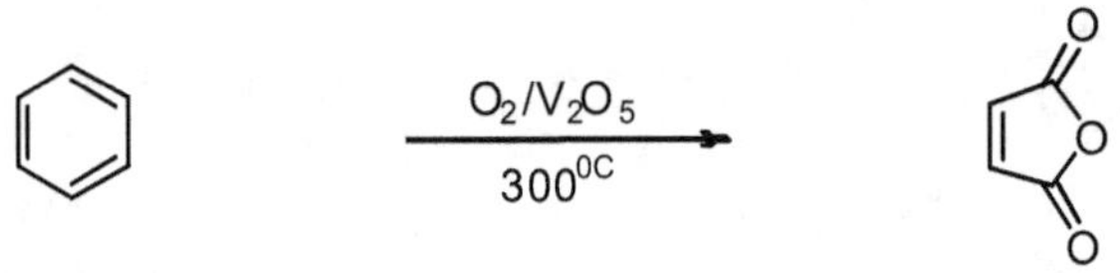

$$\xrightarrow[300^0C]{O_2/V_2O_5}$$

2)

$$\xrightarrow[300^0C]{O_2/V_2O_5}$$

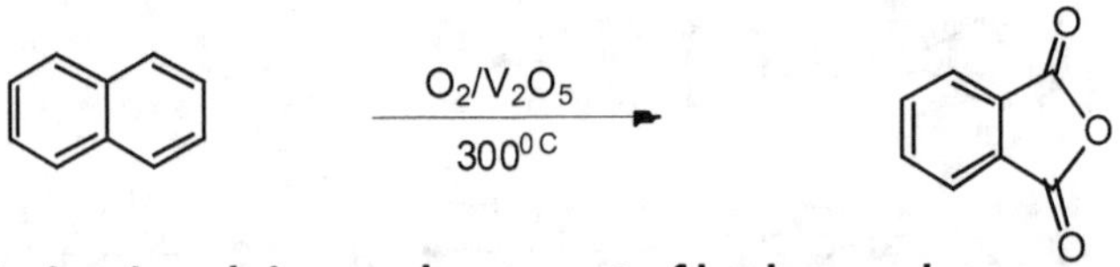

IV) Oxidation involving replacement of hydrogen by oxygen.
a) Oxidation of CH_2 to CO by using following reagents
1) SeO_2 (Riley Oxidation)

The Riley Oxidation is selenium dioxide mediated oxidation of methylene group adjacent to α-carbonyl group of aldehyde or Ketone. The oxidation of α-carbon of carbonyl compounds can only be possible if carbon has at least two hydrogens. If α-carbon is methylene ($-CH_2-$) then it is oxidized into carbonyl group ($-CO-$). If the α-carbon is $-CH_3$ group then it can be oxidizes into aldehyde ($-CHO$) group as shown in the following examples.

1)

$$\xrightarrow[\text{t-BuOOH}]{\text{SeO}_2}$$

2)

$$\xrightarrow[\text{t-BuO OH}]{\text{SeO}_2}$$

3)

$$\xrightarrow[\text{t-BuO OH}]{\text{SeO}_2}$$

4)

$$\xrightarrow[\text{t-BuOOH}]{\text{SeO}_2}$$

5)

$$\xrightarrow[\text{t-BuOOH}]{\text{SeO}_2}$$

6)

$$\xrightarrow[\text{t-BuOOH}]{\text{SeO}_2}$$

In the oxidation process SeO_2 acts as good electrophile and enol form of aldehydes or ketones can be attack very easily as shown in mechanism. The SeO_2 oxidation is convenient way to carry out the reaction in presence of only catalytic amount of SeO_2 along with co-oxidant as *t*-BuOOH (tertiary butylhydroperoxide) that re-oxidizes the selenium (II) compound formed after chemical reaction to Selenium (IV) dioxide again and this makes reagent to used in catalytic amount as the reagent is expensive, toxic and smelly. SeO_2 is a colorless solid, it exist as one dimensional polymeric chain with alternating Selenium and oxygen atom as below.

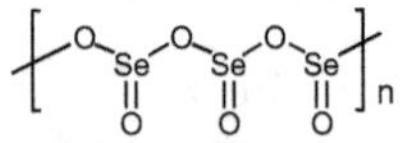

Mechanism

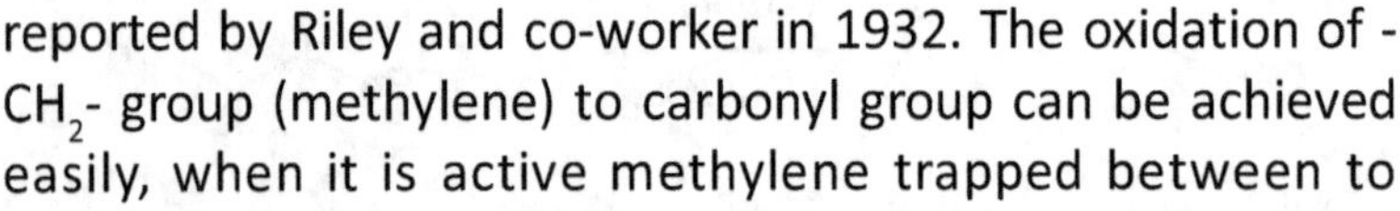

Oxidation at α-carbon of carbonyl group by selenium dioxide is known as Riley oxidation reaction. It was first reported by Riley and co-worker in 1932. The oxidation of - CH_2- group (methylene) to carbonyl group can be achieved easily, when it is active methylene trapped between to carbonyl groups. SeO_2 oxidizes ethylmalonate directly to ethyl mesoxalate.

1)

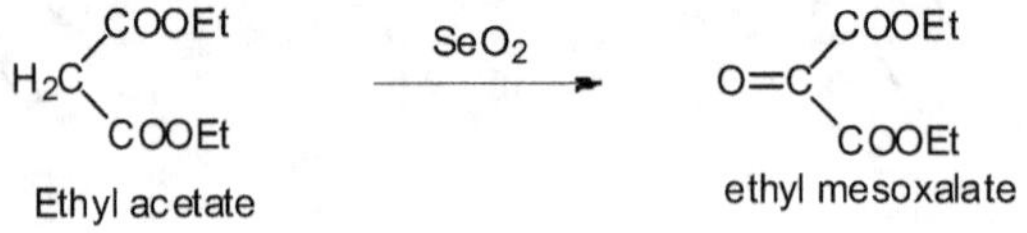

Ethyl acetate

ethyl mesoxalate

2)

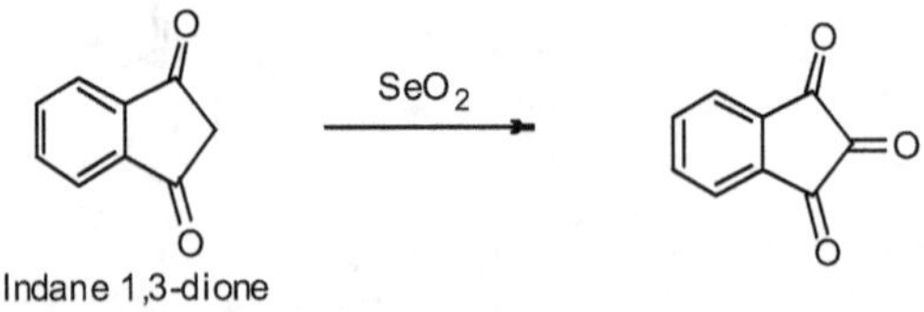

Indane 1,3-dione

Selenium dioxide is a useful oxidizing reagent for allylic oxidation of alkenes to allylic alcohols.

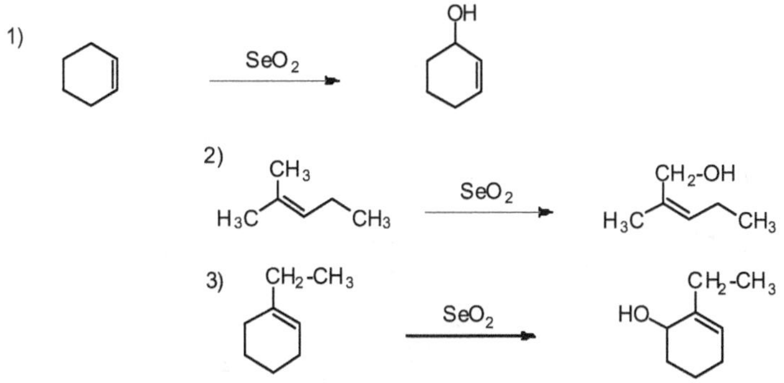

Mechanism of allylic oxidation by SeO$_2$

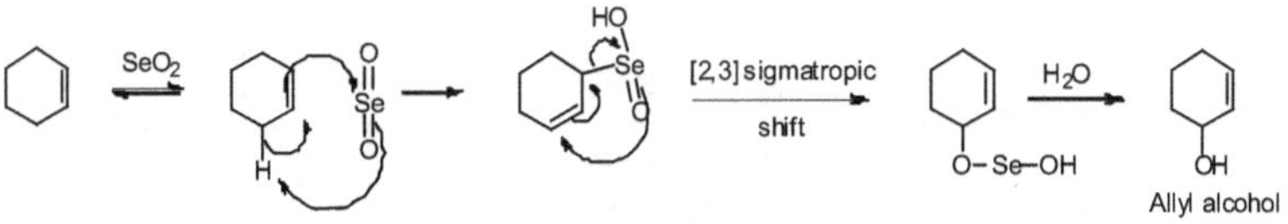

In some cases SeO$_2$ oxidation continues to give an aldehydes or ketones, when methylene group flanked between two aromatic rings convert into carbonyl group as in the following examples.

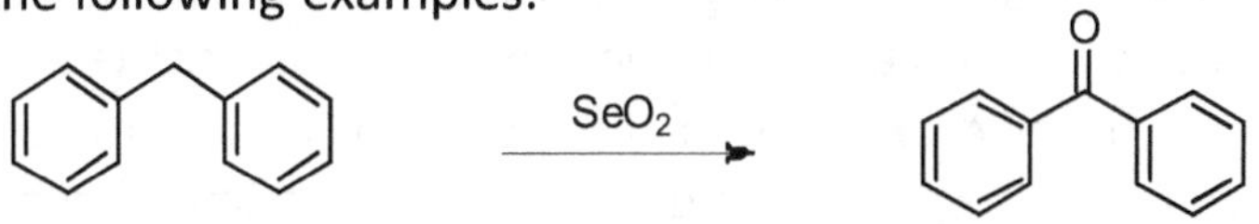

It also gives oxidation product of benzylcarbon e.g. oxidation of toluene to benzaldehyde as below.

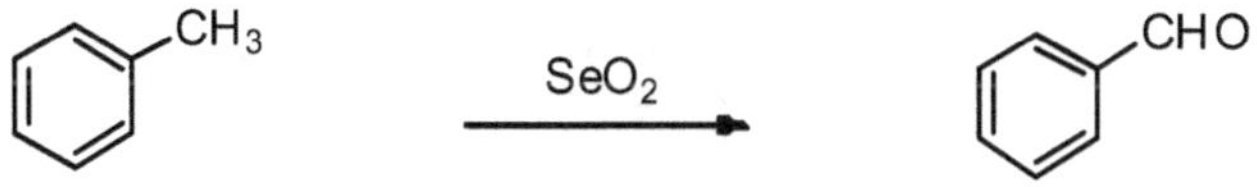

The active methylene of tropone can also easily oxidize to troponone as below.

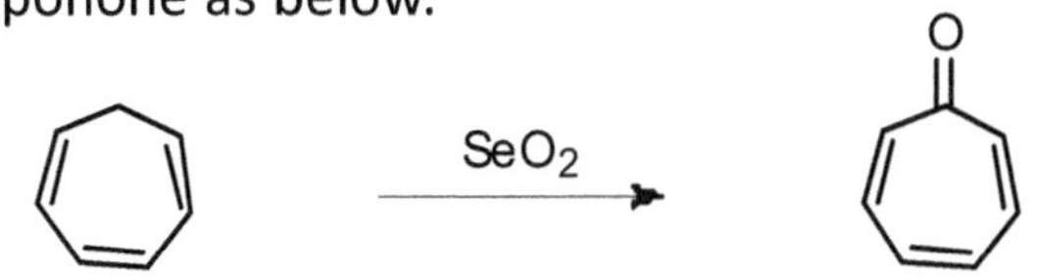

It also oxidizes alkynes into α-dicarbonyl compounds; this oxidation takes place in the presence of small amount of H_2SO_4.

1) $H-C\equiv C-H \xrightarrow[H_2SO_4]{SeO_2}$ $H-\overset{O}{\overset{||}{C}}-\overset{O}{\overset{||}{C}}-H$

2) $H_3C-C\equiv C-H \xrightarrow[H_2SO_4]{SeO_2}$ $H_3C-\overset{O}{\overset{||}{C}}-\overset{O}{\overset{||}{C}}-H$

3) $H_3C-C\equiv C-CH_3 \xrightarrow[H_2SO_4]{SeO_2}$ $H_3C-\overset{O}{\overset{||}{C}}-\overset{O}{\overset{||}{C}}-CH_3$

4) $H_3C-C\equiv C-Ph \xrightarrow[H_2SO_4]{SeO_2}$ $H_3C-\overset{O}{\overset{||}{C}}-\overset{O}{\overset{||}{C}}-Ph$

5) $Ph-C\equiv C-Ph \xrightarrow[H_2SO_4]{SeO_2}$ $Ph-\overset{O}{\overset{||}{C}}-\overset{O}{\overset{||}{C}}-Ph$

2) Alkyl Nitrite

Aldehyde and ketones having methylene group activated by the carbonyl group undergo oxidation with alkyl nitrite in the presence of acid or base. In the course of reaction nitroso compound undergo tautomerisation to the oxime which on hydrolysis results in to the formation of α-dicarbonyl compound.

1) Ph$-\overset{O}{\overset{||}{C}}-CH_2-CH_2-CH_3 \xrightarrow[ii)H_2O/H^{\oplus}]{i) CH_3-O-NO}$ Ph$-\overset{O}{\overset{||}{C}}-\overset{O}{\overset{||}{C}}-CH_2-CH_3$

2) (3,5-dimethylphenyl)$-\overset{O}{\overset{||}{C}}-CH_2-CH_2-CH_3 \xrightarrow[ii)H_2O/H^{\oplus}]{i) CH_3-O-NO}$ (3,5-dimethylphenyl)$-\overset{O}{\overset{||}{C}}-\overset{O}{\overset{||}{C}}-CH_2-CH_3$

3) Ph$-CH_2-\overset{O}{\overset{||}{C}}-H \xrightarrow[ii)H_2O/H^{\oplus}]{i) CH_3-O-NO}$ Ph$-\overset{O}{\overset{||}{C}}-\overset{O}{\overset{||}{C}}-H$

Mechanism

$$R-O-N=O \; + \; \overset{\oplus}{H} \; \rightleftharpoons \; R-\overset{\oplus}{\underset{H}{O}}-N=O \; \longrightarrow \; R\text{-}OH \; + \; \overset{\oplus}{N=O}$$

b) Oxidation of Arylmethane by using CrO_2Cl_2
1) CrO_2Cl_2 (Chromyl Chloride or Etard Oxidation)

The Etard oxidation is a chemical reaction that involves the direct oxidation of methyl group attached to aromatic or heteroaromatic ring in presence of chromyl chloride (CrO_2Cl_2) in solvent carbon disulfide (CS_2) at room temperature to aldehyde. It is name after the chemist Alexandre Leon Etard and it efficiently converts the arylmethane to aromatic aldehyde.

1) toluene $\xrightarrow[\text{CS}_2,\ \text{r.t.}]{\text{CrO}_2\text{Cl}_2}$ benzaldehyde (CHO)

2) 3-methylanisole (CH_3, OCH_3) $\xrightarrow[\text{CS}_2,\ \text{r.t.}]{\text{CrO}_2\text{Cl}_2}$ (CHO, OCH_3)

3) 4-nitrotoluene (CH_3, NO_2) $\xrightarrow[\text{CS}_2,\ \text{r.t.}]{\text{CrO}_2\text{Cl}_2}$ (CHO, NO_2)

4) chlorotoluene (CH_3, Cl) $\xrightarrow[\text{CS}_2,\ \text{r.t.}]{\text{CrO}_2\text{Cl}_2}$ (CHO, Cl)

The over-oxidation of aldehyde can be controlled by simultaneous removal of aldehyde formed in the reaction rapidly by distillation or extraction. The reactions mechanism proceeds via ENE reaction with chromyl chloride forming the precipitated Etard complex. The Etard complex is then decomposed by [2,3]-sigmatropic rearrangement which collapsed to the desired product as aldehyde as shown in the mechanism. If benzene nucleus is having more than one methyl group attached then only one is oxidised i.e *m*-xylene yield 3-methylbenzaldehyde.

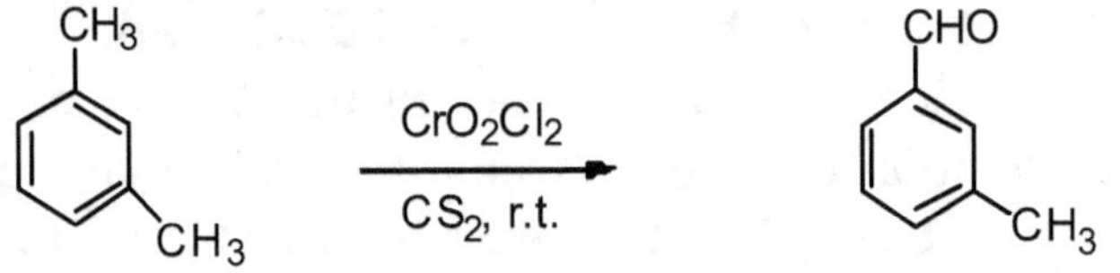

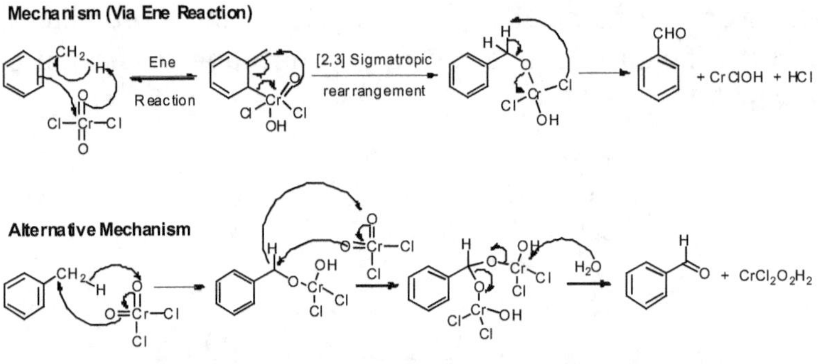

Mechanism (Via Ene Reaction)

Alternative Mechanism

However strong oxidising agents such as $KMnO_4$, $K_2Cr_2O_7$ etc. oxidize the side chain of aromatic ring into carboxylic acid as shown in the below example.

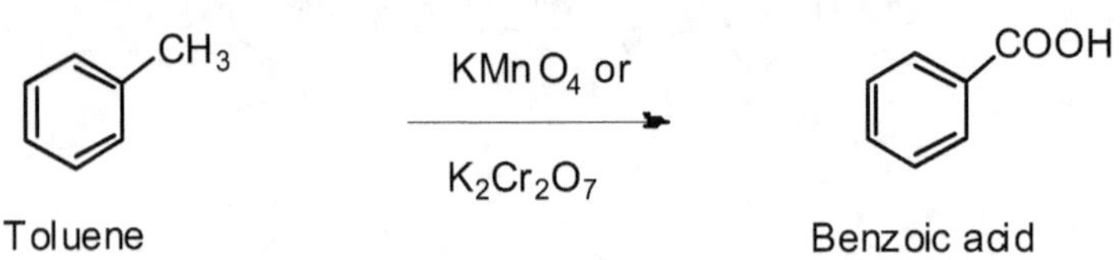

Toluene   Benzoic acid

The side chains bigger than -CH_3 can be oxidized by CrO_2Cl_2 at the end carbon atom of the side chain in to aldehyde.

Ethyl benzene → (CrO$_2$Cl$_2$/CCl$_4$, H$_2$O) → Phenyl acetaldehyde

The oxidation of *n*-propylbenzene yields a mixture of propiophenone and benzyl methyl ketone. The later compound is obtained through the involvement of a rearrangement.

n-propylbenzene → (CrO$_2$Cl$_2$/CCl$_4$, H2O) → Propiophenone → (Rearrangement) → Benzyl methyl ketone

Similar results are found for the reagent CrO$_3$/acetic anhydride in H$_2$SO$_4$, it forms initially diacetate which protect the aldehyde group against over-oxidation.

(CrO$_3$/Ac$_2$O, H$_2$SO$_4$) → diacetate (OAc, OAc) → (H$_2$O/H$^+$) → CHO

Ceric ions also readily oxidizes aromatic methyl group to aldehyde in acidic medium as in the following example.

CH$_3$ → (Ceric ammonium Nitrate, CAN) → CHO

SeO$_2$ can also be used for the similar type of oxidation as.

CH$_3$ → (SeO$_2$, Selenium dioxide) → CHO

C) Oxidation of Aldehydes/Ketones
1) H_2O_2/NaOH (Dakin Oxidation)

The Dakin oxidation is an organic redox reaction in which aromatic aldehyde or ketones containing *ortho* or *para* hydroxyl or amino group as substituents in alkaline H_2O_2 are converts into catechol or hydroquinol. The Dakin oxidation is the name of the reaction after the name Henry Drysdale Dakin.

o-hydroxylbenzaldehyde
(Salicylaldehyde) → Catechol

p-hydroxybenzaldehyde → Hydroquinone

Some more examples of Dakin oxidation for acetophenone derivatives as below.

1) o-hydroxyacetophenone → Catechol

2) p-hydroxyacetophenone → Hydroquinone

3)

$H_2O_2/NaOH$

o-hydroxyacetophenone

2-aminophenol

4)

$H_2O_2/NaOH$

p-hydroxyacetophenone

4-aminophenol

The mechanism is similar to that of the Baeyer-Villigers oxidation reaction. The Dakin oxidation starts with nucleophilic addition of hydroperoxide anion to the carbonyl carbon forming a tetrahedral intermediate. The intermediate collapses through [1,2] aryl migration with the loss of hydroxyl group. The phenyl esters then hydrolyzed to form phenol as product and carboxylic acid as by-product.

Mechanism

$$H_2O_2 + {}^{\ominus}OH \longrightarrow HO\text{-}O^{\ominus} + H_2O$$

Hydroperoxide anion

salicylaldehyde

[1,2] shift of aryl

phenyl formate as intermediate

H_2O/OH

Catechol

Ester intermediate has been isolated from the reaction mixture which confirms the mechanism. Electrophilicity of the carbonyl carbon matters the rate of reaction, hence aldehydes are more reactive than ketones. The electron donating substituents such as -OH or $-NH_2$ on ortho position gives extrastability through hydrogen bonding therefore *o*-hydroxy compounds are oxidized faster than *p*-hydroxy compounds.

Stability through H-bonding

The *m*-hydroxy benzaldehyde do not oxidize to *m*-benzenediol, whereas it rearranged through 1,2 shift of hydrogen to give *m*-hydroxy benzoic acid as shown in the following example.

[1,2] shift of H

m-Hydroxybenzaldehyde

m-Hydroxybenzoic acid

This variation in the aryl rings migration explains by electron density at the *ipso* aryl carbon bonded to carboxyl carbon. Phenyl group have low migratory aptitude but electron density at the migratory carbon increases by electron donating substituents such as -OH or $-NH_2$, which facilitated the [1,2] aryl migration. But in case of *m*-hydroxy group electron density will be low at migratory carbon, hence instead of [1,2] aryl migration hydrogen migrates leads to oxidation of carbonyl group to carboxylic acid as in above example.

Mechanism of o and p-Hydroxy substituent which facilitate migration of aryl group

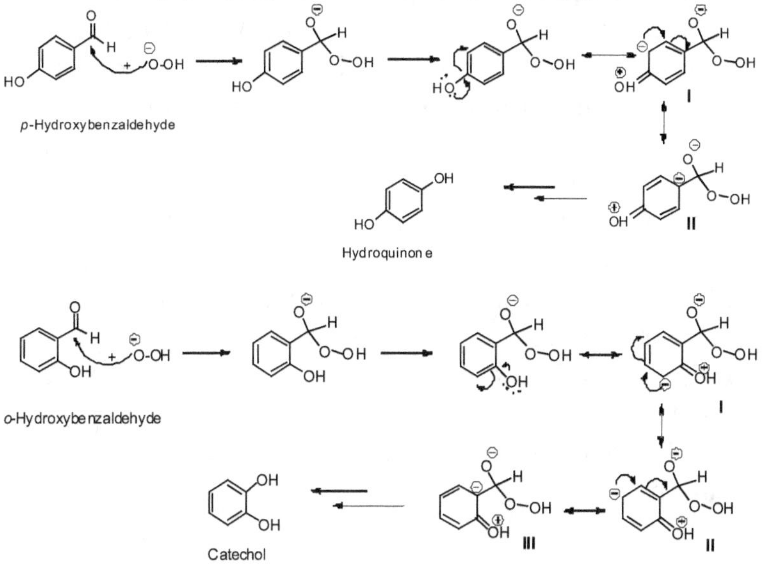

p-Hydroxybenzaldehyde

Hydroquinone

o-Hydroxybenzaldehyde

Catechol

The resonance structure (II) for *p*-hydroxy benzaldehyde and (III) for *o*-hydroxy benzaldehyde shows maximum electron density at the migratory carbon of the aromatic ring, which makes aryl group to migrate on electron deficient oxygen similar to Baeyer-Villiger rearrangement. Whereas in *m*-hydroxy benzaldehyde, it do not undergo aryl group migration but end up with hydrogen migration due to less electron density at migratory carbon of the aryl ring as shown in the resonance structures of *m*-hydroxy benzaldehyde as shown in the below examples.

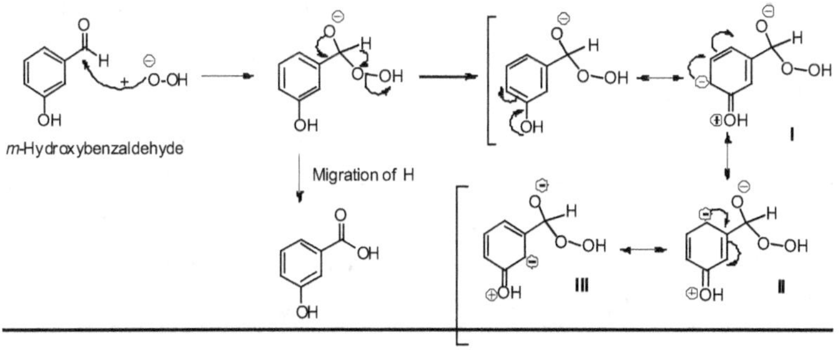

m-Hydroxybenzaldehyde

Migration of H

2) Peroxy acid (Baeyer Villiger Oxidation)

The oxidation of acyclic Ketones or cyclic ketones with peroxy acids gives esters or lactones and this reaction is known as Baeyer Villiger oxidation. In 1899 Baeyer and Villiger discovered this reaction who found that reaction of a number of cyclic ketones with Caro's acid (permonosulfuric acid) lead to the formation lactones. Better yield was obtained with organic peroxy acids such as perbenzoic acid, peracetic acid and trifluroacetic acid, although most of the chemist preferred with *meta*-chloroperbenzoic acid (*m*CPBA). This reagent is more stable than the other peracids and is commercially available.

Examples of peroxy acids oxidation or Bayer Villigers oxidation.

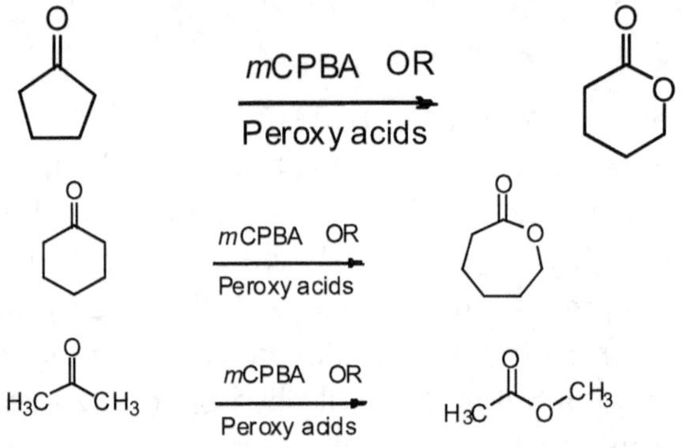

Acid catalyzed the reaction by facilitating both the addition to carbonyl group and the leaving of the carboxylate. The trifluoroperoxy acetic acid has been successfully employed in the reaction because of the most reactive peroxy acids, probably due to trifluoroacetate ion derived from a strong acid is a very good leaving group. In an unsymmetrical ketone the group migrates which is the better able to supply electrons as in the Wagner Meerwein and related rearrangements. Amongst alkyl group the ease of migration is tertiary > secondary > primary methyl.

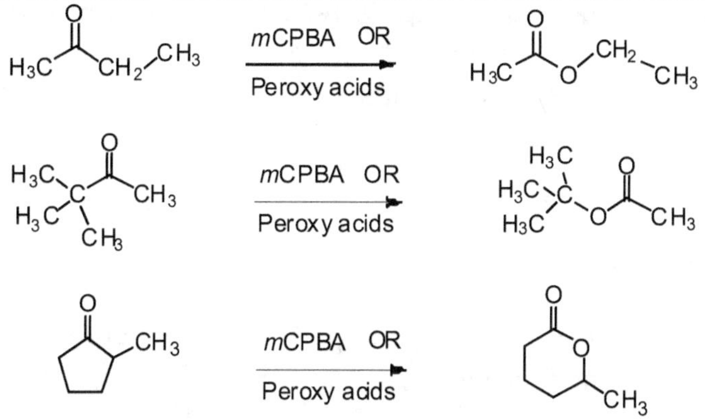

$$H_3C-CO-CH_2-CH_3 \xrightarrow{\text{mCPBA OR}\atop\text{Peroxy acids}} H_3C-CO-O-CH_2-CH_3$$

$$(CH_3)_3C-CO-CH_3 \xrightarrow{\text{mCPBA OR}\atop\text{Peroxy acids}} (CH_3)_3C-O-CO-CH_3$$

2-methylcyclopentanone $\xrightarrow{\text{mCPBA OR}\atop\text{Peroxy acids}}$ lactone (6-methyltetrahydropyran-2-one)

Amongst aryl group the order of migratory aptitude is *p*-methoxyphenyl > *p*-tolyl > phenyl > *p*-chlorophenyl and in case of aryl and alkyl group both together will give the preference to aryl group to migrate in preference of primary alkyl group. Whereas if the electron donating group is attached to aryl ring, it do migrate in preference to 2^0 and 1^0 alkyl groups as shown in the following examples.

1) $C_6H_5-CO-CH_3 \xrightarrow{\text{mCPBA OR}\atop\text{Peroxy acids}} C_6H_5-O-CO-CH_3$

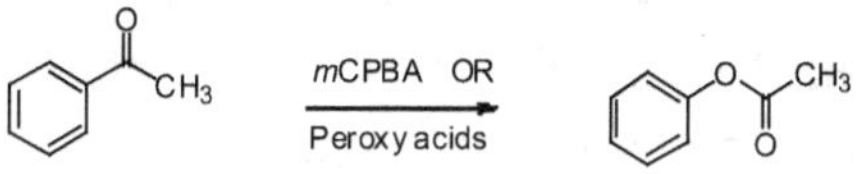

2) $\xrightarrow{\text{mCPBA OR}\atop\text{Peroxy acids}}$

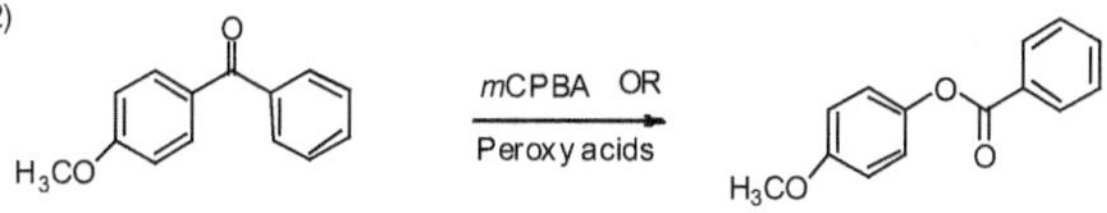

3) $\xrightarrow{\text{mCPBA OR}\atop\text{Peroxy acids}}$

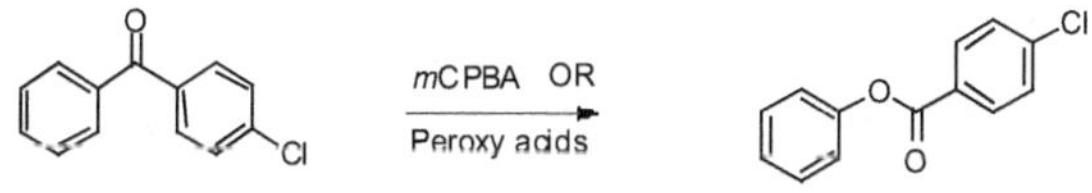

4) $\xrightarrow{\text{mCPBA OR}\atop\text{Peroxy acids}}$

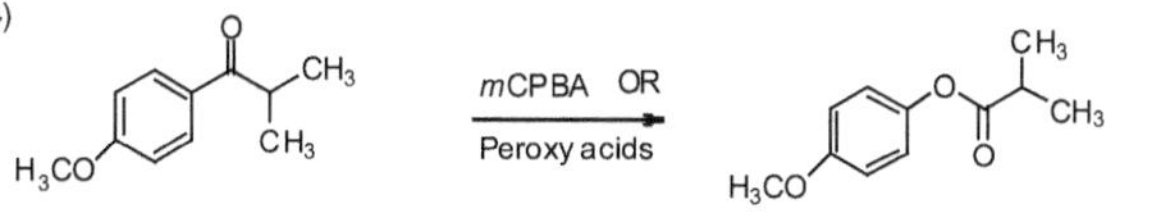

5) $\xrightarrow{\text{mCPBA OR}\atop\text{Peroxy acids}}$

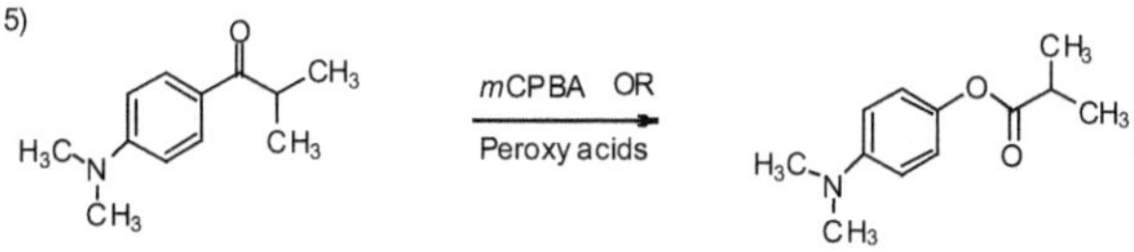

Electron withdrawing group decreases the electron density at migratory carbon of aryl ring hence its preference of migration will be low as compare to aryl or 1^0, 2^0 and 3^0 alkyl groups.

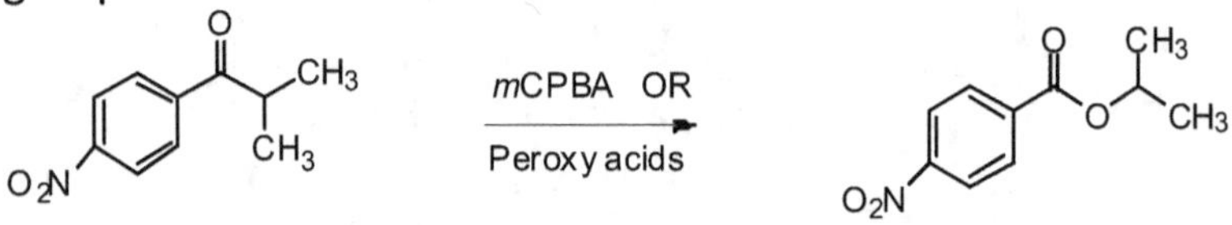

Cyclic Ketones undergo ring expansion with peroxyacid as shown in the following example.

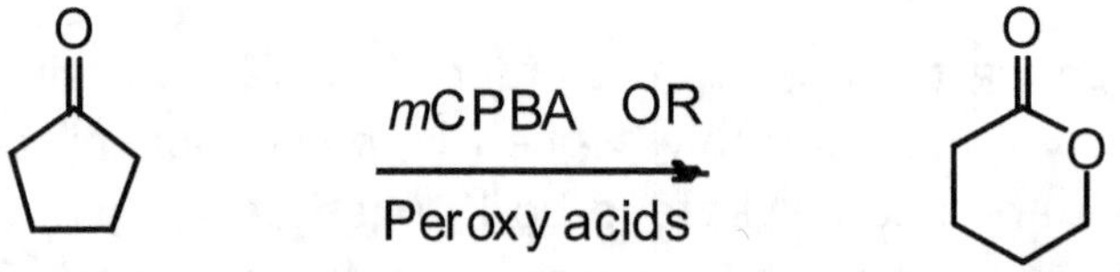

The mechanism is closely related to that of the Pinacol rearrangement in which the peroxyacid as nucleophile attack on the carbonyl group gives an intermediate which on rearrangement with removal of the anion of an acid result in the formation of ester. It is the rearrangement of electron deficient oxygen atom as shown in mechanism.

e.g

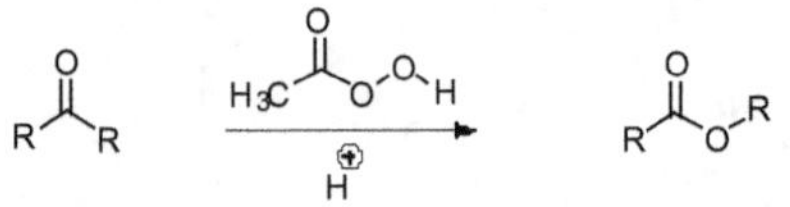

Mechanism

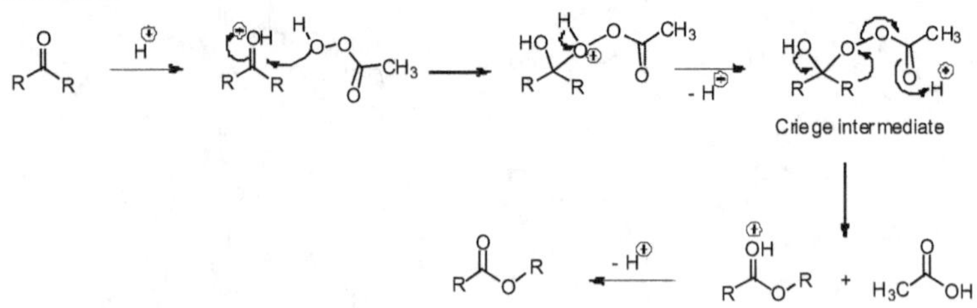

Criege intermediate

Cyclic ketones oxidations undergo similar type of mechanism as shown below.

e.g

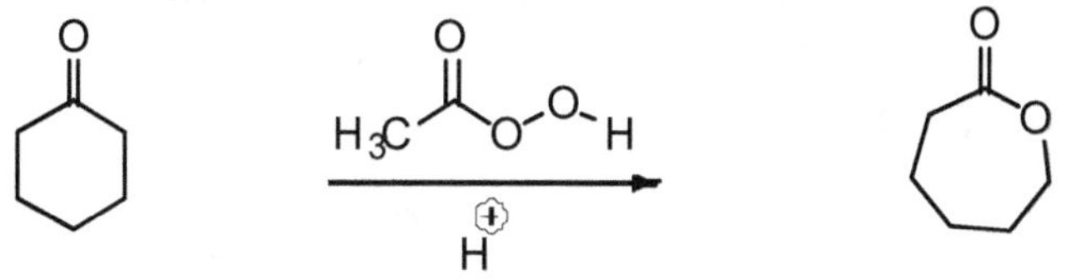

Mechanism (Cyclic ketone Oxidation)

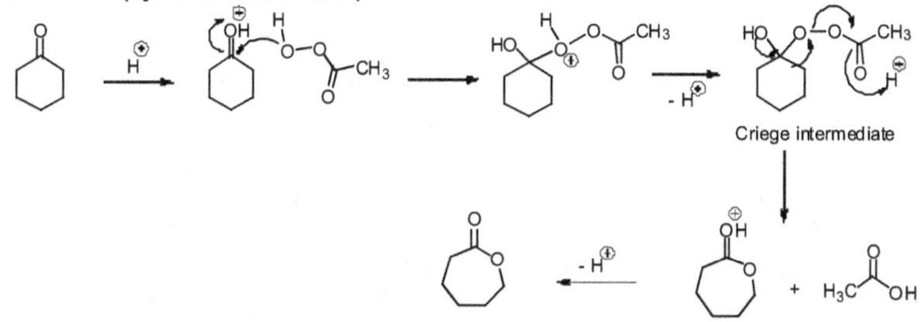

Criege intermediate

The acid catalyzed rearrangement of tertiary hydroperoxides is similar to the Baeyer-Villiger oxidation reaction.

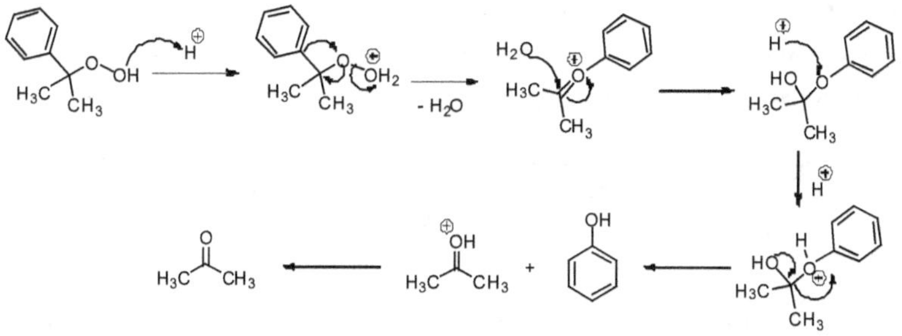

Baeyer-Villiges oxidation does not change the optical properties, when optically active ketones in which chiral carbon is directly bonded to the carbonyl group have shown that these reactions occur with retention of configuration.

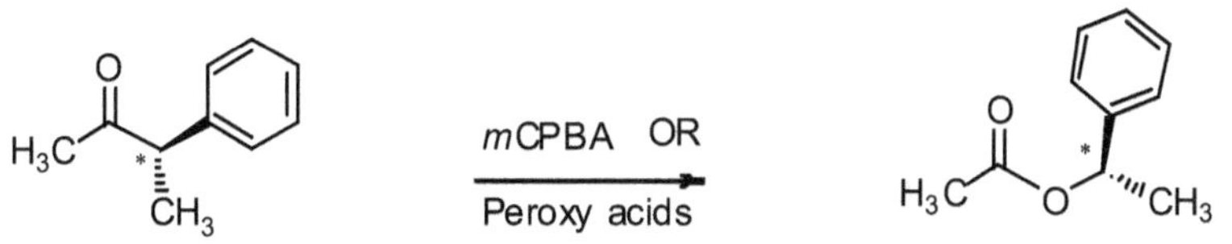

mCPBA OR

Peroxy acids

Bridged bicycle Ketones undergoes peroxyacid oxidation e.g. 1-methylnorcamphor gives the expected lactone on oxidation with peroxyacid.

$$CH_3COOOH$$

Whereas epicamphor gives only abnormal product due to stereohindrance as below.

$$CH_3CO\,OOH$$

Bayer-Villiger oxidation of bridged bicyclic Ketones is valuable in synthesis because it provides a method for preparing derivatives of cyclohexane and cyclopentane with control of stereochemistry on hydrolysis of lactones.

$$mCPBA$$

$$H_2O/NaOH$$

If the unsaturated Ketones are treated with *m*CPBA promoted preferential epoxidation however bis(trimethylsilyl) peroxide and BF_3 gave the Bayer-Villiger product as lactone.

$$mCPBA \quad DCM$$

Epoxide

$$Me_3Si\text{-}O\text{-}O\text{-}SiMe_3 \quad BF_3, DCM$$

Lactone

The Baeyer-Villiger oxidation can be carried out using isolated enzymes. Biotransformations of simple cyclic Ketones are most effective 4-methylcyclohexanone is oxidized with high enantioselectivity by using enzyme cyclohexanone-monoxygenase.

Oxidation of aldehyde with peroxyacid is not as synthetically useful as oxidation of ketones generally gives either carboxylic acid or formate esters (Dakin Oxidation).

Chapter 3

Reduction

Reductive process of the organic molecules fall into three categories i.e the removal of oxygen or the addition hydrogen or the gain of electrons. The addition of hydrogen may be sub-divided into hydrogenation or the addition of hydrogen to an unsaturated system.

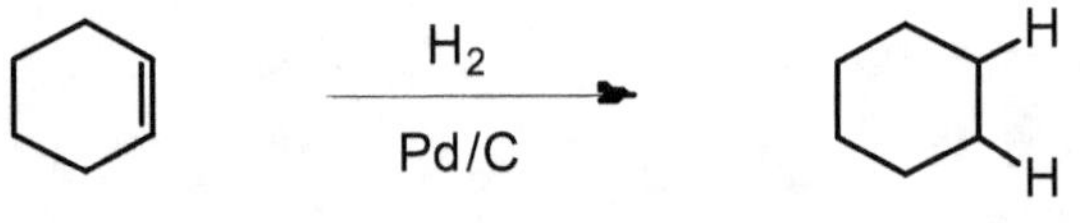

Another application is the hydrogenolysis i.e the addition of hydrogen across single bond rupture.

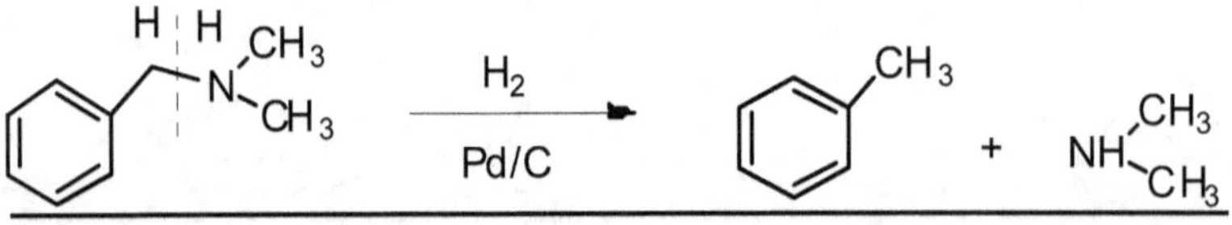

Mechanistically there are three main pathways for reduction.

1) By the addition of electrons

After addition of electron across π-bond the proton will be added as in the reduction of an alkyne by Sodium or Lithium in liquid Ammonia (Birch reduction is the best example of this kind reduction) and reductive coupling as in the case of Ketones to Pinacols.

a)   Reduction of Alkyne to *trans* alkene;

b)   Reductive coupling of ketones;

e.g.

2) By the transfer of hydride ion

The best examples are the reduction of carbonyl compounds by metal hydrides i.e. $LiAlH_4$, $NaBH_4$, $LiBH_4$, etc.

3) Catalytic Hydrogenation in presence of metal

By the catalytic addition of molecular hydrogen as in the reduction of alkene in presence of metal.

The older methods involved electron transfer such as Na/EtOH and Zn/AcOH are now supplemented by the metal-ammonia and metal-amine systems which have increased the scope of these reductions. Enzyme reduction has many merits as they are enantioselective, so that optically active compounds can be obtained from inactive reactants.

e.g.

I. Reduction of carbonyl group (–CO-) to methylene group (-CH$_2$-) in Aldehydes and Ketones.

There are several methods available for reductive removal of carbonyl group from aldehyde and Ketone to methylene group. The choice of a method depends on the sensitivity of the substrate under reducing conditions. Following are the methods available for the said transformation.

1) Zn/HCl (Clemmensen Reduction)

The Clemmensen reduction of aldehyde or Ketone to methyl or methylene group takes place by heating with amalgamated Zn (Zinc) and hydrochloric acid (HCl).

1)

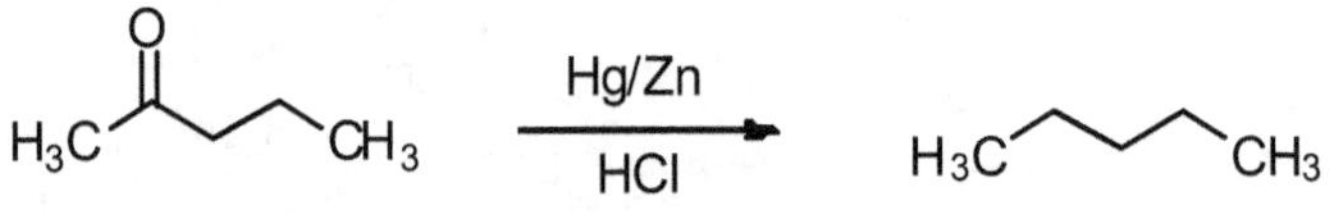

2)

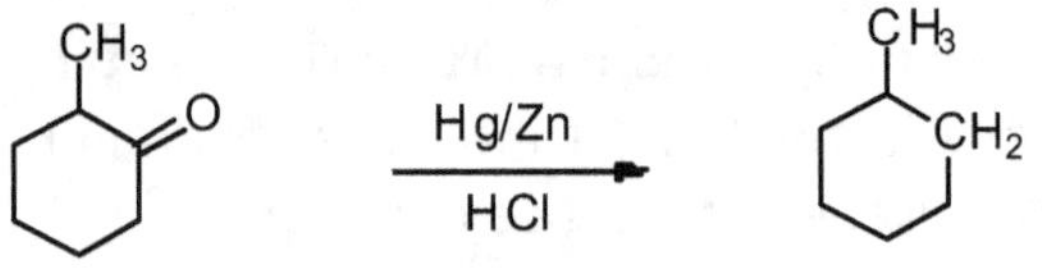

3)

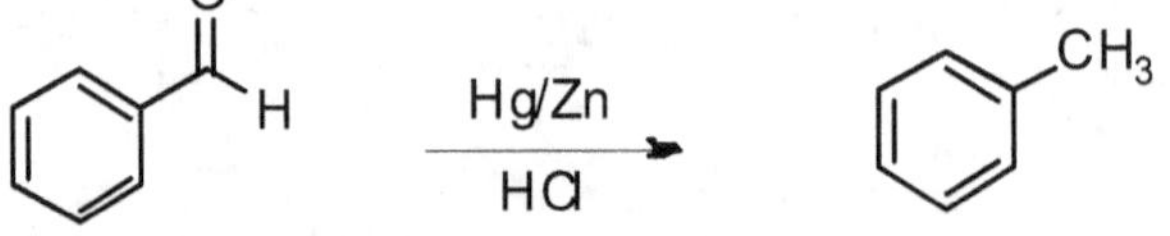

The method is particularly useful for reduction of Ketones which contain phenolic or carboxylic group.

1)

$$Ph\text{-}CO\text{-}(CH_2)_{14}\text{-}CH_3 \xrightarrow[\text{HCl}]{\text{Hg/Zn}} Ph\text{-}(CH_2)_{14}\text{-}CH_3$$

2)

$$Ph\text{-}CO\text{-}CH_2CH_2\text{-}COOH \xrightarrow[\text{HCl}]{\text{Hg/Zn}} Ph\text{-}CH_2CH_2CH_2\text{-}COOH$$

The mechanism is not certain but may be as follows:

Mechanism:

The reductions take place at the surface of the zinc catalyst.

A non-miscible solvent can be used and serves to keep the concentration in the aqueous phase low and thus prevent bimolecular condensations at the metal surface. The choice of acid is confined to the hydrogen halide, which appear to be the only strong acids whose anions are not reduced with Zn/Hg. The Clemmensen reduction reaction condition consider to be vigorous and is not suitable for the reduction of polyfunctional molecules such as 1,3 or 1,4- diketones or of sensitive compounds. However, it is effective for simple compounds that are stable in acidic condition.

The substrate must be unreactive to the strongly acidic conditions of the Clemmensen reduction. Acid sensitive substrates should be reacted in the Wolff-Kishner reduction, which utilizes strongly basic conditions.

❖In the reaction Zn metal dissolve in concentrate HCl and it gives up two electrons. In the absence of substrate as Ketone release electrons would reduce the H^+ in the acid to gives H_2 and $ZnCl_2$ but in the presence of carbonyl compounds the electrons goes to reduce the carbonyl (-CO-) bond. Thus the Clemmensens reduction is a member known as dissolving metal reduction.❖

2) NH_2-NH_2/NaOH (Wolff-Kishner Reduction)

The Wolff-Kishner reduction gives an excellent method for the reduction of the carbonyl group of many aldehyde and Ketones to a methyl or methylene group respectively in presence of hydrazine hydrate and alkali at higher temperature.

1)
$$\xrightarrow[\text{NaOH } \Delta]{NH_2\text{-}NH_2.H_2O}$$

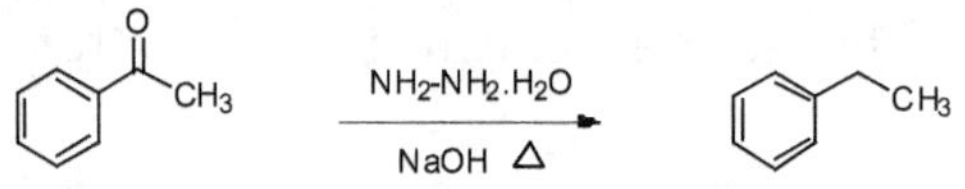

2)
$$\xrightarrow[\text{NaOH } \Delta]{NH_2\text{-}NH_2.H_2O}$$

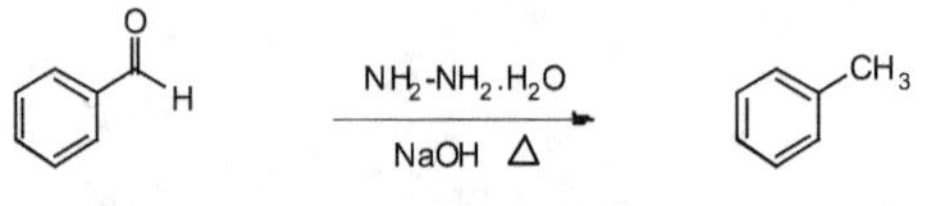

3)
$$\xrightarrow[\text{NaOH } \Delta]{NH_2\text{-}NH_2.H_2O}$$

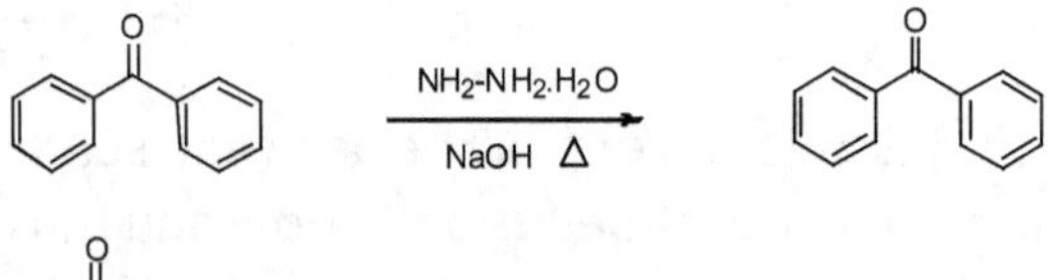

4)
$$\xrightarrow[\text{NaOH } \Delta]{NH_2\text{-}NH_2.H_2O}$$

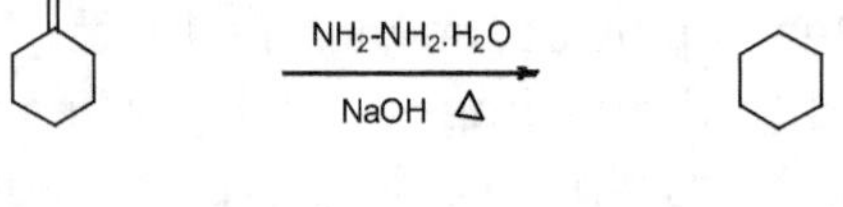

5)
$$\xrightarrow[\text{NaOH } \Delta]{NH_2\text{-}NH_2.H_2O}$$

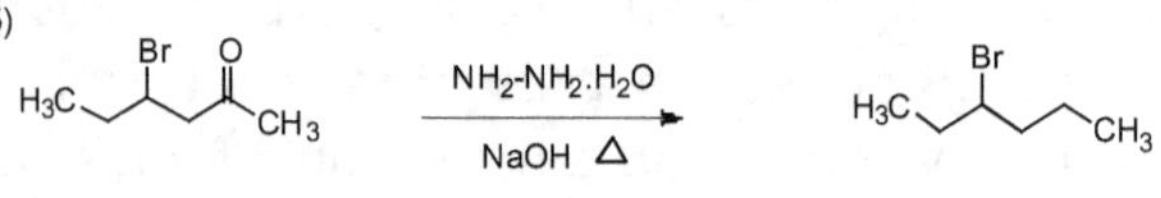

6)
$$\xrightarrow[\text{NaOH } \Delta]{NH_2\text{-}NH_2.H_2O}$$

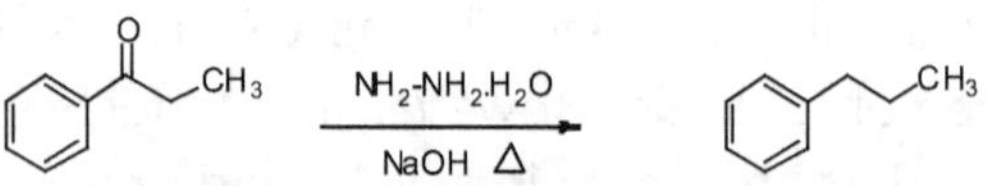

The Wolff-Kishner reduction was discovered independently by N. Kishner in 1911 and   L. Wolff in 1912. The Kishner found that addition of preformed hydrazone to hot KOH containing crushed platinized porous plate led to the formation of the corresponding hydrocarbon.

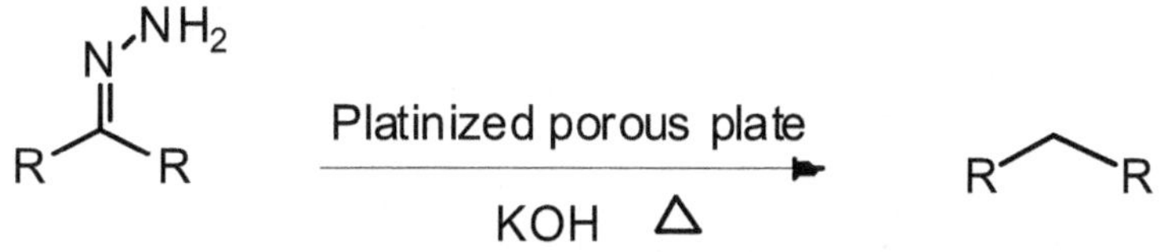

The Wolff later accomplished the same result by heating an ethanol solution of semi-carbazones or hydrazones in a sealed tube to 180^{oC} in the presence of sodium ethoxide.

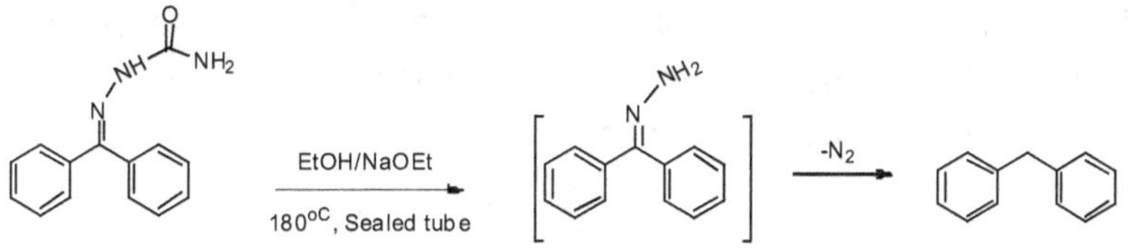

Semicarbazone

By considering both results the modified reagent has been consider as Wolff-Kishner reduction. Use of the high boiling solvent ethylene glycol promotes removal of excess hydrazine and water after hydrazone formation and requires less time for the reduction. The polar aprotic solvent DMSO increases the rate of the reaction and with potassium tertiary butoxide in DMSO reduction can even be carried out at room temperature.

1)

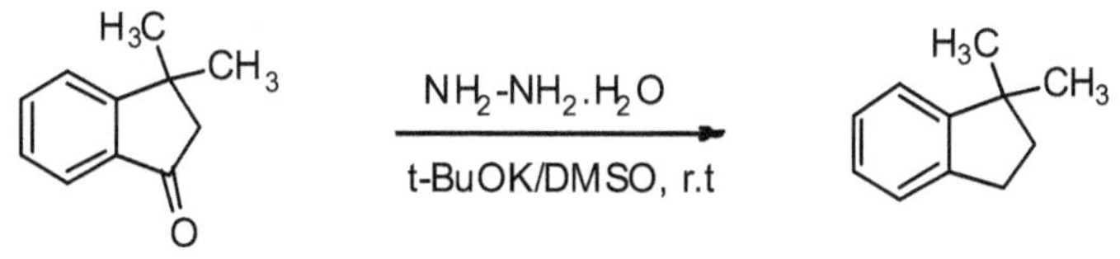

2)

$$\text{4-Br-C}_6\text{H}_4\text{-CO-CH}_2\text{CH}_3 \xrightarrow[\text{t-BuOK/DMSO, r.t}]{\text{NH}_2\text{-NH}_2.\text{H}_2\text{O}} \text{4-Br-C}_6\text{H}_4\text{-CH}_2\text{CH}_2\text{CH}_3$$

3)

$$\xrightarrow[\text{KOH/Ethylene glycol}]{\text{NH}_2\text{-NH}_2.\text{H}_2\text{O}}$$

4)

$$\xrightarrow[\text{KOH/Ethylene glycol}]{\text{NH}_2\text{-NH}_2.\text{H}_2\text{O}}$$

In general the reaction mechanism first involves the *in situ* generation of a hydrazone by condensation of hydrazine with the Ketones or aldehyde as substrate.

$$\underset{R}{\overset{O}{\underset{}{\parallel}}}\!\!\!\!\!C\!\!\!-\!\!R \xrightarrow[-\text{H}_2\text{O}]{\text{NH}_2\text{-NH}_2.\text{H}_2\text{O}} \underset{R}{\overset{N\text{-NH}_2}{\underset{}{\parallel}}}\!\!\!\!\!C\!\!\!-\!\!R \xrightarrow[-\text{N}_2]{\overset{\ominus}{\text{OH}}/\;\Delta} R\text{-CH}_2\text{-}R$$

However some time it is advantageous to use a preformed hydrazone as substrate. The hydrazone is deprotonated by base followed by a concerted rate determining step in which alkyl diimide anion is formed. The alkyl diimide anion collapse to alkyl anion with the loss of N_2 gas which can be further protonated by solvent to give the desired product as alkane.

Mechanism

Diimide anion

alkyl anion

Alkane

The Wolff-Kishner reduction requires highly basic conditions; it is unsuitable for base- sensitive substrates. However this method can be superior over the related Clemmensen reduction for acid-sensitive compounds such as pyrroles and for higher molecules weight compounds.

3) NH_2-NH_2/KOH/Ethylene glycol (Huang-Minlon Modification)

The Huang-Minlon modification is name after Huang Minglon. It was the first time that a Chinese chemist name appeared in an organic chemical reaction.This is the modification of Wolff-Kishner reduction and involves heating the carbonyl compounds as Ketones or aldehydes, KOH or NaOH and hydrazine hydrate together in ethylene glycol in a one-pot synthesis result to the formation hydrocarbon. This reduction was modified method of Wolff-Kishner reduction discovered in the year 1946.

$$\underset{\text{Ketone}}{R-\underset{\overset{\|}{O}}{C}-R} \quad \xrightarrow[\Delta \ \text{Ethylene glycol}]{NH_2\text{-}NH_2, \ H_2O/KOH} \quad \underset{\text{Alkane}}{R-\underset{\overset{H \quad H}{}}{C}-R}$$

In the modified procedure as Huang-Minlon reduction of Ketone in which excess hydrazine and water were removed by distillation after hydrazone formation. The temperature lowering effect of water that was produced in hydrazone formation usually resulted in long reaction time and harsh reaction conditions even if anhydrous hydrazine was used in the formation hydrazone. The modified procedure consists of refluxing the carbonyl compound in 85% hydrazine hydrate with 3 equivalent of sodium hydroxide followed by distillation of water and excess hydrazine and elevation of the temperature to 200^{0C}. It significantly reduced reaction times and improved yields can be obtained using this Huang-Minlon modification method.

1)

85% NH$_2$-NH$_2$.H$_2$O/KOH
Δ Ethylene glycol

1) Removal of Excess of NH$_2$-NH$_2$ and water by Distillation
2) temp. 180-200°C

2)

85% NH$_2$-NH$_2$.H$_2$O/KOH
Δ Ethylene glycol

1) Removal of Excess of NH$_2$-NH$_2$ and water by Distillation
2) temp. 180-200°C

II. Metal Hydride Reduction

The metal hydride reagents are widely used in organic synthesis for reduction of carbonyl compounds to alcohols as well other functional groups too and the reagents with various reducing strengths and properties are known. The following reducing reagents mostly based on Boron (B) and Aluminium (Al) as metal hydride used commonly depends upon the practical qualities such as availability and ease of handling.

a) Boron based Reagents : NaBH$_4$, NaCNBH$_3$, B$_2$H$_6$, 9BBN, Na(OAc)$_3$BH.

b) Aluminium Based Reagents : LiAlH$_4$, DIBALH, Red Al, L and K selectrides.

a) Boron based Reagents

1) NaBH$_4$ (Sodium Borohydride)

Sodium Borohydride (NaBH$_4$) is less reactive than Lithium Aluminium Hydride (LiALH$_4$) hence it becomes selective over it and most extensively used as metal hydride reducing reagent. It reduces aldehydes and ketones to 1^0 and

2^0 alcohols respectively as the products with methanol or ethanol is used as the solvent for the solubility reasons. It cannot reduces esters, amides and carboxylic acids but esters containing a heteroatom at the α-position are the exceptions that can be reduced due to neighbouring group participation. $NaBH_4$ is mild reducing reagents has no effect on C=C, C≡C, N=N, -C≡N, and $-NO_2$ as functional groups. Following are some examples of $NaBH_4$ selective reduction of aldehydes and ketones to primary and secondary alcohols in presence of other functional groups.

1) 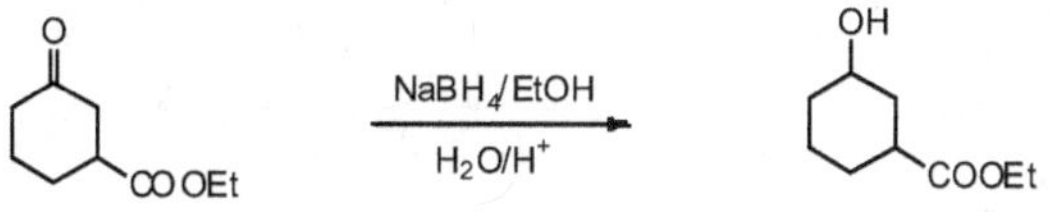 $\xrightarrow[\text{H}_2\text{O/H}^+]{\text{NaBH}_4/\text{EtOH}}$

2) $\xrightarrow[\text{H}_2\text{O/H}^+]{\text{NaBH}_4/\text{EtOH}}$

3) $\xrightarrow[\text{H}_2\text{O/H}^+]{\text{NaBH}_4/\text{EtOH}}$

4) $\xrightarrow[\text{H}_2\text{O/H}^+]{\text{NaBH}_4/\text{EtOH}}$

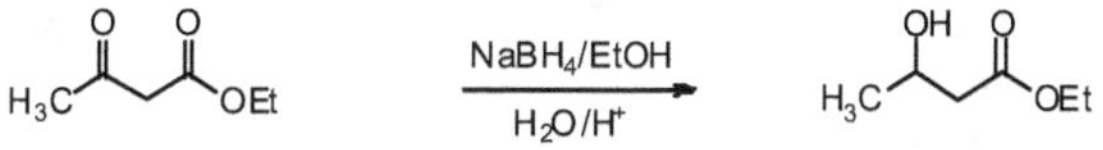

5) 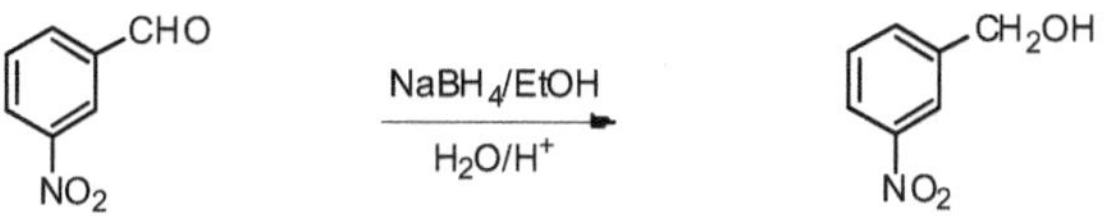 $\xrightarrow[\text{H}_2\text{O/H}^+]{\text{NaBH}_4/\text{EtOH}}$

6) 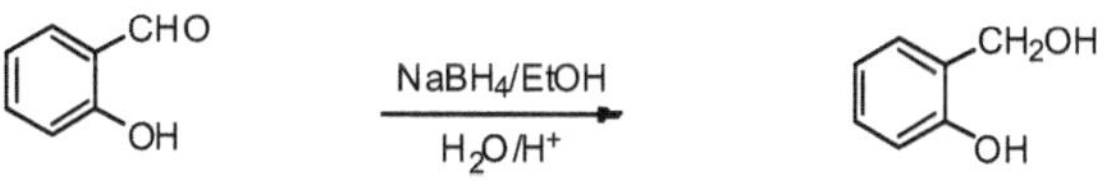 $\xrightarrow[\text{H}_2\text{O/H}^+]{\text{NaBH}_4/\text{EtOH}}$

7) 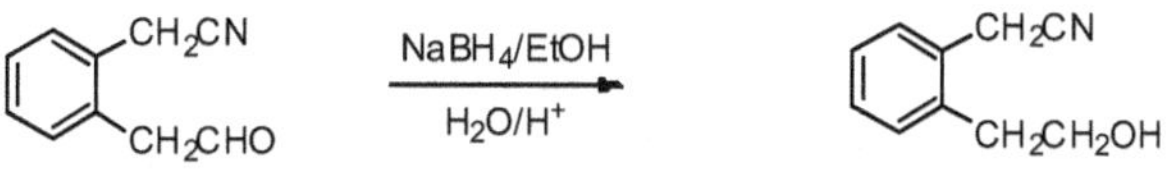 $\xrightarrow[\text{H}_2\text{O/H}^+]{\text{NaBH}_4/\text{EtOH}}$

8) 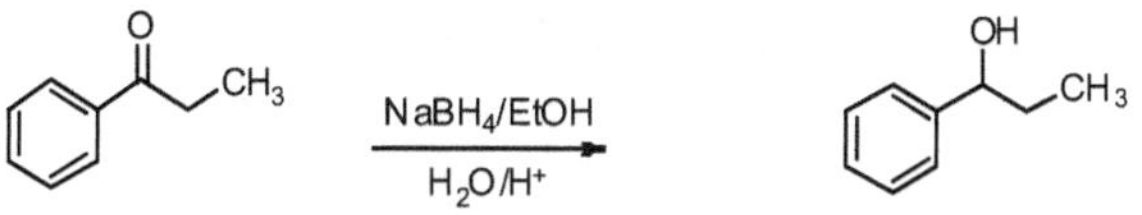 $\xrightarrow[\text{H}_2\text{O/H}^+]{\text{NaBH}_4/\text{EtOH}}$

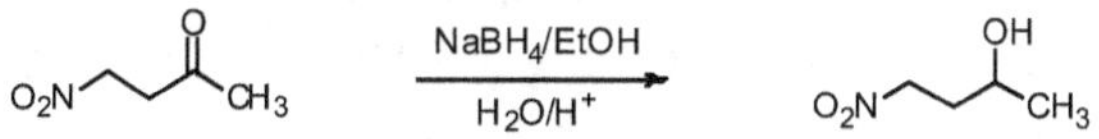

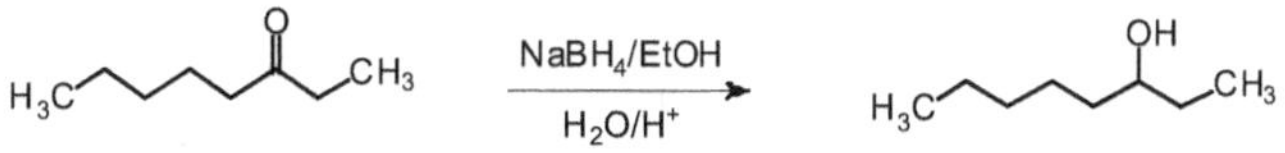

Heteroatom at the α-position to the ester functional group can be reduced by $NaBH_4$ to primary alcohol. $NaBH_4$ is selective in between conjugated and non-conjugated aldehydes and ketones reduction, as the non-conjugated compounds can be easily reduced to alcohol and conjugated carbonyl will not get reduced by the $NaBH_4$ reduction.

9)

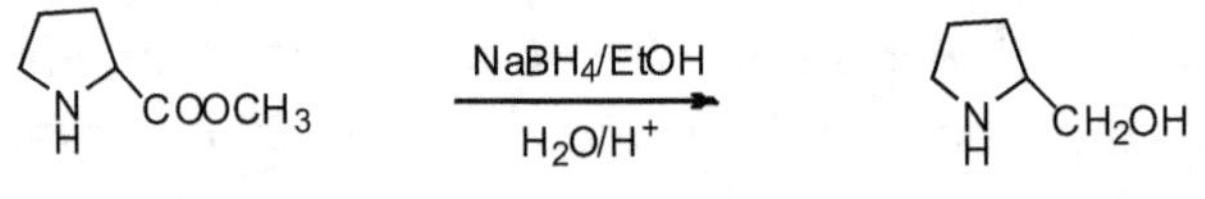

10)

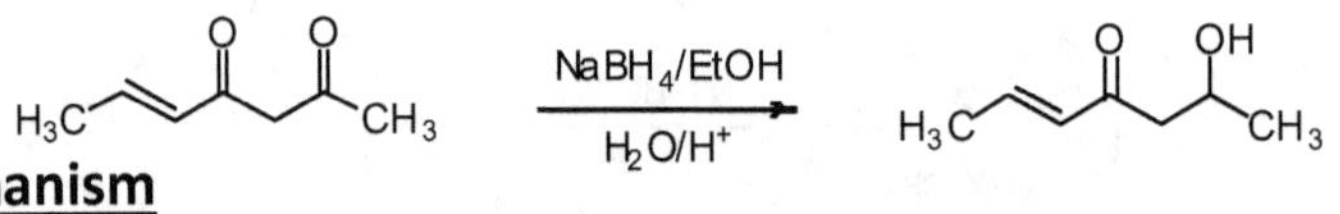

Mechanism

The precise mechanism surprisingly is still not clear but follows a course something like this with the dotted lines representing some association, perhaps coordination or bond formation.

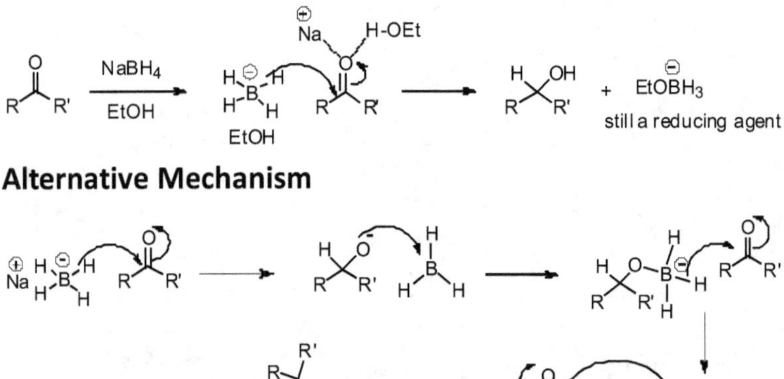

Alternative Mechanism

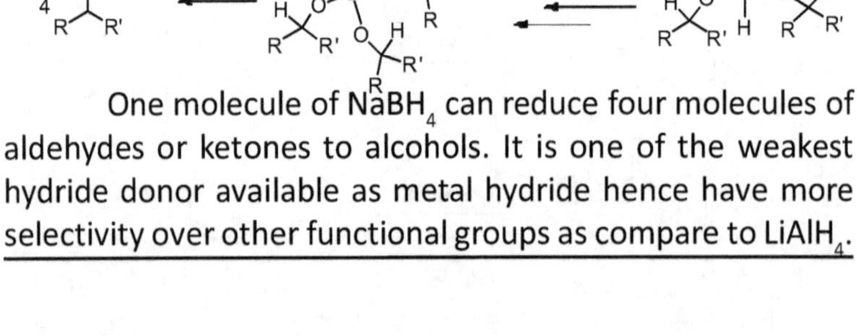

One molecule of $NaBH_4$ can reduce four molecules of aldehydes or ketones to alcohols. It is one of the weakest hydride donor available as metal hydride hence have more selectivity over other functional groups as compare to $LiAlH_4$.

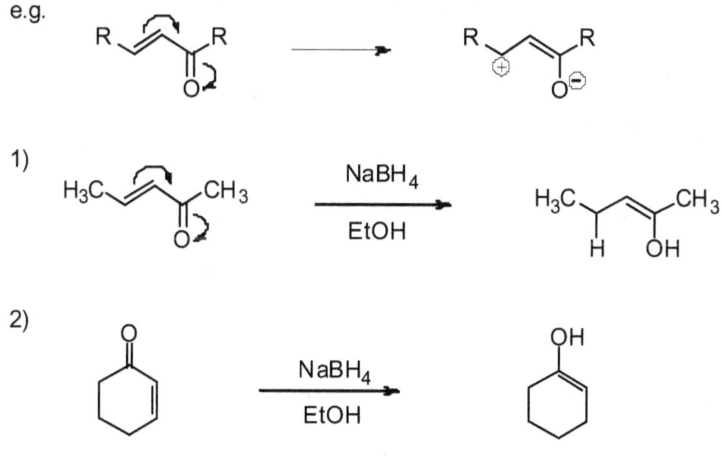

The α-β-unsaturated ketones and aldehydes on reduction with NaBH$_4$ can gives 1,4-addition of hydride and proton due to delocalisation in the conjugated systems to enol formation.

When the reduction of α-β-unsaturated ketones and aldehydes with $NaBH_4$ is carried out in presence of catalytic amount of $CeCl_3$ then 1,2 addition product favours because complex formation with $CeCl_3$ restrict the delocalisation of double bond electron.

$$\xrightarrow[\text{CH}_3\text{OH}]{\text{NaBH}_4/\text{CeCl}_3}$$

\ Remarkably $NaBH_4$-$CeCl_3$ can differentiate between different aldehydes or ketones group by reducing selectively less reactive carbonyl group as α-β-unsaturated aldehydes or ketones in presence of other carbonyl as aldehydes or ketones.

1)

$$\xrightarrow[\text{EtOH}]{\text{NaBH}_4/\text{CeCl}_3}$$

2)

$$\xrightarrow[\text{EtOH}]{\text{NaBH}_4/\text{CeCl}_3}$$

3)

$$\xrightarrow[\text{EtOH}]{\text{NaBH}_4/\text{CeCl}_3}$$

Reduction by $NaBH_4$ without $CeCl_3$.

$$\xrightarrow[\text{EtOH}]{\text{NaBH}_4}$$

$NaBH_4$ also reduces acid chlorides to primary alcohols.

e.g.

$$R\text{-COCl} \xrightarrow[\text{EtOH}]{\text{NaBH}_4} R\text{-OH}$$

1)

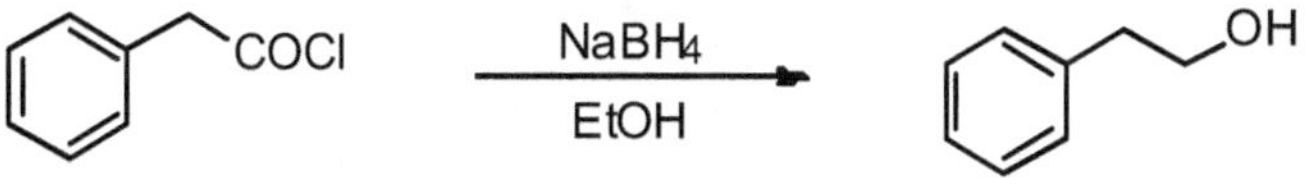

$$\text{PhCH}_2\text{COCl} \xrightarrow[\text{EtOH}]{\text{NaBH}_4} \text{PhCH}_2\text{CH}_2\text{OH}$$

2) NaCNBH$_3$ (Sodium cyanoborohydride)

The sodium cyanoborohydride (NaCNBH$_3$) is a reducing agent derived from sodium borohydride (NaBH$_4$) by replacing one of the hydrogen atom by electron withdrawing cyano (-CN) group. Due to the electron withdrawing effect of -CN group the NaCNBH$_3$ is far less reactive 11as compare to NaBH$_4$ and more selective in reduction process.

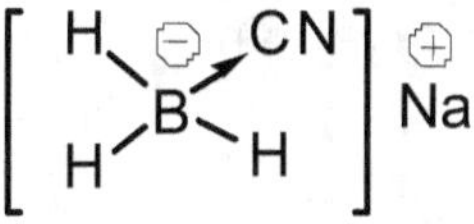

$$\left[\begin{array}{c} H \quad \ominus \quad CN \\ B \\ H \qquad H \end{array} \right] \overset{\oplus}{Na}$$

The iminium group are more easily reduced to amine than carbonyl group in the acid solution and this has been exploited as method for reductive amination of aldehyde and ketones by the way of the iminium salt formation from the carbonyl compound and a primary or secondary amines.

1)

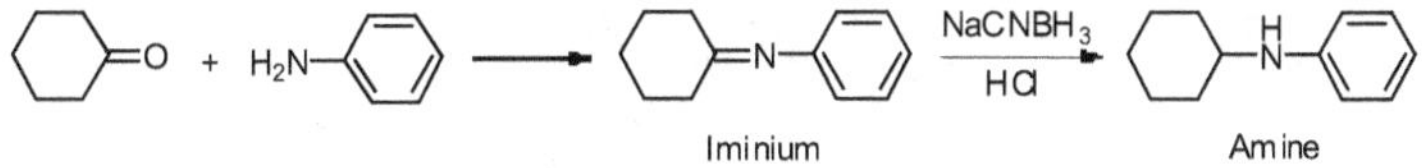

Iminium · · · · · · Amine

2)

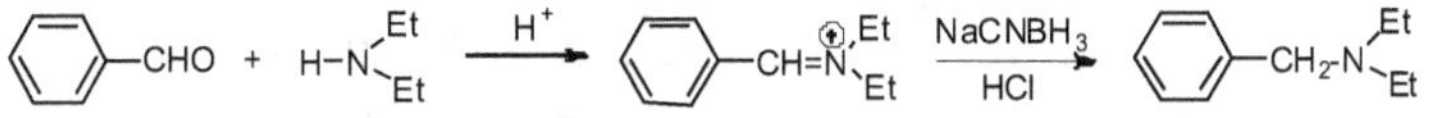

3)

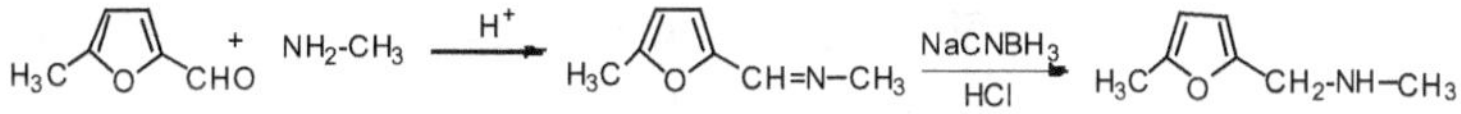

4)

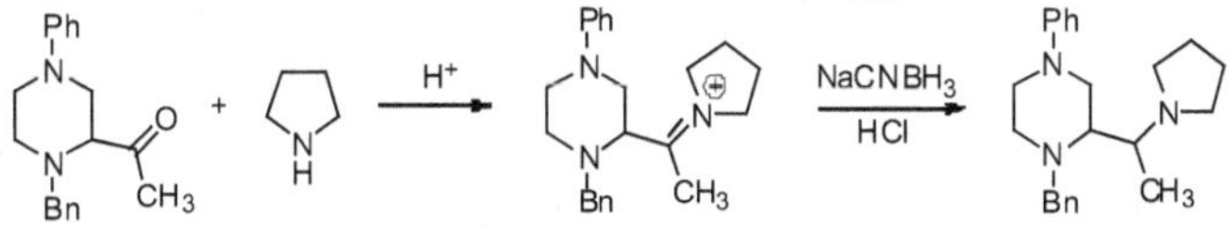

5)

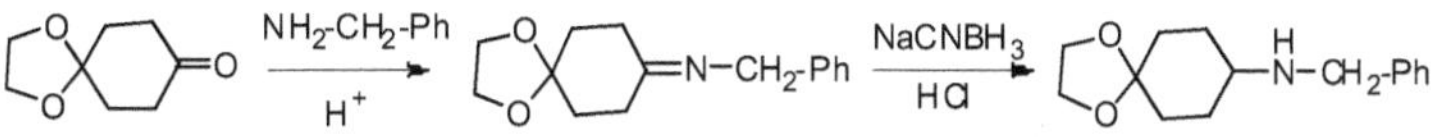

6)

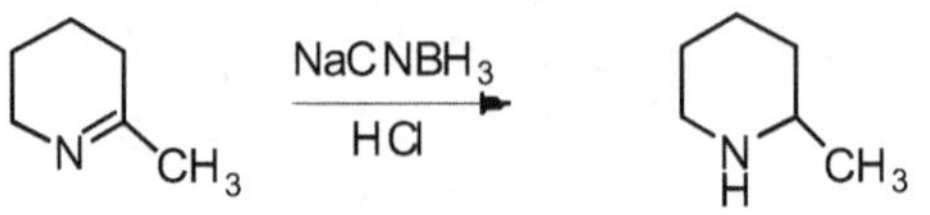

7)

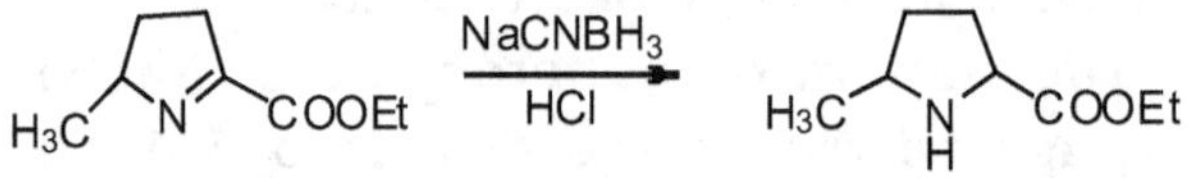

❖ **Reductive Amination:** Reductive amination with formaldehyde and NaCNBH$_3$ in acidic condition provides a convenient method for methylation of secondary amines and dimethylation of primary amines.

1)

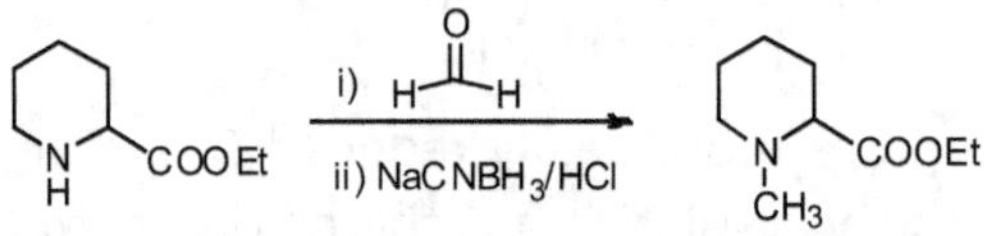

2)

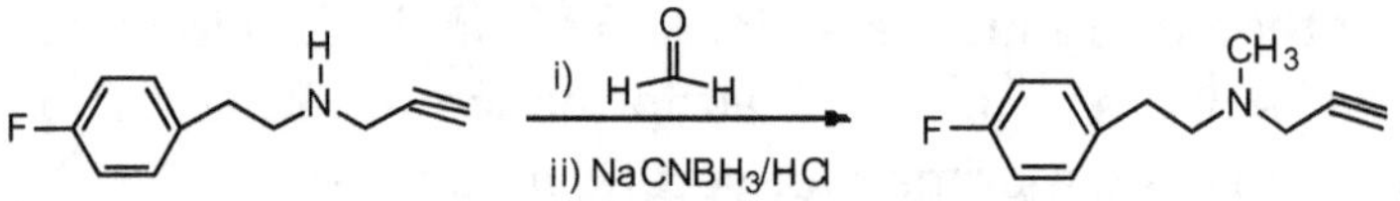

3)

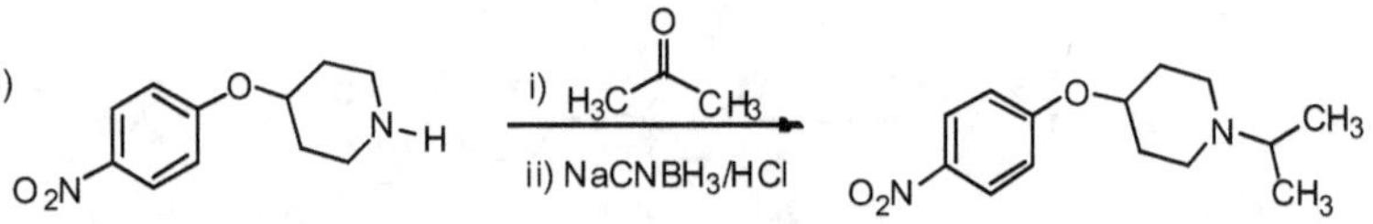

Improvement in the yield of the reduction to amine as product can be achieved by the addition of Lewis acids such as Ti(O*i*Pr)$_4$, TiCl$_4$ or ZnCl$_2$ with NaCNBH$_3$. In the process of reduction by NaCNBH$_3$ aldehyde and ketones are unaffected in neutral solution but they can be readily reduced to corresponding alcohols in acidic solution with *pH* 3-4 by the way of the protonation of carbonyl groups.

Mechanism

Intramolecular reductive amination can results in the cyclic amines shown in the following example.

NaCNBH$_3$ have some limitation as it is highly toxic and avoid the toxic effect due to cyano group the similar application of iminium reduction to amine or reductive amination can be achieved by alternative reducing agent as sodium triacetoxyborohydride [NaBH(OAc)$_3$]. Owing to the steric and electronic effect of the three acetoxy groups [NaBH(OAc)$_3$] is milder reducing reagent than NaBH$_4$ or even NaCNBH$_3$, but [NaBH(OAc)$_3$] is water sensitive nor compatible with methanol as solvent.

3) NaBH(OAc)$_3$ (Sodium triacetoxyborohydride)

Sodium triacetoxyborohydride [NaBH(OAc)$_3$] is especially suitable for reductive aminations, since the reaction rate for the reduction of iminium ion is much faster than ketones and even aldehydes. The reductive amination can be carried out as a one-pot synthesis by adding the reducing agent, carbonyl compound and amine together. The presence of catalytic amount of acetic acid helps in the iminium ion formation. Secondary amine can also undergo the reaction but the rate of reaction will be slow.

1) Cyclohexanone $\xrightarrow[\text{iii)CH}_3\text{COOH}]{\substack{\text{i) NH}_2\text{-CH}_2\text{CH}_3 \\ \text{ii) NaBH(OAc)}_3}}$ N-ethylcyclohexylamine (cyclohexyl–NH–CH$_2$–CH$_3$)

2) $\text{H}_3\text{C}\!-\!\!\text{CH}_2\text{CH}_2\!-\!\text{CO}\!-\!\text{CH}_3 \xrightarrow[\text{iii)CH}_3\text{COOH}]{\substack{\text{i) CH}_3\text{NHCH}_3 \\ \text{ii) NaBH(OAc)}_3}}$ product (H$_3$C–CH$_2$CH$_2$–CH(CH$_3$)–N(CH$_3$)$_2$)

Due to the steric and electronic effect of the acetoxy group [NaBH(OAc)$_3$] is milder reducing agent than NaBH$_4$ or even NaCNBH$_3$ and reduces iminium salt of aldehydes and ketones in the solvent 1,2-dichloroethane (DCM) but the reaction can be carried out in THF and occasionally in acetonitrile. Acid sensitive functional groups such as acetal and ketals, reducible functional groups such as C-C multiple bonds, cyano and nitro groups are tolerated in this reduction.

1) (cyclohexenyl-methyl ketone) $\xrightarrow[\text{iii)CH}_3\text{COOH/THF}]{\substack{\text{i) NH}_3 \\ \text{ii) NaBH(OAc)}_3}}$ (1-(cyclohex-3-enyl)ethylamine, NH$_2$–CH(CH$_3$)–)

2) $\text{H}_3\text{C}\!-\!\text{CO}\!-\!\text{CH}_2\!-\!\text{COOH} \xrightarrow[\text{iii)CH}_3\text{COOH/THF}]{\substack{\text{i) NH}_3 \\ \text{ii) NaBH(OAc)}_3}}$ $\text{H}_3\text{C}\!-\!\text{CH}(\text{NH}_2)\!-\!\text{CH}_2\!-\!\text{COOH}$

3) (benzyl CHO) $\xrightarrow[\text{iii)CH}_3\text{COOH/THF}]{\substack{\text{i) NH}_3 \\ \text{ii) NaBH(OAc)}_3}}$ (phenyl–CH$_2$–CH$_2$–NH$_2$)

4) (3-nitroacetophenone, CH$_3$–CO– with NO$_2$) $\xrightarrow[\text{ii)CH}_3\text{COOH/THF}]{\substack{\text{i) NH}_3 \\ \text{ii) NaBH(OAc)}_3}}$ (1-(3-nitrophenyl)ethylamine, NH$_2$–CH(CH$_3$)– with NO$_2$)

Sodium triacetoxyborohydride can reduce aldehyde selectively in the presence of ketone.

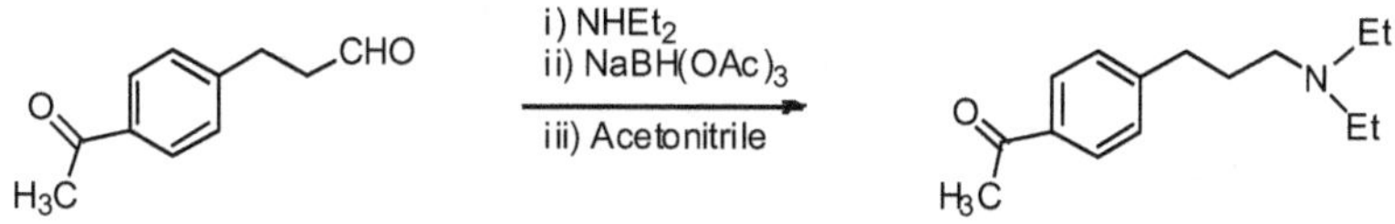

However α- and β-hydroxy ketones are reduced with this reagent. The reduction occur stereoselectively to give predominantly the *anti* diol as product.

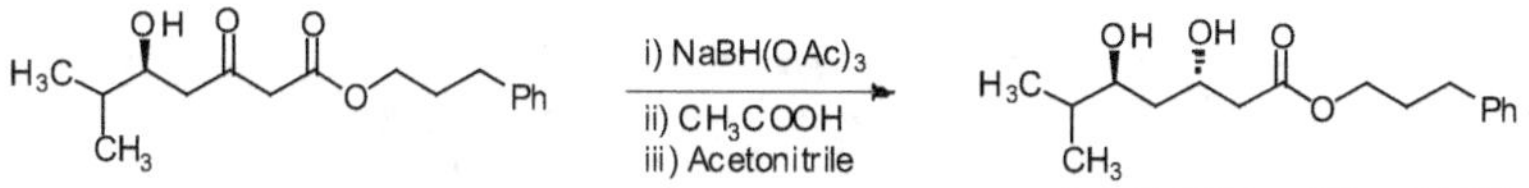

Anti diol 95% and *Syn* diol 5%

Though the application of NaCNBH$_3$ and NaBH(OAc)$_3$ are almost similar but the organic chemist prefer to used NaBH(OAc)$_3$ as reducing reagent due to the safe and non toxic where as NaCNBH$_3$ in acidic condition produces by-product as HCN.

4) B$_2$H$_6$ (Diborane)

Borane BH$_3$ exit as the gaseous dimmer as diborane B$_2$H$_6$ as a powerful reducing agent and reduces a variety of unsaturated functional groups including aldehyde, ketones, carboxylic acids to alcohols, Nitriles to amines, epoxides to alcohols, alkenes to alkanes or alcohols. When B$_2$H$_6$ combines with H$_2$O$_2$ it acts as oxidising agent and very well known for the hydroxylation of olefinic compounds. Reduction of esters to alcohols is quite slow reaction while acid chloride and nitro compounds are not reduced by diborane.

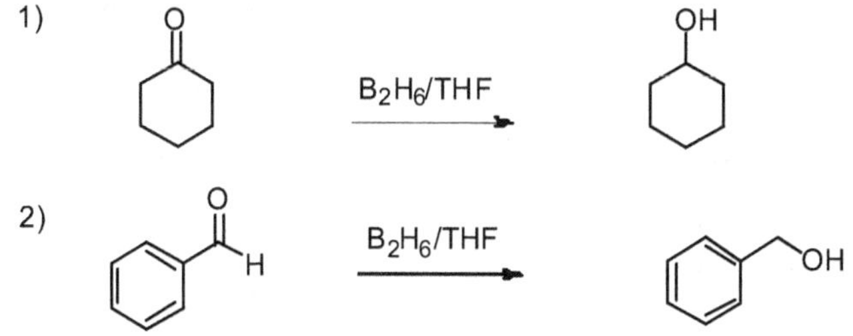

1)

B$_2$H$_6$/THF

2)

B$_2$H$_6$/THF

3)

[reaction] benzoic acid $\xrightarrow{B_2H_6/THF}$ benzyl alcohol

4)

[reaction] phenylacetonitrile (PhCH$_2$CN) $\xrightarrow{B_2H_6/THF}$ phenethylamine (PhCH$_2$CH$_2$NH$_2$)

5)

[reaction] N,N-diethylbutanamide $\xrightarrow{B_2H_6/THF}$ N,N-diethylbutylamine

6)

[reaction] ethyl 3-methylbutanoate $\xrightarrow[\text{very slow}]{B_2H_6/THF}$ 3-methylbutan-1-ol

7)

[reaction] H_3C—CH=CH—CH_3 $\xrightarrow{B_2H_6/THF}$ trialkylborane

8)

[reaction] 2-methyloxirane (propylene oxide) $\xrightarrow{B_2H_6/THF}$ propan-2-ol

Diborane (B$_2$H$_6$) is Lewis acid due to vacant *p*-orbital, the way of reaction is exactly different than that of NaBH$_4$. Where in case of NaBH$_4$ the hydrides are nucleophilic and attacked to the electrophilic carbonyl carbon on the other hand borane as Lewis acid attacked to electron rich carbonyl group oxygen gives the complex intermediate. In the complex irreversible transfer of hydride ion from boron to carbonyl carbon reduced the carbonyl group as shown in the mechanism below.

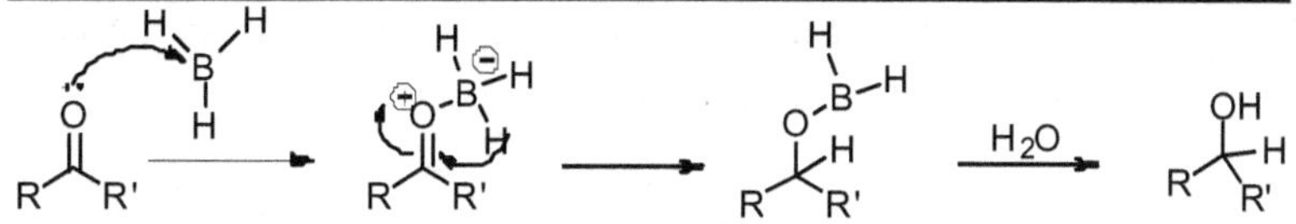

In case of acid chloride electron withdrawing effect of halide is more, so reaction does not occurred and similar reason for very slow reduction of esters by diborane. A useful reaction of diborane is the reduction of carboxylic acids to primary alcohols, which occurs very readily and can be achieved selectivity in the presence of other functional group including ester.

1)

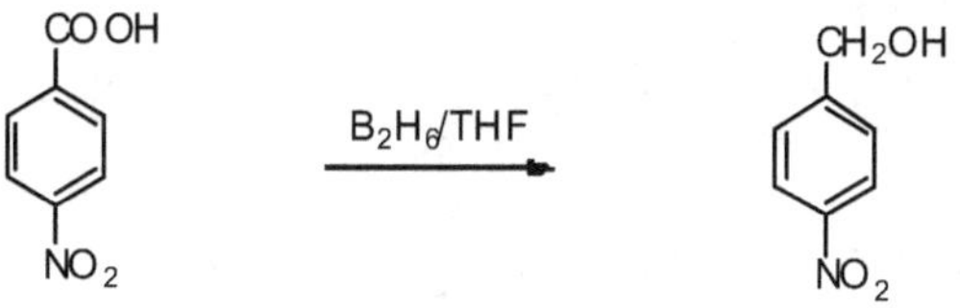

2)

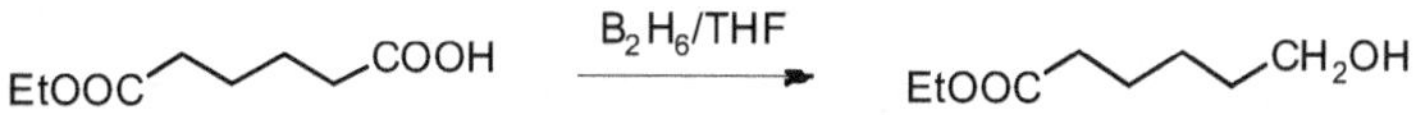

Amides and lactones are also good functional group for reduction by borane and give amines because being electron deficient react with most nucleophilic carbonyl oxygen. It is therefore selective reduction in the presence of other functional groups as below.

1)

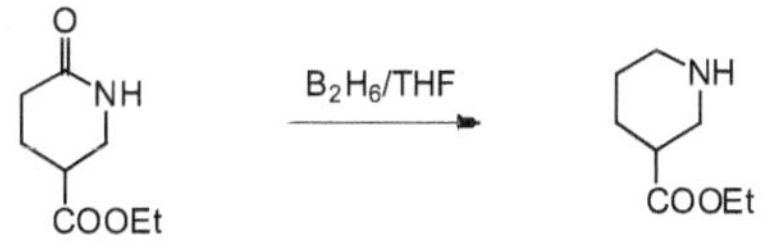

2)

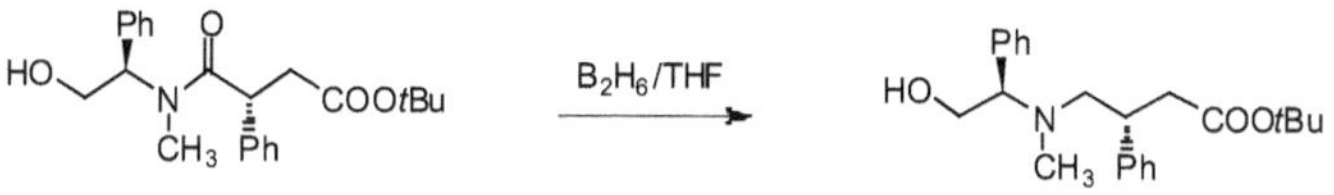

The reduction of epoxide with borane is noteworthy as it gives to the less substituted alcohol as the major product.

$$\text{(benzyl 2-methyl-2,3-epoxide)} \xrightarrow{\text{B}_2\text{H}_6/\text{THF}} \text{(4-phenyl-3-methyl-2-butanol)}$$

Mechanism:

i) Reduction of carboxylic acid by diborane (B_2H_6).

$$\text{(benzoic acid)} \xrightarrow{\text{B}_2\text{H}_6/\text{THF}} \text{(benzyl alcohol)}$$

ii) Nitrile reduction by diborane (B_2H_6).

$$\text{(benzonitrile)} \xrightarrow{\text{B}_2\text{H}_6/\text{THF}} \text{(benzylamine)}$$

iii) Amide reduction by diborane (B_2H_6).

$$\text{(N,N-dimethylbenzamide)} \xrightarrow{\text{B}_2\text{H}_6/\text{THF}} \text{(N,N-dimethylbenzylamine)}$$

iv) Epoxide reduction by diborane (B_2H_6).

The diborane is a useful regent with many applications but it is pyrophoric, gaseous and not convenient to handle. Hence it is stored in THF or dimethyl sulphide (DMS) as solvent and name as Borane-tetrahydrofuran (BTHF) and borane-dimethylsulfide (BMS, DMCB) are often used as a borane source. Both reagents are available in solution (e.g. 1M in THF) are therefore easier to handle than diborane.

Borane-tetrahydrofuran (BTHF)   Borane-dimethylsulfide (BMS, DMCB)

BMS is more stable than BTHF but has an unpleasant odder and volatility and flammability are always a drawback with borane.

❖ **Hydroboration oxidation** can also be achieved by diborane in presence of alkaline H_2O_2, where the alkenes can be converted into alcohols. The less substituted carbon get boranated and on more substituted carbon hydride ion added regioselectively and on treatment with alkaline H_2O_2 hydroboration oxidation take place to give less substituted alcohol.

5) 9-BBN (9-Borobicyclo[3,3,1] nonane)

The 9-BBN is colourless solid used in organic synthesis as a hydroboration reagent. The compound exists as a hydride-bridge dime, which easily cleaves in the presence of reducible substrates. It is prepared by the action of 1,5-cyclooctadiene with borane usually in ethereal solvent as THF as shown in the following reaction.

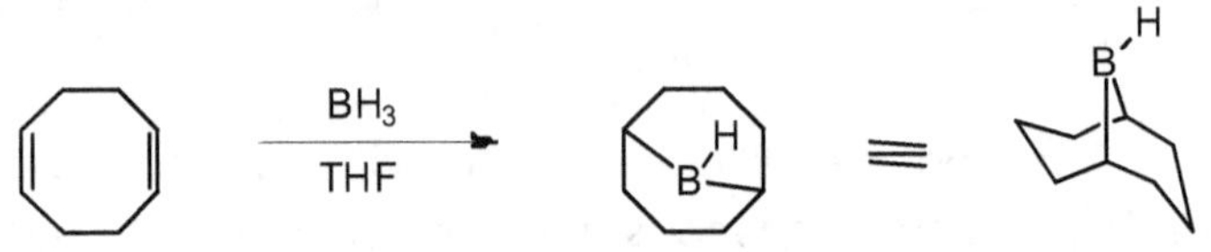

1,5-Cyclooctadiene   9-BBN   Hydride Bridge

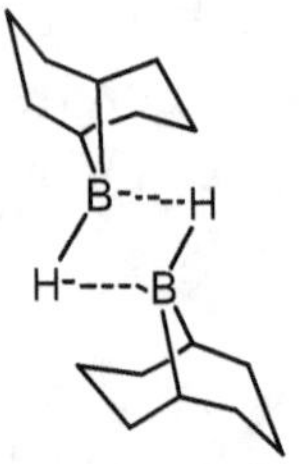

9-BBN as dimer 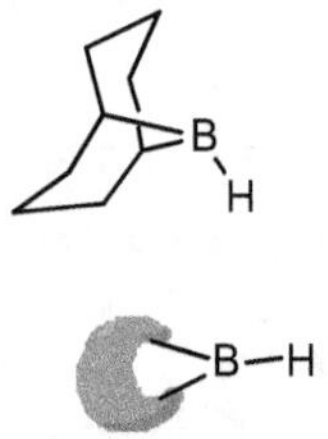   9-BBN is also known as banana borane

It is highly regioselective due to the steric bulky structure of the reagent and preferred to attack on less substituted carbon of alkene and reduced the carbon by hydride which is more substituted.

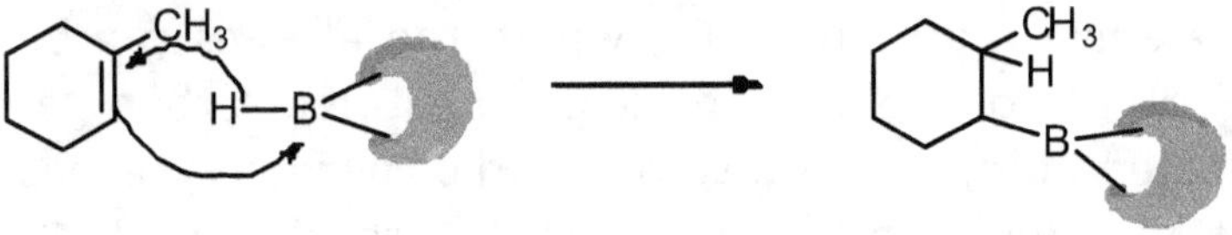

Hydroboration of mono and disubstituted alkene with borane gives typically to trialkyl-borane as product.

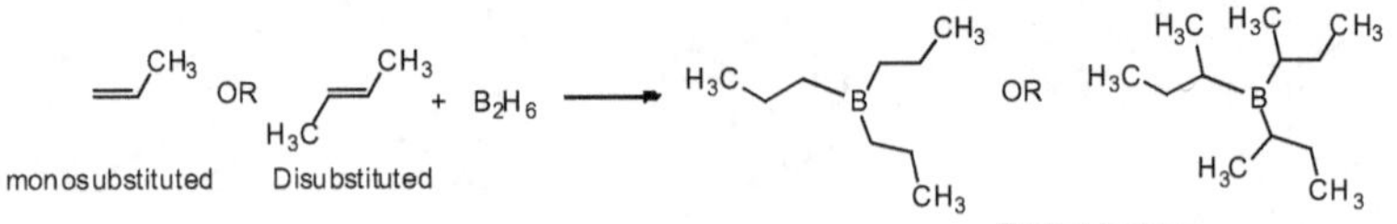

monosubstituted   Disubstituted   Trialkyl boranes

However trisubstituted alkene normally gives a dialkylborane and tetrasubstituted alkene form only the monoalkylboranes as below.

Trisubstituted alkene + B_2H_6 → Dialkyl boranes (Disiamylborane)

Tetrasubstituted alkene + B_2H_6 → monoalkyl borane (Thexyl borane)

This stoichiometry of alkene and borane has been exploited in the preparation of a number of mono and dialkylboranes that are less reactive and more selective than diborane in organic synthesis for reduction of alkenes. 9-BBN is bicyclic dialkylated borane and used to hydroborated less hindered alkenes.

1,5-Cyclooctadiene $\xrightarrow[\text{THF}]{B_2H_6}$ 9-BBN ≡ 9-BBN

Hydroboration is readily effective with alkenes containing many types of functional groups, where using 9-BBN the other functional groups is not reduced due to less reactive nature than B_2H_6. In reduction with B_2H_6 esters react very slowly, whereas with 9-BBN it is remain un-reactive. The carbonyl group of aldehydes, ketones and carboxylic acid are readily reacted with B_2H_6, however must be protected as their acetals and carboxylic ester which are tolerated by the reduction of 9-BBN.

1)

2)

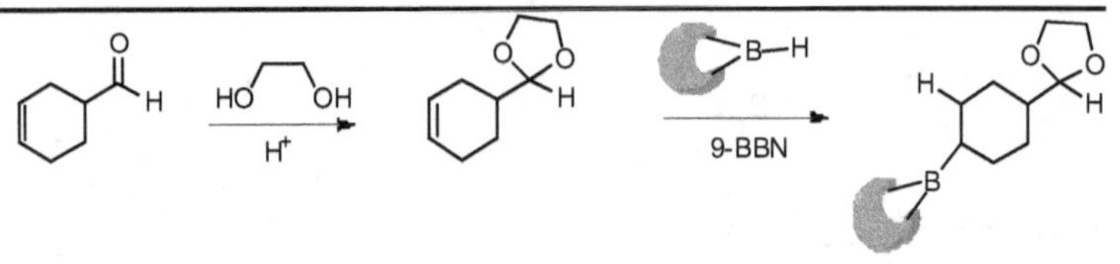

Addition of borane (9-BBN) to an unsymmetrical alkene could give two different products by addition of boron at either end of the double bond as below.

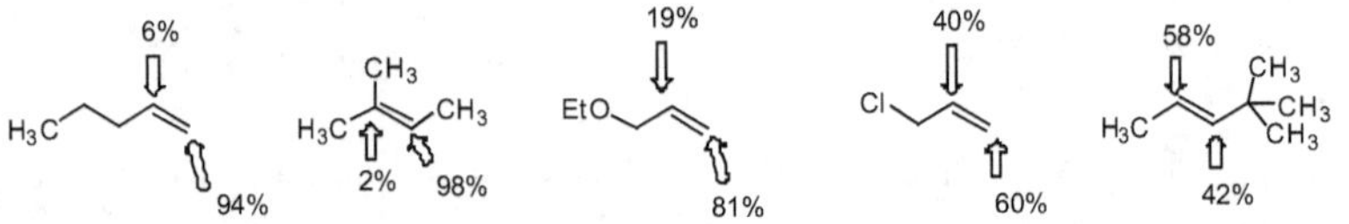

The less hindered end of the alkene double bond is also the more electron rich and therefore interacts better with the electron deficient boron atom. However the selectivity is decreases with increasing electronegativity of the substituents. The terminal alkenes react with 9-BBN more rapidly than internal alkene as well the Z-alkenes more rapidly than E-alkenes.

1)

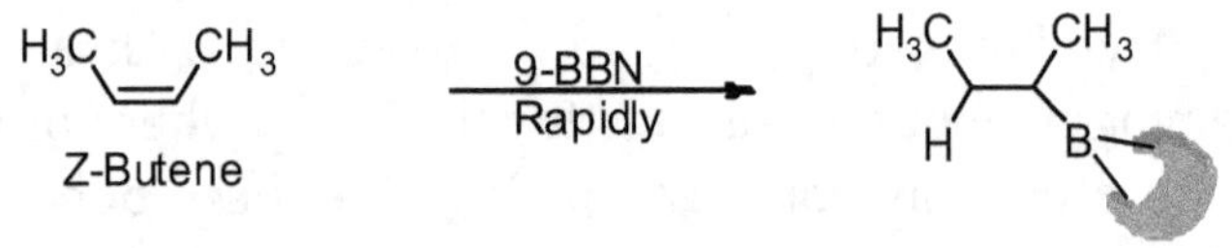

Z-Butene   9-BBN / Rapidly

2)

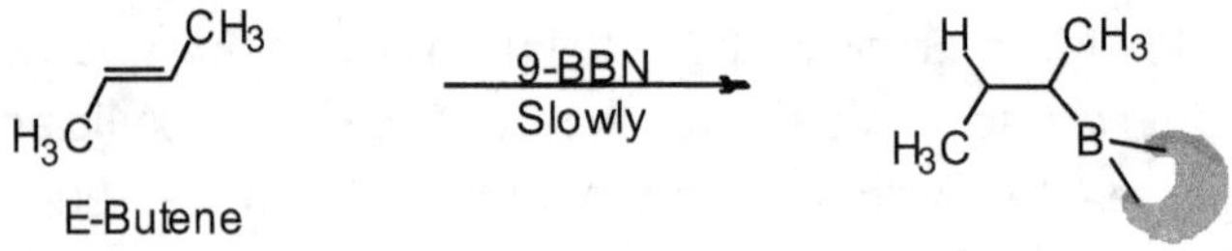

E-Butene   9-BBN / Slowly

3)

9-BBN

4)

9-BBN

CH₃ · · · B · H · CH₃

Hydroboration Oxidation can be achieved by using alkaline H_2O_2 as shown in below reaction.

9-BBN

B

H_2O_2

NaOH

OH

Applications of borane
1) Preparation of Alkanes from Alkenes

1)

3 · · · B_2H_6 · · · B₃ · · · propionic acid · · · 3 · · · CH₃

2)

9-BBN · · · B · · · propionic acid · · · CH₃

3)

O_2N · · · CH₂ · · · 9-BBN or / B_2H_6/H^+ · · · O_2N · · · CH₃

2) Preparation of Alkenes from Alkynes

9-BBN · · · H · B · *syn* addition · · · CH_3COOH · · · H · H · *Cis* stilbene

3) Preparation of Amines

e.g.

3 H_3C · · · BH_3 · · · H_3C · B · CH₃ · CH₃ · Cl-NH-CH₂-CH₃ · · · H_3C · B⁻ · ⁺NH-CH₂-CH₃ · Cl · CH₃ · CH₃

-H⁺

H_3C · B · OH + H_3C · N-CH₂-CH₃ · H · · · H_2O/H^+ · · · H_3C · B-N · CH₂-CH₃ · H₃C · · · 1,2-trasfer of alkyl group · · · H_3C · B⁻-N · CH₂-CH₃ · Cl · CH₃

1)

$$\text{(methyl bicyclic alkene)} \xrightarrow[\text{2) } NH_2SO_3]{\text{1) } B_2H_6} \text{(methyl bicyclic amine, } NH_2)$$

4) Preparation of Alcohols

1)

$$\text{(vinylcyclohexane)} \xrightarrow[\text{2) } H_2O_2/NaOH]{\text{1) } B_2H_6} \text{(2-cyclohexylethanol, } OH)$$

2)

$$\text{(1-methylcyclohexene)} \xrightarrow[\text{2) } H_2O_2/NaOH]{\text{1) } B_2H_6} \text{(2-methylcyclohexanol)}$$

5) Preparation of Aldehydes and Ketones

1)

$$3 \text{(cyclohexene)} \xrightarrow[\text{THF}]{B_2H_6} \text{(tricyclohexylborane)}_3 \xrightarrow{K_2Cr_2O_7} \text{(cyclohexanone)}$$

2)

$$\text{(cyclopentyl-CH=CH}_2) \xrightarrow[\text{2) PCC}]{\text{1) 9-BBN}} \text{(cyclopentyl-CH}_2\text{-CHO})$$

3)

$$H_3C-\!\!\equiv\!\!-CH_3 \xrightarrow[\text{2) } H_2O_2/NaOH]{\text{1) 9-BBN}} \underset{\text{enol}}{\overset{H_3C}{\underset{H}{\diagup}}\overset{CH_3}{\underset{OH}{\diagdown}}} \rightleftharpoons \underset{\text{keto}}{H_3C-CO-CH_3}$$

6) Carbonylation of Organoboranes

$$3 \text{(cyclohexene)} \xrightarrow[\text{THF}]{B_2H_6} \text{(tricyclohexylborane)}_3 \xrightarrow{\bar{C}\equiv\overset{+}{O}} \cdots$$

$$\cdots \xrightarrow{H_2O_2/NaOH} \text{(tricyclohexylcarbinol, HO–C)}$$

If carbonylation reaction is carried in the presence of small amount of water then it inhibits the migration of the third alkyl group from boron to carbon and this lead to the formation of ketone and phenol as shown below reaction.

7) Reaction of borane with carbanions.

b) Aluminium Based Reagents

1) LiAlH$_4$ (Lithium Aluminium Hydride [LAH] or Lithium tetrahydroaluminate III)

LiAlH$_4$ is a strong reducing agent commonly used in organic synthesis and it reduces almost all functional functional groups.

Preparations: It is prepared by the reaction between lithium hydride and aluminium chloride in ether as solvent as diethyl ether or THF and in the same solvent is normally used in reaction.

$$4LiH + AlCl_3 \longrightarrow LiAlH_4 + 3LiCl_3$$

It is highly reactive hence the solvent must be dry as the hydride is destroyed by water.

$$LiAlH_4 \longrightarrow LiOH + Al(OH)_3 + 4H_2$$

It must be handled with great care since it may inflame spontaneously and explodes violently on heating. The compounds containing hydroxyl, amino or thiol group react with $LiAlH_4$ and liberate hydrogen.

$$4EtOH + LiAlH_4 \longrightarrow (EtO)_4Al\,Li + 4H_2$$

It is nucleophilic reducing reagent and best used to reduce aldehydes to primary alcohols, ketones to secondary alcohols, carboxylic acids to primary alcohols, esters to primary alcohols, amides and nitriles to amines, epoxides to alcohols, lactones to diols, acid chlorides to primary alcohols and nitro compounds to amines as shown in the following examples.

1)

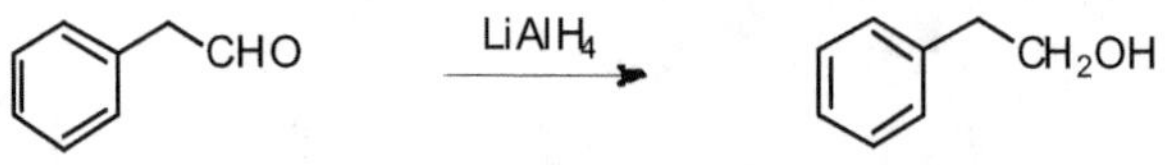

2)

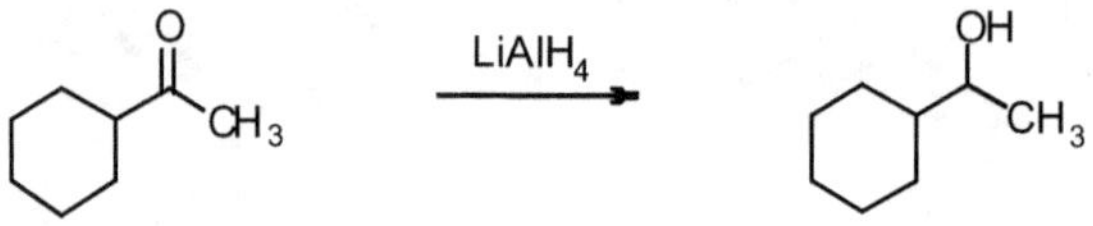

3)

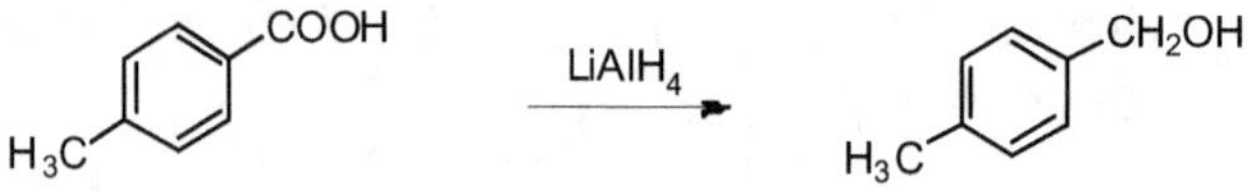

4)

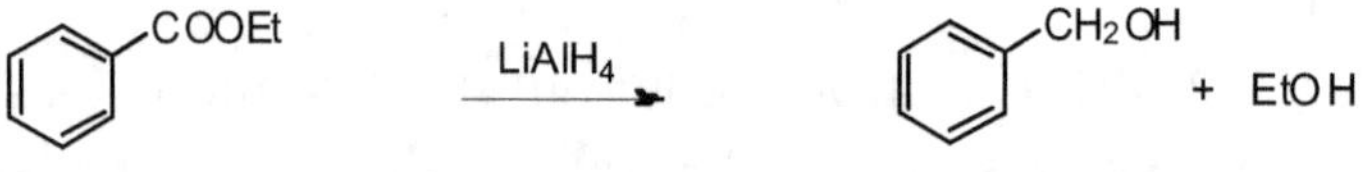

5)

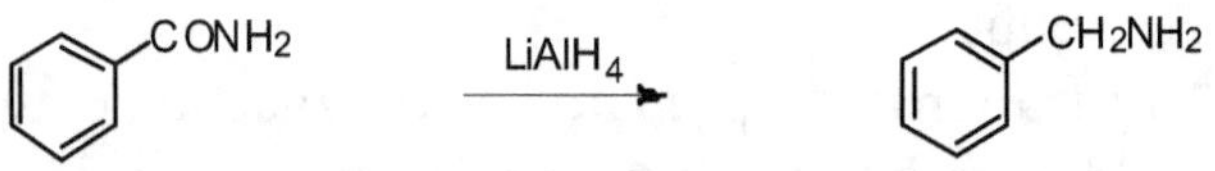

6)

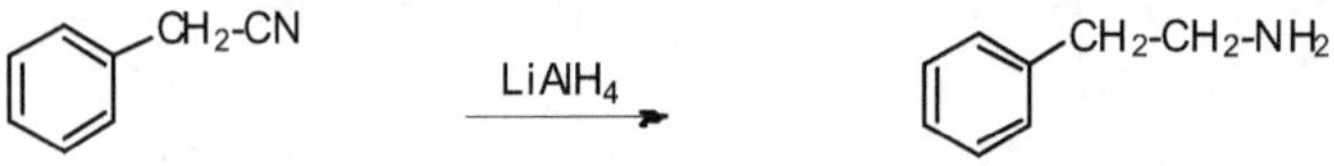

7)

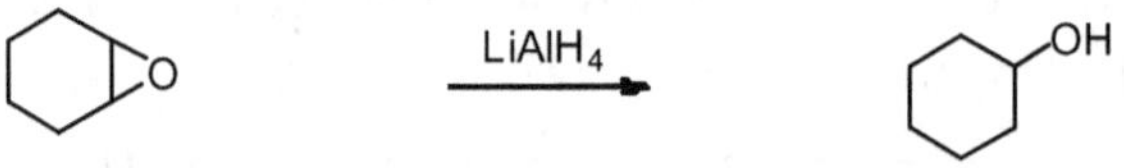

8)

$$\text{(lactone)} \xrightarrow{\text{LiAlH}_4} \text{(diol, OH, OH)}$$

9)

$$C_6H_5CH_2COCl \xrightarrow{\text{LiAlH}_4} C_6H_5CH_2CH_2OH$$

10)

$$C_6H_5NO_2 \xrightarrow{\text{LiAlH}_4} C_6H_5NH_2$$

$LiAlH_4$ can not reduce an isolated non-polar double bonds or triple bonds. However the double bonds or triple bonds in conjugation with aromatic ring can reduce but lowering the temperature of the reaction can selectively reduce only carbonyl group.

1)

$$H_3C-CH=CH-CO-CH_3 \xrightarrow[35^0c]{\substack{\text{excess of} \\ \text{LiAlH}_4}} H_3C-CH=CH-CH(OH)-CH_3$$

2)

$$H_3C-C\equiv C-CH_2-CO-CH_3 \xrightarrow[35^0c]{\substack{\text{excess of} \\ \text{LiAlH}_4}} H_3C-C\equiv C-CH_2-CH(OH)-CH_3$$

3)

$$\xrightarrow[35^0c]{\substack{\text{excess of} \\ \text{LiAlH}_4}}$$

4)

$$\xrightarrow[35^0c]{\substack{\text{excess of} \\ \text{LiAlH}_4}}$$

5)

$$\xrightarrow[35^0c]{\substack{\text{excess of} \\ \text{LiAlH}_4}}$$

6) 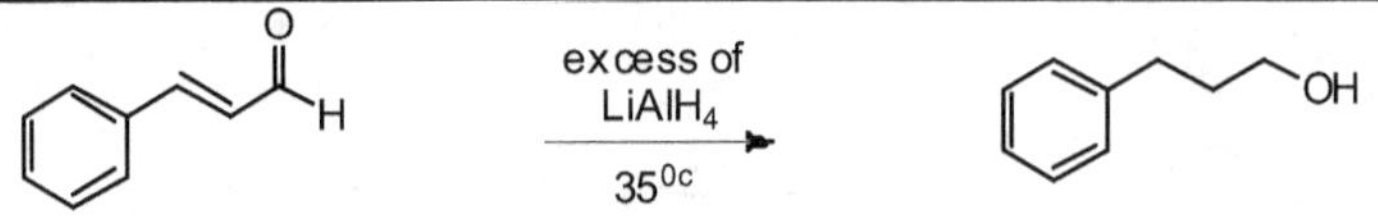

7) 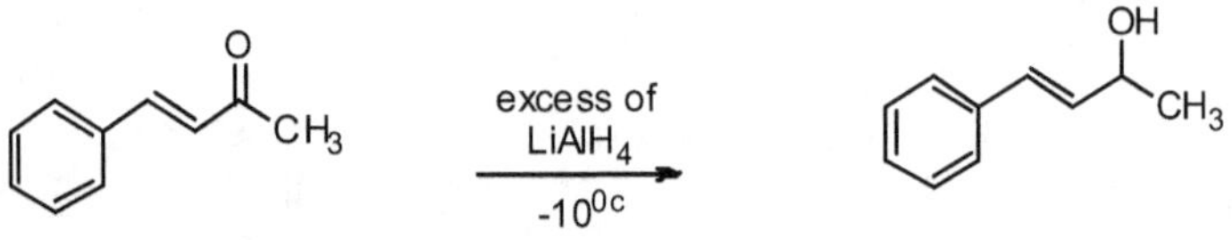

8) 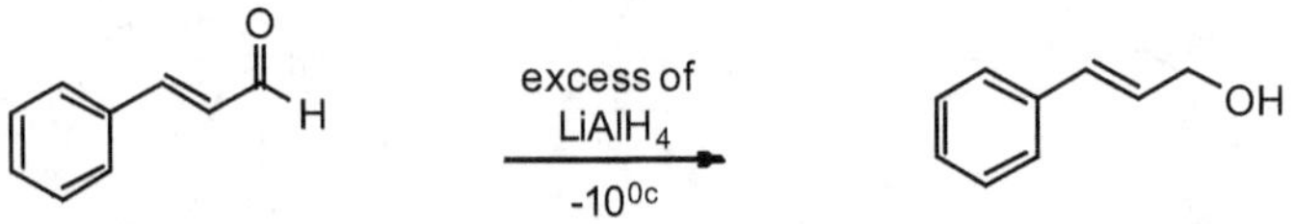

In this process of reduction first of all α,β-unsaturated carbonyl (aromatic) convert into allyl alcohol. The reduction of double bond takes place by formation of cyclic organoaluminium compound as an intermediate which collapses on hydrolysis to saturated alcohol as product.

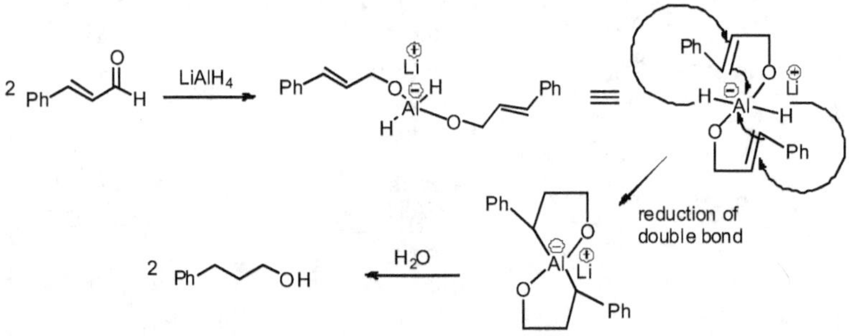

Mechanism (Aldehydes/ketones)

Each of the four hydride of $LiAlH_4$ is available for transfer to carbonyl groups as the reduction process shown below.

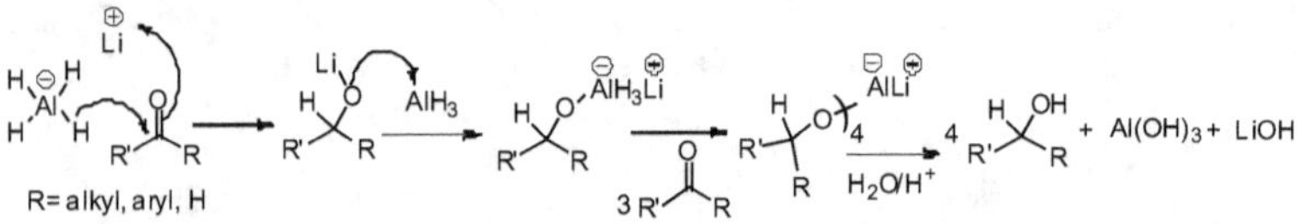

While adding the second, third and fourth molecule of carbonyl compound to the reagent, it is less rapidly react than the first molecule. The alkoxy group give less reactivity and become more selective reducing reagent. Finally hydrolysis of the aluminium alkoxide gives the four moles of alcohol form one mole of reagent as $LiAlH_4$.

Mechanism (Reduction of Ester)

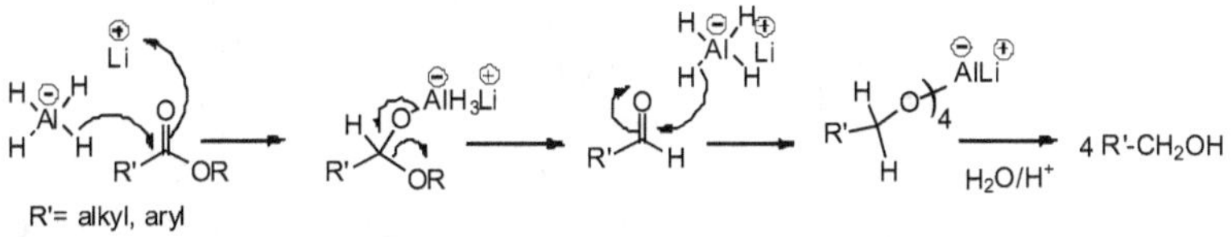

R'= alkyl, aryl

Mechanism (Reduction of Amide)

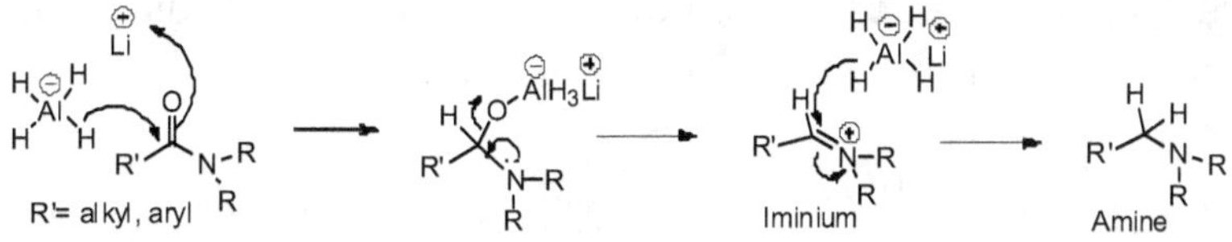

R'= alkyl, aryl

Iminium   Amine

$LiAlH_4$ can also reduced primary and secondary alkyl halides to corresponding hydrocarbons and tertiary alkyl halides give mostly alkenes. Tosylates resemble to halides and can be reduced to alkanes.

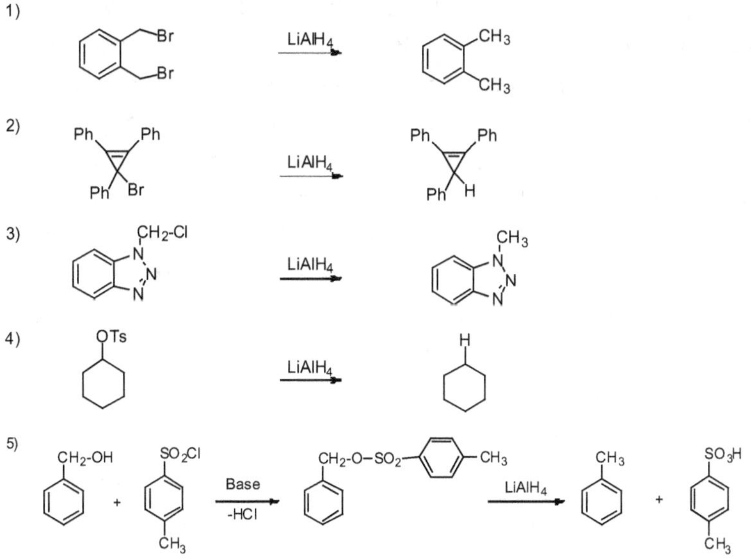

1)

2)

3)

4)

5)

Stereochemistry of Reduction of Ketones

The normal reduction of the carbonyl group of an unsymmetrical ketone such as ethyl methyl ketone leads to the formation of racemic alcohol.

Where as ketones that contains any symmetric (Chiral) centre gives the two diastereomers of the alcohols in different proportion as shown in below example.

In the above example optically active ketone on reduction with $LiAlH_4$ give *anti*-stereoisomer of the alcohol as predominantly major product, it can be predicted on the basis of the Felkin-Anh model also called Cram's rule. The diastereomer which predominates is that formed by approach of the reagent to the less hindered side of the carbonyl group when the rotational conformation of the molecule is such that largest group on the adjacent chiral centre is perpendicular to the carbonyl group. This has been shown using Newman's projections, where S, M, L represent small, medium and large substituents. Thus the reduction of ketones, major *anti*-alcohol arises by the attack of metal hydride on the less hindered side of the carbonyl group in the conformation shown below.

In the α-hydroxy or α-amino ketones reduction proceed through a relatively rigid chelate formation. Hence reduction of such compounds usually proceeds with a comparatively high degree of stereoselectivity by attack on the chelate from the less hindered side but not necessarily according to Cram's approach. Thus reaction of this kind leads to the diol formation with *Anti:Syn* (80:20) ratio.

Anti 80%   *Syn* 20%

Stereochemistry of reduction of cyclic ketones

When less hindered cyclohexanone reduced with LiAlH$_4$ more stable equatorial product predominates, where the attack of hydride to carbonyl group in an axial direction leading to the equatorial alcohol as product as shown in below reactions.

90%   10%

Axial attack

90%

Equatorial attack

10%

In the above reaction 1,4-interaction is very less, if any substituent is present on third position the 1,3-interaction will change the path of reaction. For example the reduction of 3,3,5-trisubstituted cyclohexanone a hindered cyclic ketone by LiAlH$_4$ gives the axial alcohol as the major product. In hindered ketones however axial approach of hydride may be hampered by steric factor (1,3-interaction) there by favouring equatorial approach and gives the axial alcohol as the product.

3,3,5-trimethyl cyclohexamone   major   minor

The selectivity of reduction can be improved to almost only product by changing to more hindered reducing reagent as L-Selectride [LiBH(Bu)$_3$] or modified LiAlH4 to lithium hydro-tri-tertiary butoxyaluminate [LiAlH(OtBu)$_3$].

3,3,5-trimethyl cyclohexamone   99%   Equatorial attack

Reduction of Epoxides

Reduction of unsymmetrical epoxides reaction takes place at the less substituted carbon atom to give the more substituted alcohols.

The same reaction can be revert by using Lewis acid and NaCNBH$_3$ through backside attack of hydride on epoxide-Lewis acid complex. The direction of ring opening is now dictated by the formation of the more stable carbocation intermediate.

Reduction of Bicycloketones

Reduction of norcamphor and camphor with LiAlH$_4$ gives different products as endo norborneol and exo isoborneol.

1)

Less stable endo product

2)

$$\xrightarrow{\text{LiAlH}_4}$$

Exo product

In general there is tendency for approach of the reagent to the carbonyl carbon from less hindered side to have product although it is less stable due to substituent interaction.

1)

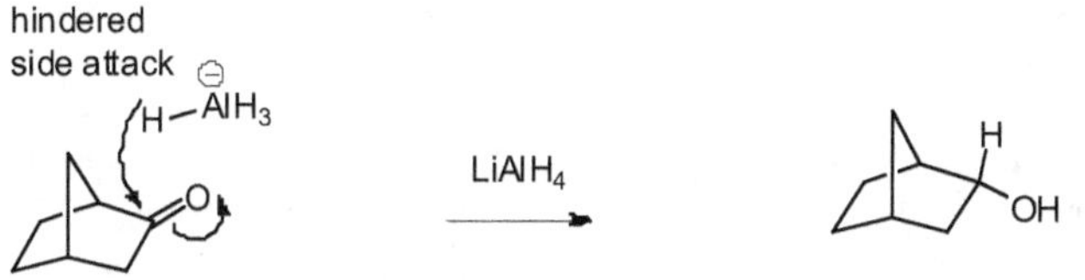

hindered side attack

$$\xrightarrow{\text{LiAlH}_4}$$

Less stable endo product

2)

less hindered side attack

$$\xrightarrow{\text{LiAlH}_4}$$

less stable exo product

$LiAlH_4$ and $AlCl_3$ in combination reduce ester in THF selectively keeping other functional group unreacted. Hence it is selective reducing agent as shown below examples.

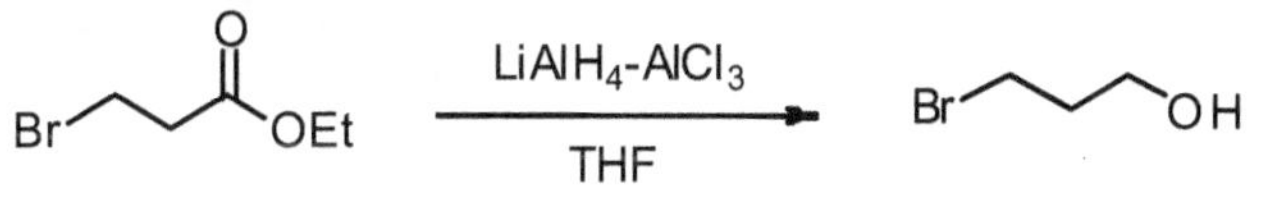

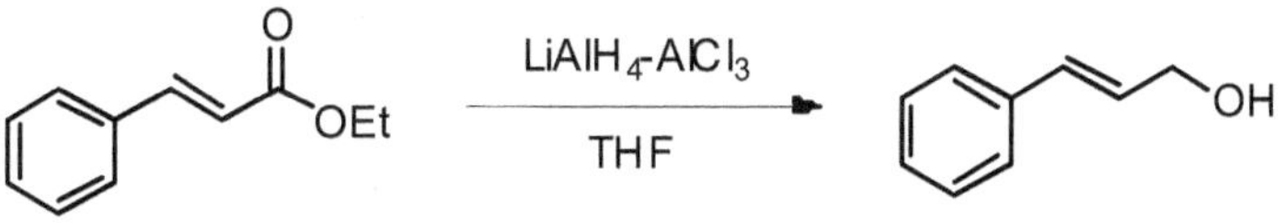

$$\xrightarrow[\text{THF}]{\text{LiAlH}_4\text{-AlCl}_3}$$

$$\xrightarrow[\text{THF}]{\text{LiAlH}_4\text{-AlCl}_3}$$

Examples of reduction of following functional groups:
Reduction of carboxylic acids

1)

H_3C~~~~~COOH $\xrightarrow{LiAlH_4}$ H_3C~~~~~CH_2-OH

2)

HOOC~~~~~COOH $\xrightarrow{LiAlH_4}$ HO-H_2C~~~~~CH_2-OH

3)

Ph-CH_2-COOH $\xrightarrow{LiAlH_4}$ Ph-CH_2-CH_2-OH

4)

Ph-C(Ph)(Ph)-COOH $\xrightarrow{LiAlH_4}$ Ph-C(Ph)(Ph)-CH_2-OH

Reduction of Esters

1)

Ph-CH(CH_3)-COOEt $\xrightarrow{LiAlH_4}$ Ph-CH(CH_3)-CH_2OH + EtOH

2)

o-C_6H_4(COOEt)$_2$ $\xrightarrow{LiAlH_4}$ o-C_6H_4(CH_2-OH)$_2$ + 2 EtOH

3)

pyrrolidine-N-CH(CH_3)-COOEt $\xrightarrow{LiAlH_4}$ pyrrolidine-N-CH(CH_3)-CH_2-OH + EtOH

4)

δ-valerolactone (H_3C) $\xrightarrow{LiAlH_4}$ H_3C-CH(OH)~~~~~OH

5)

$\xrightarrow{LiAlH_4}$ + 2 EtOH

Reduction of acid Anhydrides

1)

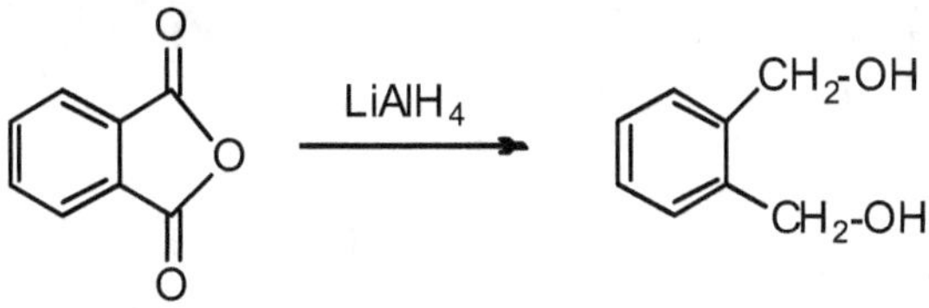

(phthalic anhydride) $\xrightarrow{\text{LiAlH}_4}$ (o-benzene with $CH_2\text{-OH}$ and $CH_2\text{-OH}$)

2)

$\xrightarrow{\text{LiAlH}_4}$ 2 $BuCH_2\text{-OH}$

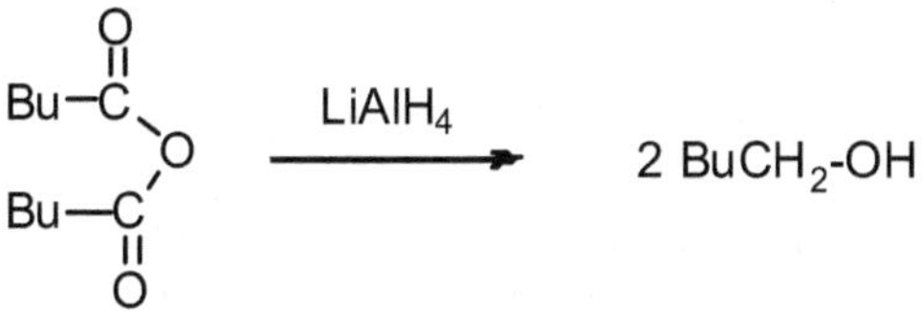

Reduction of amides

1)

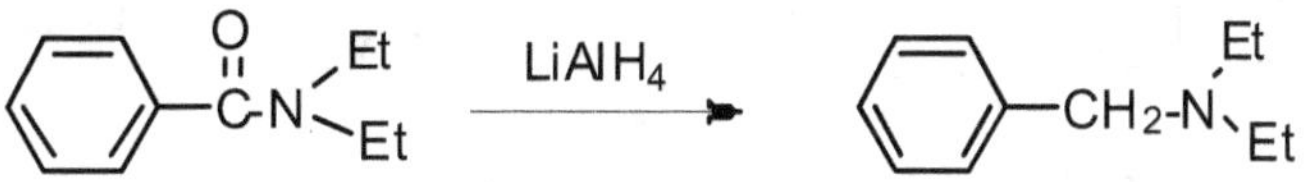

$\xrightarrow{\text{LiAlH}_4}$

2)

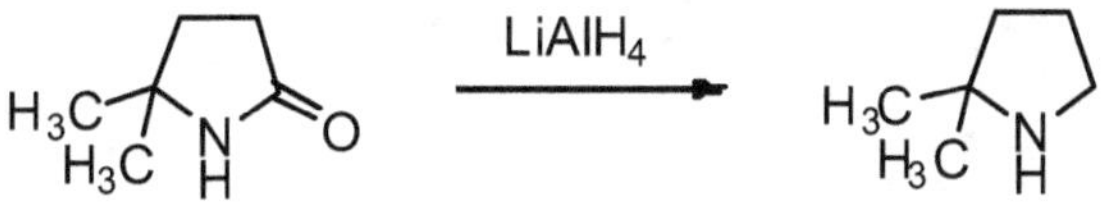

$\xrightarrow{\text{LiAlH}_4}$

3)

$\xrightarrow{\text{LiAlH}_4}$

Reduction of epoxides

1)

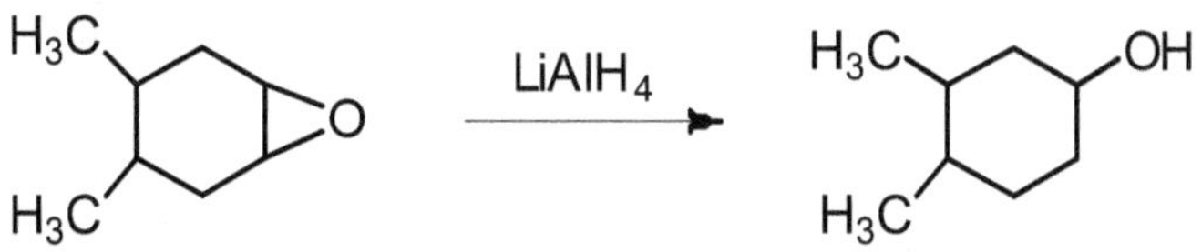

$\xrightarrow{\text{LiAlH}_4}$

2) 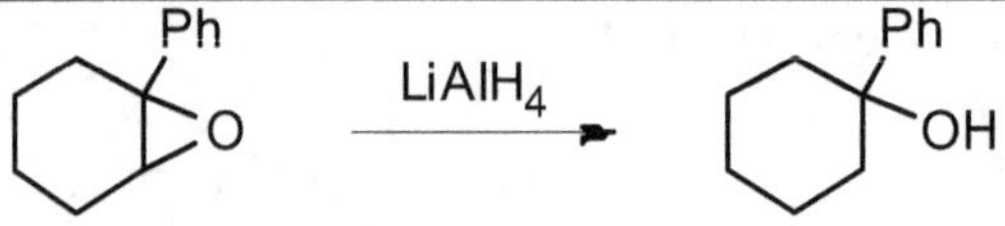

3) 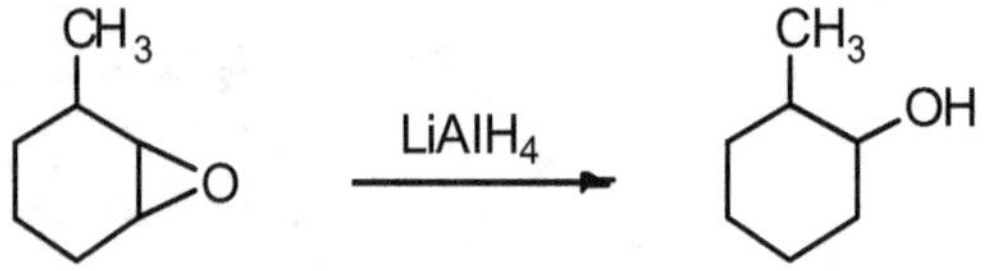

4) 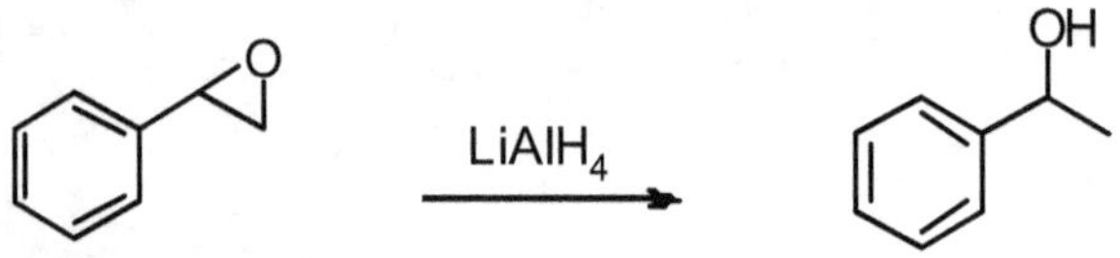

Reduction of halides

1) 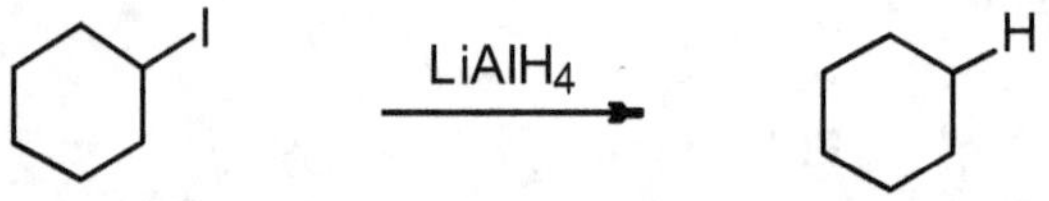

2) 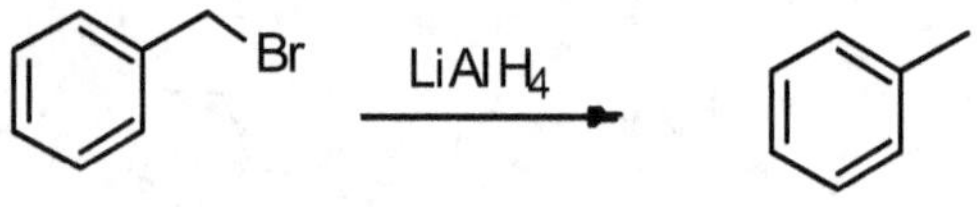

Reduction of aldehydes and ketones

1) 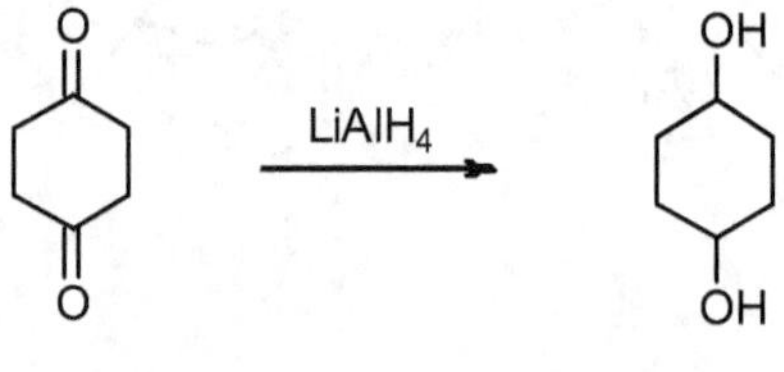

2) 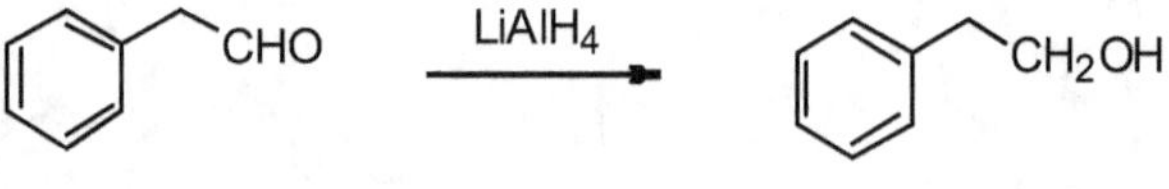

3) 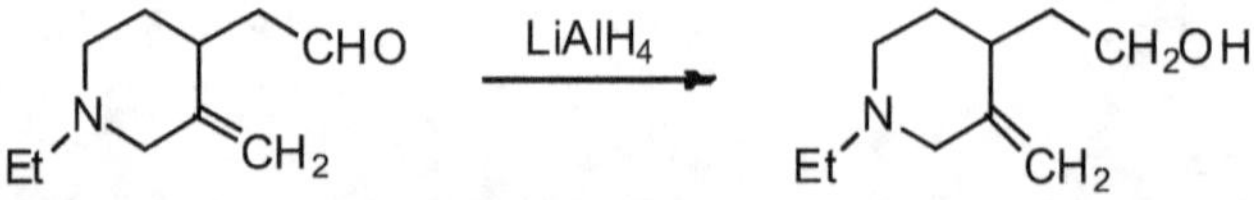

4)

$$H_3C\text{-CO-CH}_2\text{-COOEt} \xrightarrow{\text{LiAlH}_4} H_3C\text{-CH(OH)-CH}_2\text{-CH}_2\text{-OH}$$

Non selective reduction

5)

LiAlH$_4$

Reduction of nitriles

1)

$$C_6H_5\text{-CN} \xrightarrow{\text{LiAlH}_4} C_6H_5\text{-CH}_2\text{-NH}_2$$

2)

LiAlH$_4$

3)

$$NC\text{-} \cdots \text{-CN} \xrightarrow{\text{LiAlH}_4} H_2N\text{-H}_2C\text{-} \cdots \text{-CH}_2\text{-NH}_2$$

Reduction of nitro Compounds

1)

$$C_6H_{11}\text{-NO}_2 \xrightarrow{\text{LiAlH}_4} C_6H_{11}\text{-NH}_2$$

2)

LiAlH$_4$

3)

$$C_6H_5\text{-NO}_2 \xrightarrow{\text{LiAlH}_4} C_6H_5\text{-N=N-}C_6H_5$$

Azobenzene

4)

$$C_6H_5\text{-NO}_2 \xrightarrow[\text{FeCl}_3]{\text{LiAlH}_4} C_6H_5\text{-NH-NH-}C_6H_5$$

Hydrazobenzene

2) Red-Al

Sodium bis (2-methoxyethoxy) aluminium hydride

Red-Al is the trade name refers as **Red**ucing **Al**uminium compound. Red-Al is a versatile hydride reducing agent similar to LiAlH$_4$ it reduces aldehydes, ketones, carboxylic acids, esters, acid chlorides and acid anhydrides to alcohols, lactones to diols, nitriles and amides to amines as shown below reactions.

1) H$_3$C—CHO $\xrightarrow{\text{Red-Al}}$ H$_3$C—CH$_2$OH

2) (Phenyl)—CO—CH$_3$ $\xrightarrow{\text{Red-Al}}$ (Phenyl)—CH(OH)—CH$_3$

3) (Phenyl)—CH$_2$—COOH $\xrightarrow{\text{Red-Al}}$ (Phenyl)—CH$_2$—CH$_2$OH

4) (Phenyl)—COOEt $\xrightarrow{\text{Red-Al}}$ (Phenyl)—CH$_2$OH

5) (Cyclohexyl)—COOH $\xrightarrow{\text{SOCl}_2}$ (Cyclohexyl)—COCl $\xrightarrow{\text{Red-Al}}$ (Cyclohexyl)—CH$_2$OH

6) (Benzoic anhydride) $\xrightarrow{\text{Red-Al}}$ 2 (Phenyl)—CH$_2$OH

7) (4-methyl-γ-butyrolactone) $\xrightarrow{\text{Red-Al}}$ HO—CH$_2$—CH$_2$—CH(CH$_3$)—CH$_2$—OH

8) H$_3$C—CH(CH$_3$)—CH$_2$—CN $\xrightarrow{\text{Red-Al}}$ H$_3$C—CH(CH$_3$)—CH$_2$—CH$_2$NH$_2$

9)

10)

11)

depending on reaction conditions

Red-Al exhibits similar reducing application as that of LiAlH$_4$ but does not have any problem while handling. While using LiAlH$_4$ encounters many issues as it is pyrophoric in nature, short shelf life and limited solubility. Red-Al react exothermically but does not ignite like LiAlH$_4$ and tolerates temperature up to 200$^{\circ C}$. Red-Al is soluble in aromatic solvents where as LiAlH$_4$ is only soluble in ethers. Red-Al in toluene under reflux has been used to reduce aliphatic *p*-toluenesulfonamide (TsNR$_2$) to the corresponding free amine and it is one of the few reagents that can carry out this challenging reduction. LiAlH$_4$ does not reduce this functional group unless forcing condition of temperature is not used.

Red-Al reduces lactones in presence of bulky ester.

1)

Red-Al reduces epoxide through chelation.

e.g.

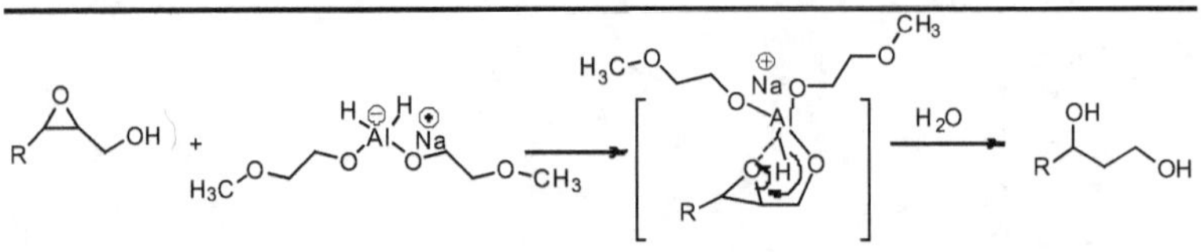

Intermediate as chelate

1)

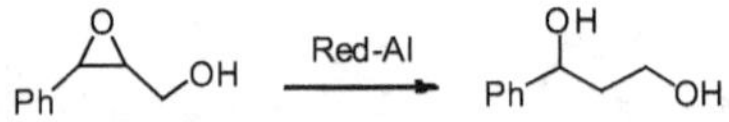

Ph — epoxide — OH → Red-Al → Ph — OH — OH

2)

BnO — epoxide — OH → Red-Al → BnO — OH — OH

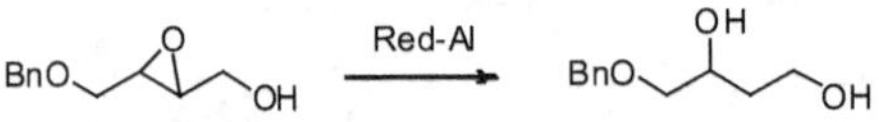

Alkynes particularly propargylic alcohol reduced to allylic alcohol with *E*-isomer with Red-Al

1)

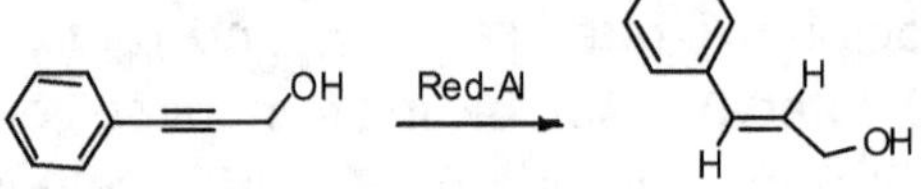

Red-Al

E-isomer

2)

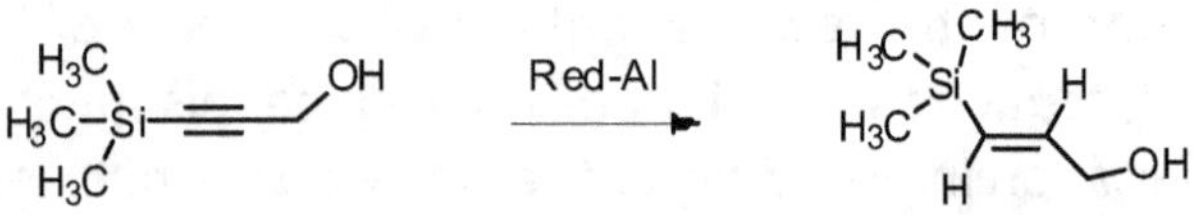

Red-Al

E-isomer

3)

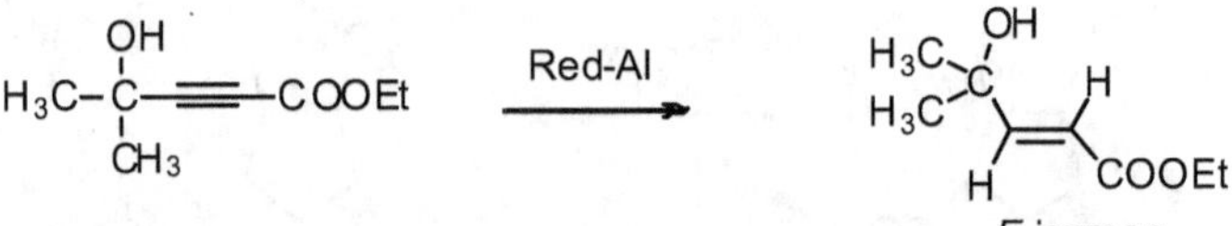

$H_3C-C(OH)(CH_3)-C\equiv C-COOEt$ → Red-Al → *E*-isomer

Mechanism

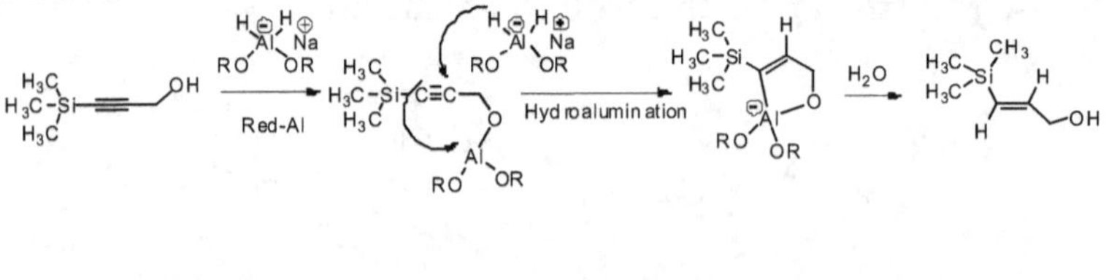

Red-Al → Hydroalumination → H_2O

Reduction of ketones/aldehydes

1) (cyclohexanone) → Red-Al → (cyclohexanol)

2) (benzaldehyde) → Red-Al → (benzyl alcohol)

Mechanism

R= alkyl, aryl, H

3) DIBAL-H (Diisobutylaluminium Hydride)

Diisobutylaluminium Hydride

Diisobutylaluminium Hydride (DIBAL-H or DIBAL or iBu$_2$AlH) is a very useful reducing agent as a derivative of aluminium hydride and available commercially as a solution in a variety of solvents. DIBAL-H is in some ways like borane, it exists as a bridged dimmer.

Bridged dimer

DIBAL-H becomes a reducing agent only after it has formed a Lewis acid-base complex with electron rich carbonyl group in the reaction. At ordinary temperature aldehydes, ketones and esters are reduces to alcohols, nitriles gives amines and epoxides are cleaved to alcohols but however DIBAL-H is particularly used for the reduction of esters, nitriles and amides to aldehyde at very low temperature i.e $-78^{\circ C}$. In the aqueous workup the excess of DIBAL-H has been destroyed so that no further reduction of aldehyde is possible.

At Ordinary Temperature (room Temp.)

1) $C_6H_5COOEt \xrightarrow[\text{room Temp}]{\text{DIBAL-H}} C_6H_5CH_2OH$

2) $C_6H_5CONEt_2 \xrightarrow[\text{room Temp}]{\text{DIBAL-H}} C_6H_5CH_2NEt_2$

3) $C_6H_5CH_2CN \xrightarrow[\text{room Temp}]{\text{DIBAL-H}} C_6H_5CH_2CH_2-NH_2$

4) $C_6H_5CHO \xrightarrow[\text{room Temp}]{\text{DIBAL-H}} C_6H_5CH_2OH$

At very low Temperature (-78^{0C})

1) $C_6H_5COOEt \xrightarrow[-78^{\circ C}]{\text{DIBAL-H}} C_6H_5CHO$

2) 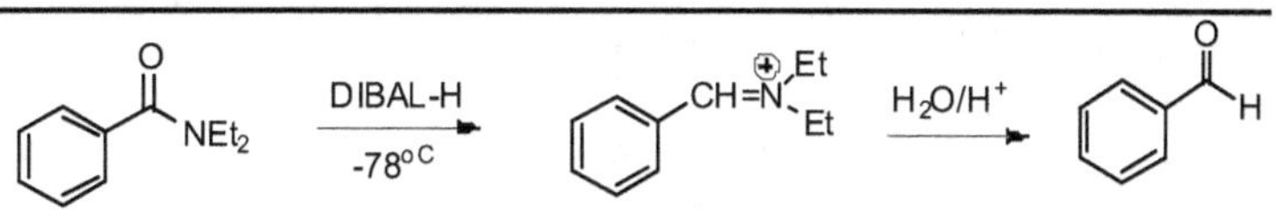 [reaction scheme: benzamide (PhCONEt₂) + DIBAL-H, -78°C → iminium intermediate + H₂O/H⁺ → benzaldehyde]

3) 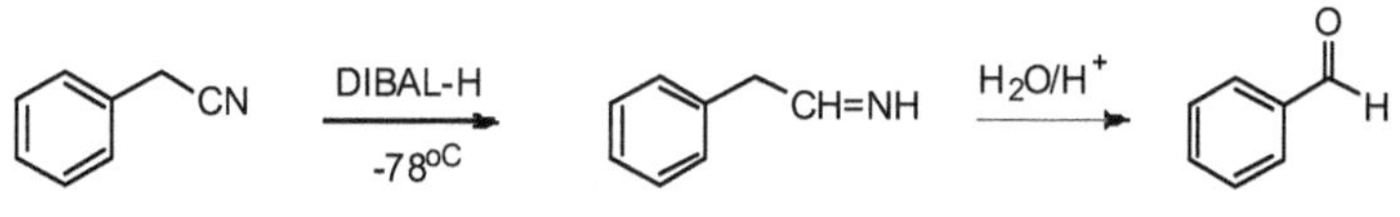 [reaction scheme: phenylacetonitrile (PhCH₂CN) + DIBAL-H, -78°C → PhCH₂CH=NH + H₂O/H⁺ → benzaldehyde]

Mechanism

[reaction mechanism scheme: ester RCOOEt + H–Al(iBu)₂, -78°C → Lewis acid-base complex → Tetrahedral intermediate stable at -78°C + H₂O/H⁺ → RCHO]

Lewis acid-base complex

Tetrahedral intermediate
stable at -78°C

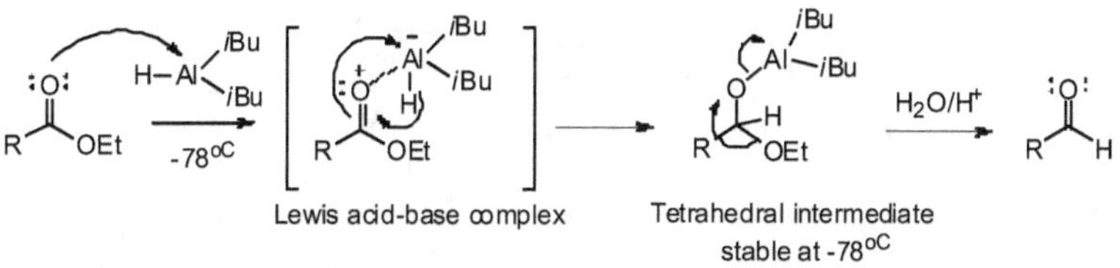

At low temperature (-78°C) esters and lactones are reduced directly to aldehyde and lactols. The nitriles and amides give imines which are readily converted into the aldehydes on hydrolysis.

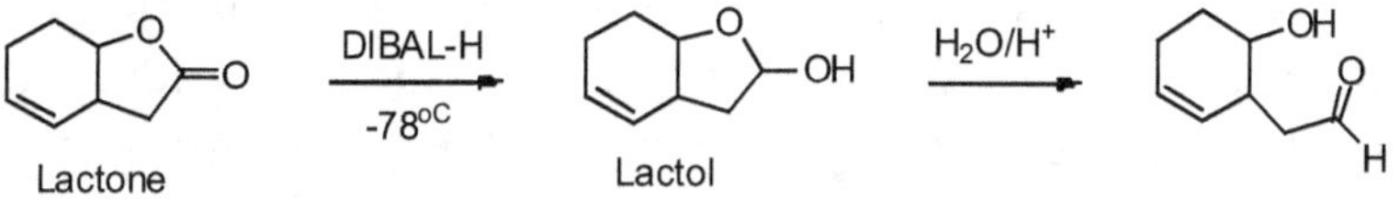

[reaction scheme: Lactone + DIBAL-H, -78°C → Lactol + H₂O/H⁺ → hydroxy aldehyde]

Lactone

Lactol

Mechanism of lactone reduction

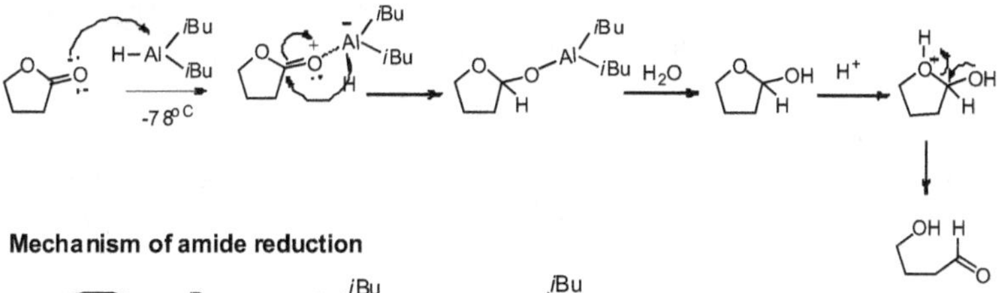

[mechanism scheme]

Mechanism of amide reduction

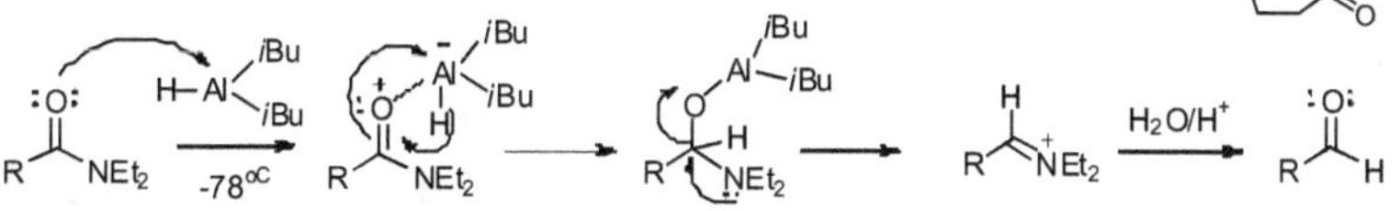

[mechanism scheme: RCONEt₂ + H–Al(iBu)₂, -78°C → ... → R–CH=N⁺Et₂ + H₂O/H⁺ → RCHO]

Mechanism of nitrile reduction

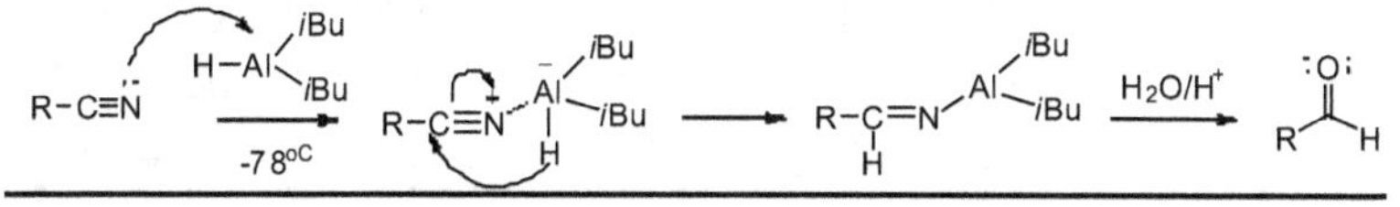

[mechanism scheme: R–C≡N + H–Al(iBu)₂, -78°C → R–C≡N–Al(iBu)₂ → R–CH=N–Al(iBu)₂ + H₂O/H⁺ → RCHO]

Examples of DIBAL-H reduction

1) [structure: methyl epoxycyclohexane] → DIBAL-H, -78^oC → [structure: 1-methylcyclohexanol]

2) [structure: 4-MeO-benzyl ether with COOEt] → DIBAL-H, -78^oC → [structure: 4-MeO-benzyl ether with CHO]

3) [structure: cyclohexane with H, CN and isopropenyl CH₃] → DIBAL-H, -78^oC → [structure: cyclohexane with H, CHO and isopropenyl CH₃]

4) [structure: Ph–N(Boc)–chain–COOEt] → DIBAL-H, -78^oC → [structure: Ph–N(Boc)–chain–CHO]

Examples of DIBAL-H reduction

Reduction of lactones to aldehyde-hemiacetals is of the most important reaction in carbohydrates chemistry. The old method converting aldolactones to aldose by reducing Na/Hg gives very poor yield but DIBAL-H gives very good results.

[reaction scheme: Aldolactone → DIBAL-H, -78^oC → Aldehyde hemiacetal ⇌ aldose (D-Allose)]

Aldolactone   Aldehyde hemiacetal   aldose (D-Allose)

DIBAL-H reacts slowly with electron poor compounds and faster with electron rich compounds as Lewis acid. Thus it is an electrophilic reducing agent where as $LiAlH_4$ can be thought of as a nucleophilic reducing agent. Due to this DIBAL-hydride has found considerable use for the selective reduction of α,β-unsaturated ester to allylic alcohols as shown below example.

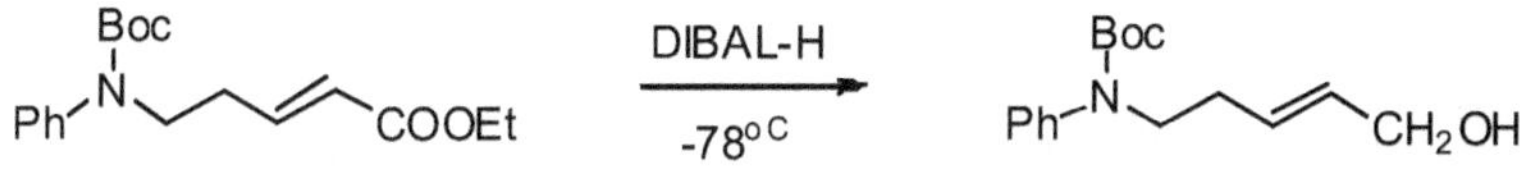

DIBAL-H like most alkylaluminium compound ($LiAlH_4$) reacts violently with air and water potentially leading to fire.

4) L and K Selectrides

L- and K-selectrides are the trade name of organoborane compounds as a reducing reagent used in organic synthesis. L-Selectride is known as lithium *tris-sec.butyl* borohydrides and K-Selectride as potassium *tris-sec.butyl* borohydride.

L-Selectride

L-Selectride is bulky reducing reagent reduces diastereoselectively the carbonyl group of aldehydes or ketones in good yield and not reducing carboxylic acids and its derivatives. Addition of hydride to carbonyl is 1,2-addition.

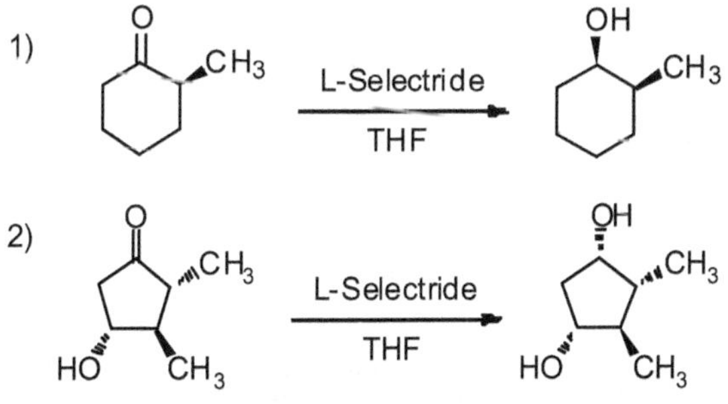

It shows high stereoselectivity in the reduction reaction of cyclohexanone with L-selectride where as $LiAlH_4$ exactly reverse as shown below examples.

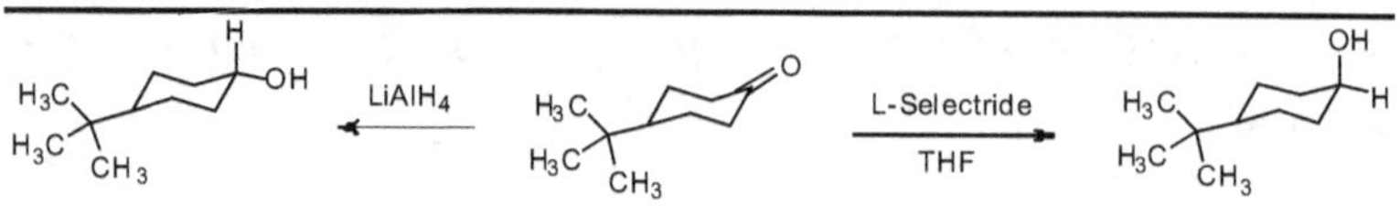

Attack of Nucleophile
due to small size and
steric hinderance side

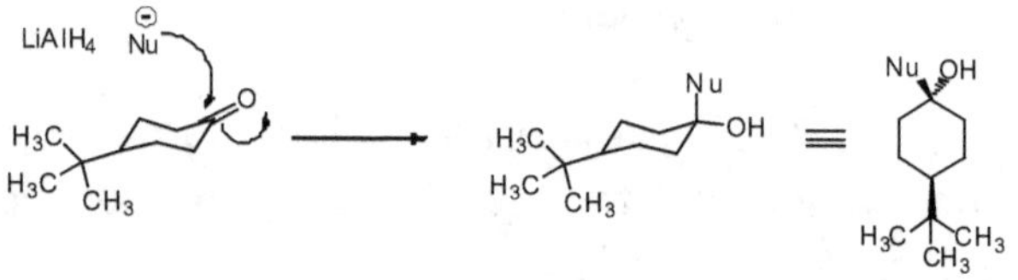

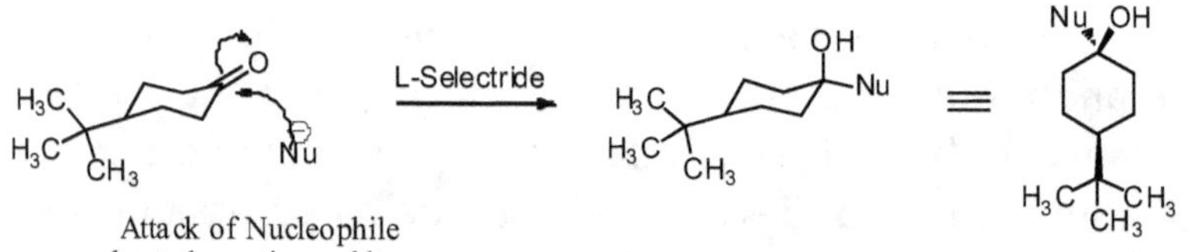

Attack of Nucleophile
due to large size and less
steric hinderance side

Due to the bulk of L-selectride the attack preferred through less hindered side i.e equatorial side whereas $LiAlH_4$ can attack through axial side due less bulky and afforded exactly different path of nucleophilic attack and results into different product stereochemically.

Similar results are for the reduction of 2-methyl cyclopentanone with L-Selectride and $LiAlH_4$ as follows.

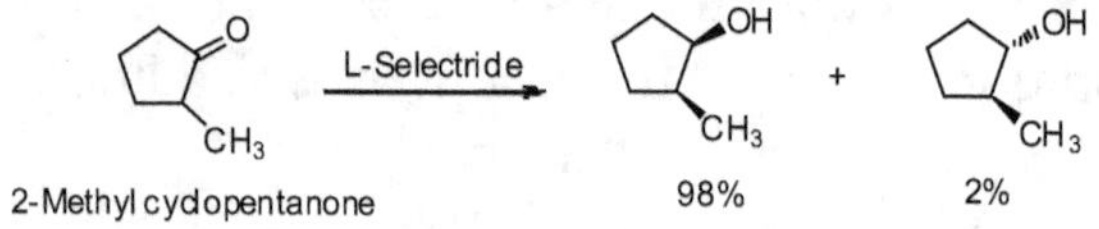

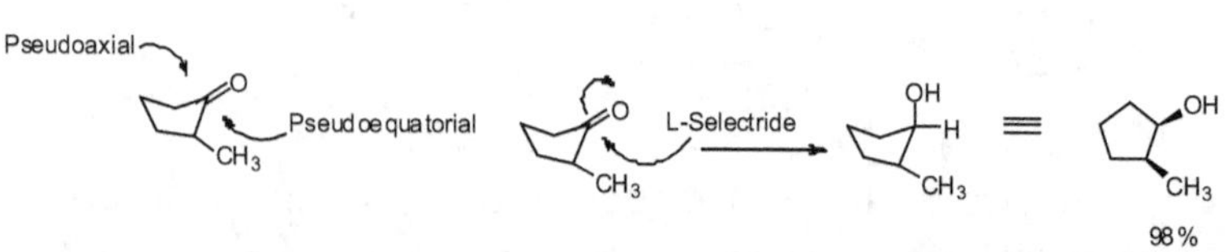

2-Methyl cyclopentanone

98%   2%

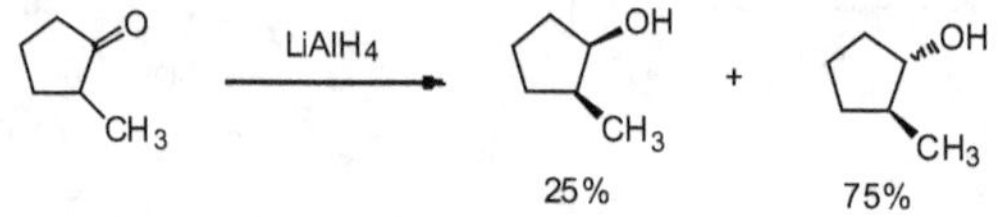

25%   75%

Pseudoaxial

Pseudoequatorial

98%

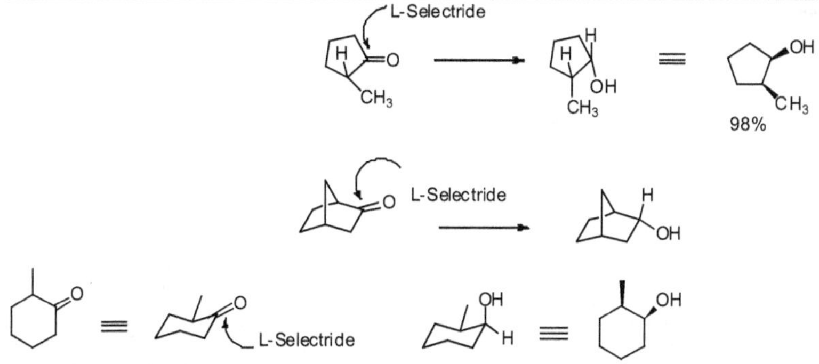

K-Selectride

K-Selectride is also bulky reducing reagent which preferentially reduce the enone to an enonate by 1,4-addition keeping the other double bond tolerant in the reduction reaction. The enonate formed in the reaction can be alkylated if any electrophile added, otherwise on hydrolysis the enolate changes to enol and give more stable product as ketone.

1)

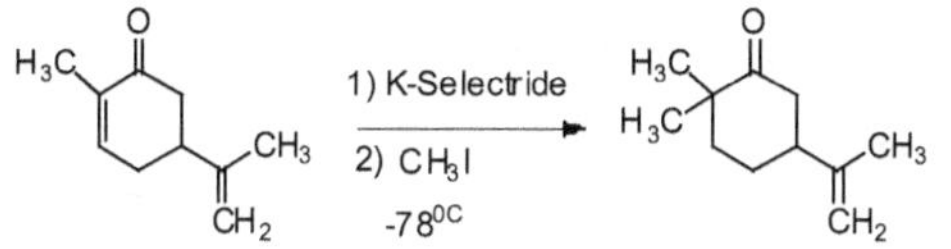

Mechanism

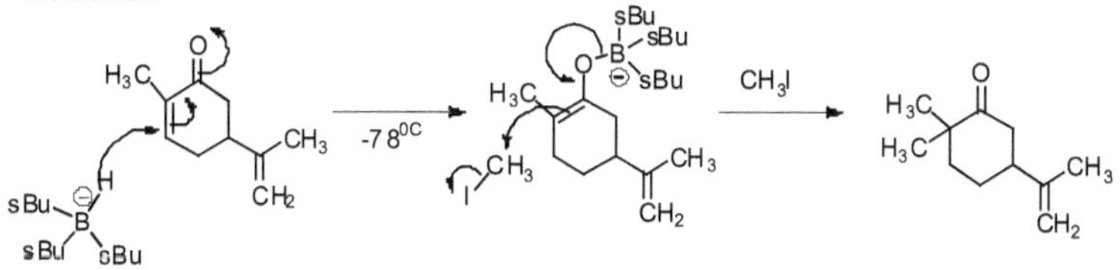

2)

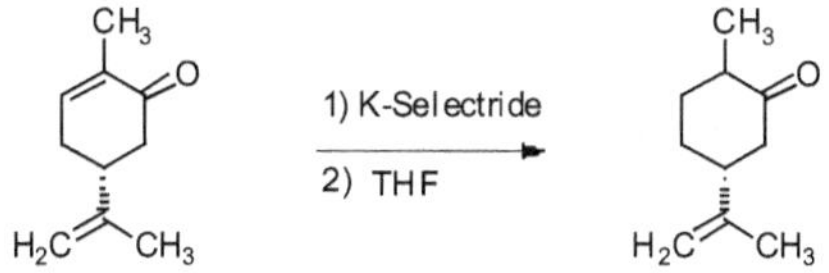

Mechanism

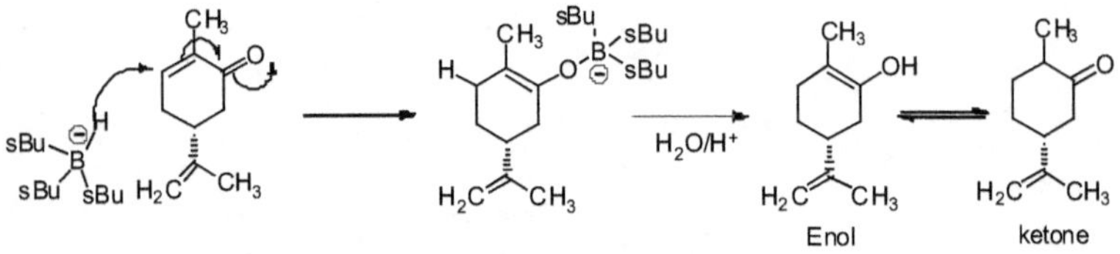

Enol   ketone

3)

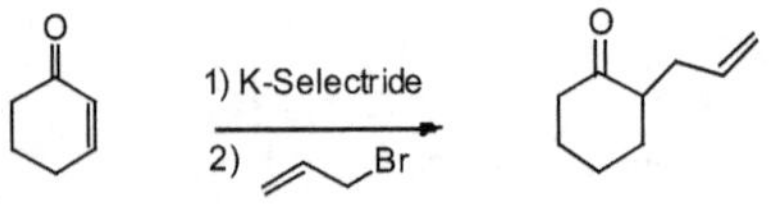

1) K-Selectride

2) Br

4)

K-Selectride

THF

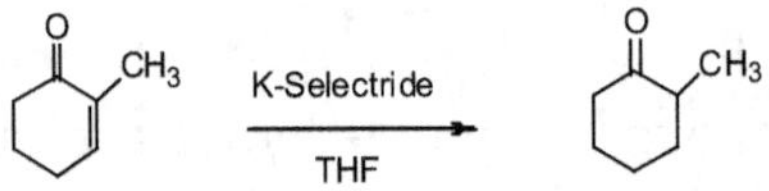

Chapter 4

III. Non-metal based agents including organic reducing agents

1) NH=NH (Diimide)

Diimide is most effective and highly selective reducing reagent used for the reduction of unpolarized carbon cabon double bond or triple bonds without affecting the polarized bond i.e C=O, C=N, N=N, O=O etc. The diimide is unstable compound and prepared *in situ* usually by the oxidation of hydrazine with H_2O_2 or by thermal decomposition of *p*-toluenesulphonyl hydrazine or azodicarboxylic acid.

Preparation of Diimide

1)

$$NH_2\text{-}NH_2 \xrightarrow{\ H_2O_2/CuCl_2\ } NH=NH$$

Hydazine　　　　　　　　　Diimide

2)  H_3C—⬡—SO_2-NH-NH$_2$ ⟶ NH=NH + H_3C—⬡—SO_2H
Diimide

p-toluenesulphonyl hydrazine

3) HOOC−N=N−COOH ⟶ NH=NH + $2CO_2$
Azodicarboxylic acid
Diimide

Diimide reduction proceeds through the *syn*-addition of hydrogen to the substrate as alkenes or alkynes. It is also proposed that the mechanism of the reduction involves concerted hydrogen transfer from *cis*-diimide to the substrate. Although the *cis*-diimide isomer is less stable but equilibrium speeds up by addition of acid as catalyst. The mechanism explains the high stereospecificity of the reaction and couples the driving force of nitrogen formation with the addition reaction.

Examples diimide reduction:

1) 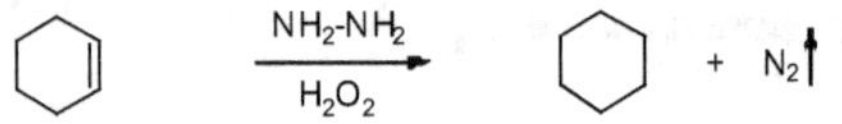 ⬡ $\xrightarrow[\text{H}_2\text{O}_2]{\text{NH}_2\text{-NH}_2}$ ⬡ + $N_2\uparrow$

2) $\xrightarrow[\text{H}_2\text{O}_2]{\text{NH}_2\text{-NH}_2}$ meso form + $N_2\uparrow$

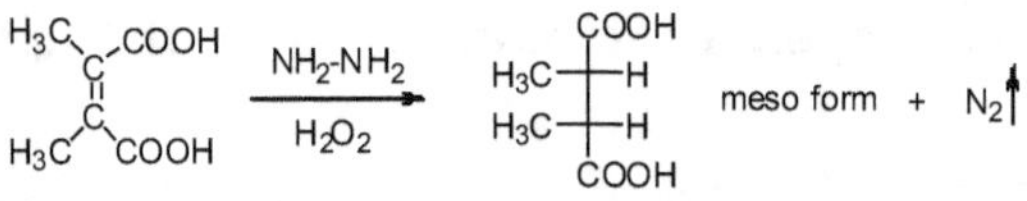

3) 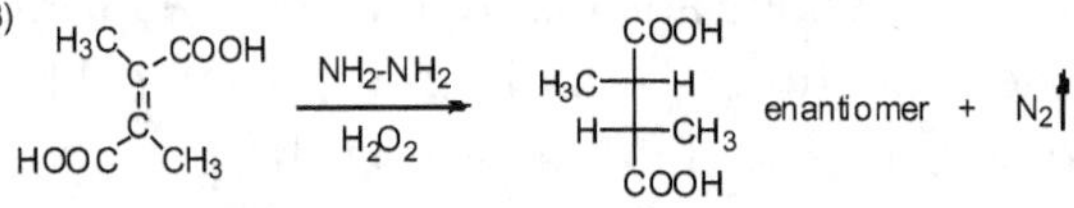 $\xrightarrow[\text{H}_2\text{O}_2]{\text{NH}_2\text{-NH}_2}$ enantiomer + $N_2\uparrow$

Mechanism

⟶ [ ] ⟶ + $N_2\uparrow$

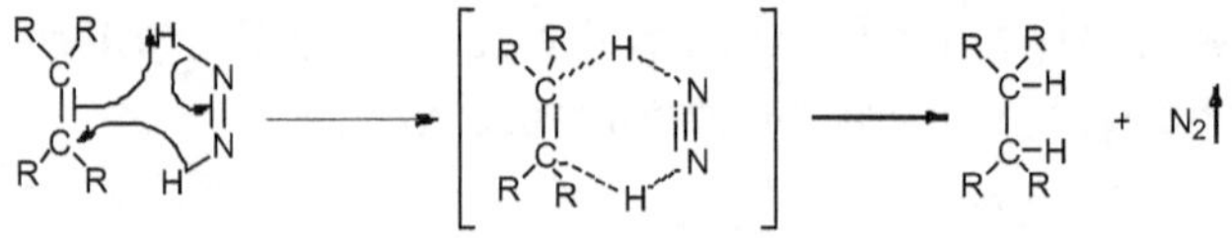

Syn addition of reagent

The order of reactivity of unsaturated substrate is alkynes > allenes > terminal or strained alkene, *trans*-alkene react more rapidly than *cis*-alkene.

4) $\xrightarrow[\text{H}_2\text{O}_2]{\text{NH}_2\text{-NH}_2}$ + $N_2\uparrow$

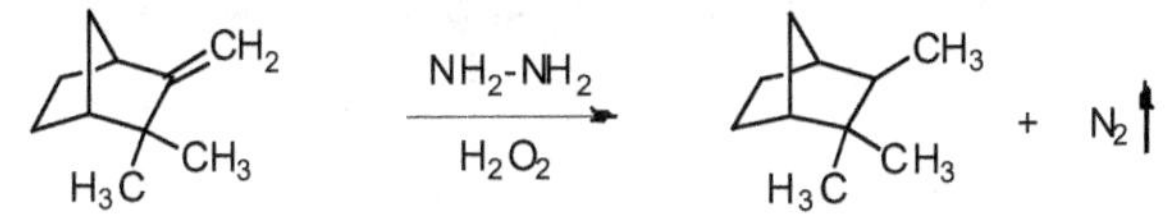

5) $\xrightarrow[\text{H}_2\text{O}_2]{\text{NH}_2\text{-NH}_2}$ + $N_2\uparrow$

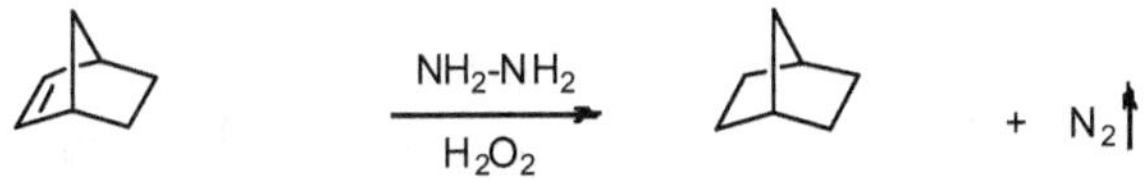

6) $\xrightarrow[\text{H}_2\text{O}_2]{\text{NH}_2\text{-NH}_2}$ + $N_2\uparrow$

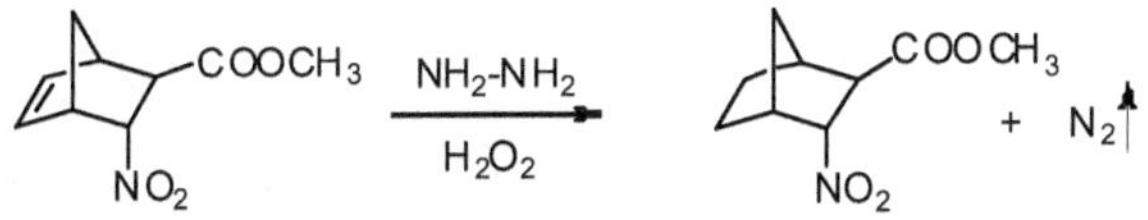

7) $\xrightarrow{\text{HOOC}-\text{N}=\text{N}-\text{COOH}}$ + $2CO_2\uparrow$

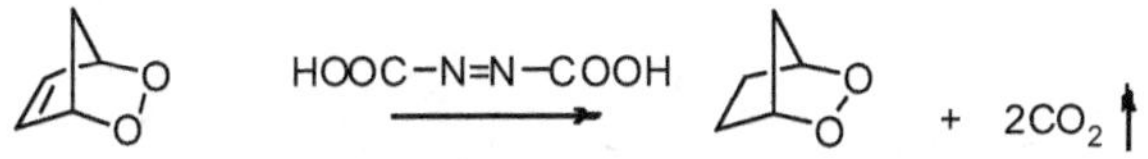

8) $\xrightarrow[\text{H}_2\text{O}_2]{\text{NH}_2\text{-NH}_2}$ + $N_2\uparrow$

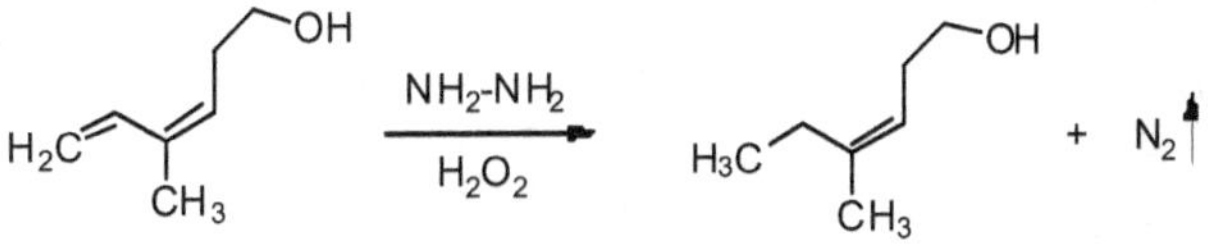

9) $\xrightarrow[\text{Base } \Delta]{\text{Ts}-\text{NH-NH}_2}$

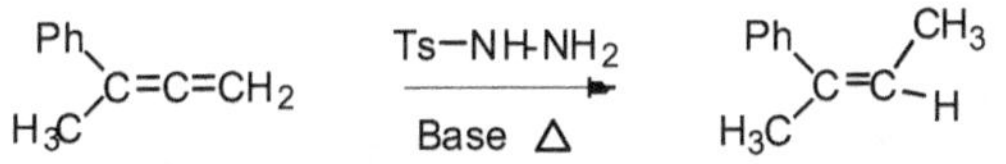

10) $\xrightarrow{\text{HOOC}-\text{N}=\text{N}-\text{COOH}}$ + $2CO_2\uparrow$

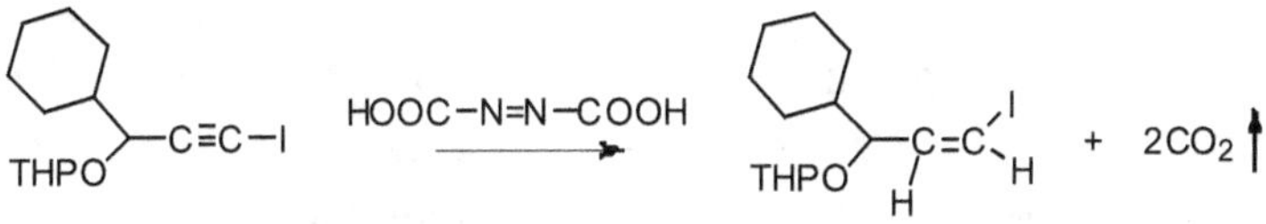

11) $\xrightarrow[\text{H}_2\text{O}_2]{\text{NH}_2\text{-NH}_2}$ + $N_2\uparrow$

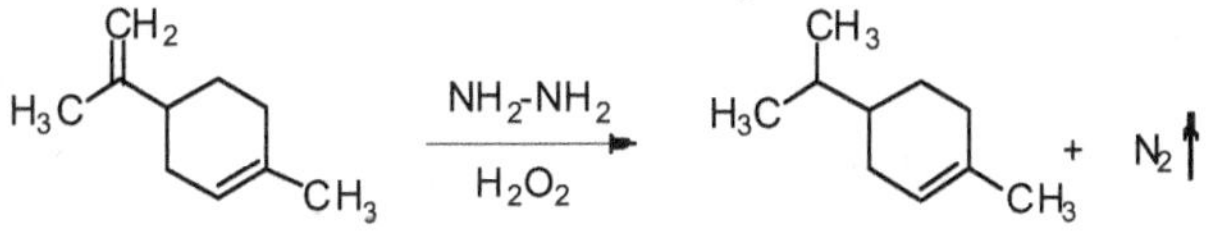

12) $\xrightarrow[\text{H}_2\text{O}_2]{\text{NH}_2\text{-NH}_2}$ + $N_2\uparrow$

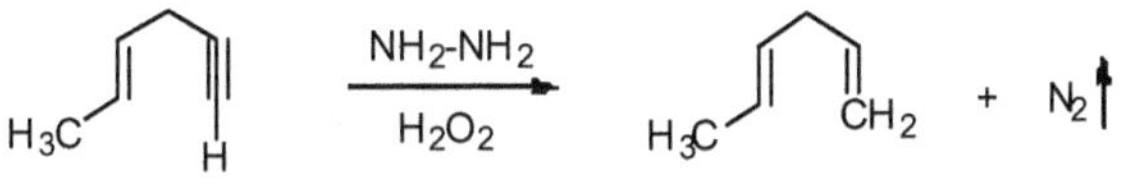

13) $\xrightarrow[\text{H}_2\text{O}_2]{\text{NH}_2\text{-NH}_2}$ + $N_2\uparrow$

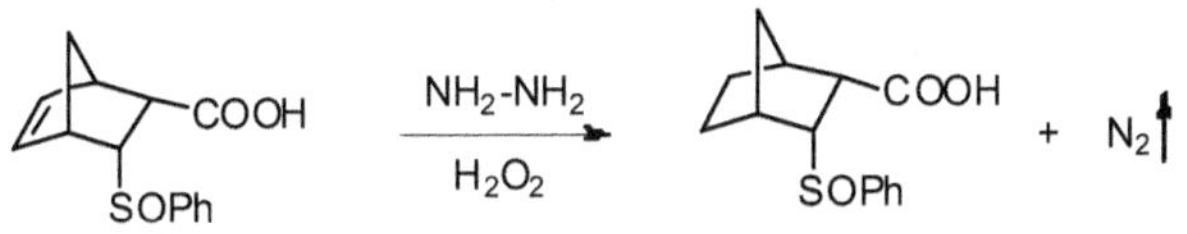

Diimide was used in 1929 for the conversion of oleic acid to stearic acid in the presence of hydrazine but it was not used in the reductive process until 1960.

2) Hantzsch dihydropyridine

The Hantzsch dihydropyridine has been synthesized by the condensation of ethylacetoacetate, aldehyde and ammonia as shown below reaction.

Dihydropyridine

Dihydropyridine easily gives out hydrogen to form stable pyridine and the same hydrogen can be used for the reduction of alkene and activated ketones such as pyruvic acid.

1)

Pyruvic acid   Lactic acid

2)

3)

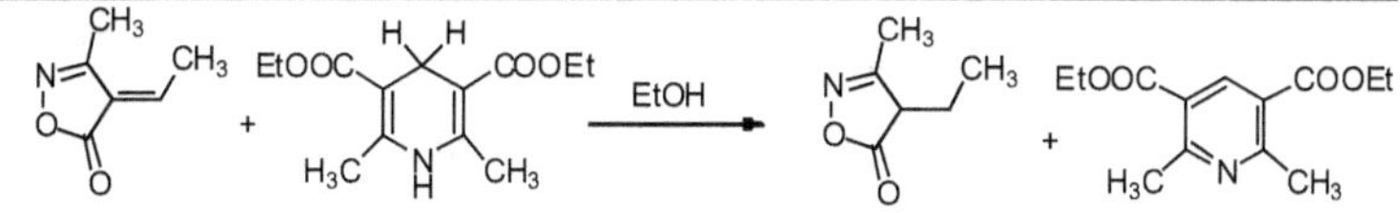

4)

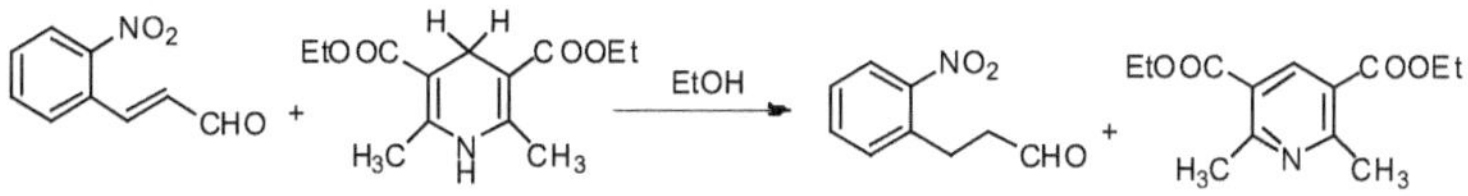

5)

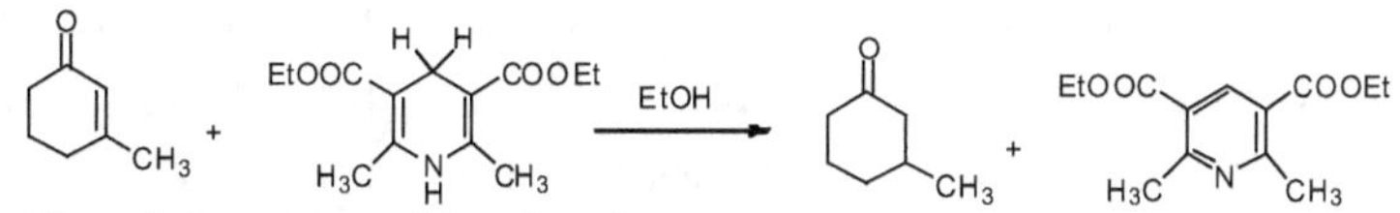

IV) Dissolving Metal Reduction

When metal dissolved in solvent like liquid ammonia metal loses electrons, which are solvated by solvent (ammonia) are called as solvated electrons.

$$Na \ (metal) \ + \ Liq. \ NH_3 \ (Solvent) \longrightarrow \overset{\oplus}{Na} \ + \ \overset{\ominus}{e} \ (NH_3) \ (Solvated \ electron)$$

The reduction of organic compounds using solution of electron in ammonia (solvated electron) is known as dissolving metal reduction. It reduces carbonyl compound such as aldehydes or ketones into alcohols or diols through dimerisation of two radicals as shown below general examples.

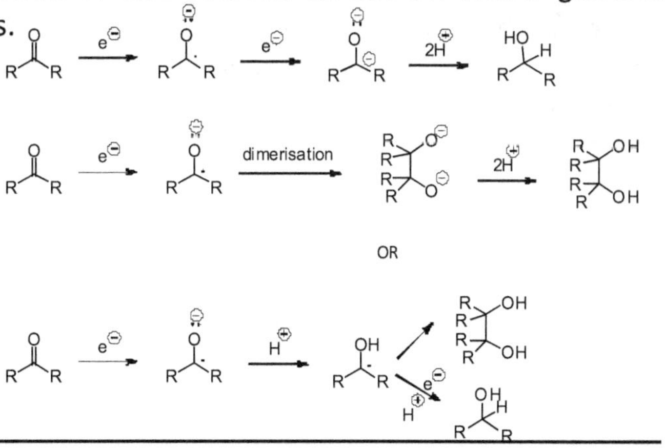

OR

OR

Dissolving metal reductions were reported very early in organic synthesis. A variety of organic functional groups are reduced by reaction with metal in neutral or acidic conditions. The metals commonly used are alkali metal such as Li, Na, K, as well Zn, Mg, Al, Fe, Sn, and Ca.

1) Zn- metal (Reduction by zinc metal or Clemmensen reduction)

Zinc metal is the most abundantly used in the process of reduction of organic compounds. It is used as zinc duct or mossy zinc in chemical reactions. Zinc dust is frequently covered with a thin layer of ZnO which deactivates its surface. Zinc dust can be activated by very dilute HCl, anhydrous $ZnCl_2$ or $ZnBr_2$ in alcohol, ether or THF. Another way of activation of zinc duct is by its conversion to Zn-Cu couple. Mossy zinc is activated by conversion to zinc amalgam this type of activation is especially used in the Clemmensen reduction which converts carbonyl group into methylene group. This reduction reaction commonly carried out in hot concentrated HCl and ethanol as co-solvent. (Detail explained in the Clemmensen reduction).

Examples

1)

2)

Ketone + Zn/Hg, Conc.HCl, Ethanol → cyclohexane

Mechanism

Zn/HCl (Clemmensen reduction) is particularly useful for ketones containing phenolic or carboxylic groups.

1)

$\text{Ph-CO-CH}_2\text{CH}_2\text{-COOH}$ + Zn/Hg, Conc.HCl, Ethanol → $\text{Ph-CH}_2\text{CH}_2\text{CH}_2\text{-COOH}$

2)

Zn/HCl can also reduces carbon carbon double bond in α,β- unsaturated ketones.

Zinc is one of the most common metal used for the reduction of aromatic nitro compounds. The different reaction condition gives entirely different results of the reduction of nitro compounds as shown in the following examples.

1)

$\text{C}_6\text{H}_5\text{-NO}_2$ + Zn/Hg, Conc.HCl, Ethanol → $\text{C}_6\text{H}_5\text{-NH}_2$

2) Ph–NO$_2$ $\xrightarrow[\text{OR Zn/CaCl/H}_2\text{O}]{\text{Zn/NH}_4\text{Cl/H}_2\text{O}}$ Ph–NH–OH

3) Ph–NO$_2$ $\xrightarrow[\text{CH}_3\text{OH/H}_2\text{O}]{\text{Zn/NaOH}}$ Ph–N=N–Ph

4) Ph–NO$_2$ $\xrightarrow[\Delta]{\text{Zn dust/NaOH}}$ Ph–NH–NH–Ph

Vicinal dihalo compounds undergo dehalogenation in the presence of Zn/C$_2$H$_5$OH. This reaction is used for the preparation of alkenes.

1) $\xrightarrow[\text{Ethanol } \Delta]{\text{Zn}}$

Mechanism

$\xrightarrow{}$ $\xrightarrow[\text{}]{-\text{ZnCl}_2}$

α-Halo alcohol, ether and esters also give the similar type of results.

1) $\xrightarrow[\text{Ethanol/H}_2\text{O}]{\text{Zn}}$ H$_3$C–CH=CH–CH$_3$

2) $\xrightarrow[\text{Ethanol/H}_2\text{O}]{\text{Zn}}$ C$_3$H$_7$–CH=CH–C$_3$H$_7$

3) $\xrightarrow[\text{Ethanol/H}_2\text{O}]{\text{Zn}}$

Mechanism

2) Li (Lithium) and Na (Sodium)

Alkali metals such as Lithium (Li) or Sodium (Na) readily gives up single outer most shell electron as they dissolve in solvent such as liquid ammonia or ethanol. Electrons are the simplest reducing agents and they will reduce carbonyl compounds,
alkynes or aromatic ring.

$$Li \xrightarrow[\text{Fast}]{\text{liq. } NH_3} Li^{\oplus} + e^{\ominus}[NH_3]_n \xrightarrow[NH_3]{\text{Slow}} \overset{\ominus}{N}H_2 + 1/2\, H_2$$

Blue solution   Colour less solution

1)

$$\xrightarrow[\text{EtOH or } NH_3]{Li/Na}$$

Mechanism (Ketone)

2)

$$R-\!\!\equiv\!\!-R \xrightarrow[\text{EtOH or } NH_3]{Li/Na}$$

Mechanism (Alkyne)

3)

$$\xrightarrow[\text{EtOH or } NH_3]{Li/Na}$$

Mechanism (Aromatic ring)

The reducing power of alkali metal depends on the reduction potential. Less will be the value of reduction potential higher will be the reducing power of alkali metals as below.

Li^+/Li -3.05 Volts   and Na^+/Na -2.73 Volts

Thus alkali metals are very powerful reducing agents and are able to reduce almost all functional groups even carbon-carbon multiple bonds.

Reduction of Conjugated systems

The isolated carbon-carbon double bonds are not reduced by Na/Li in liquid NH_3 reagent alone but in the presence of an alcohol terminal double bonds may be reduced. The conjugated dienes are readily reduced to 1,4-dihydro derivatives with Na/Li in liquid NH_3 only but without proton donor solvent (EtOH) and the product formation takes place by formation of radical anion. The proton required to complete the reduction are supplied by ammonia (NH_3).

e.g

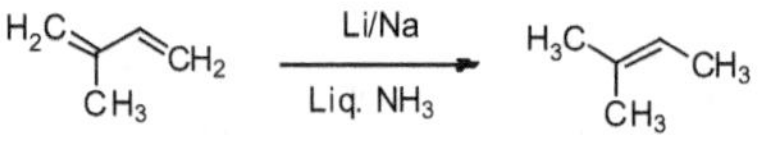

Mechanism

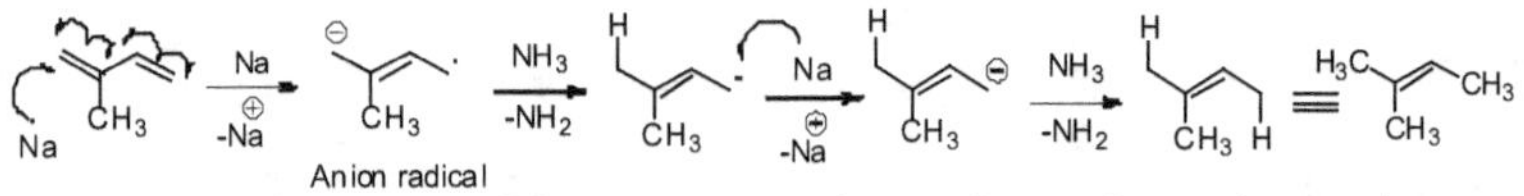

Reduction of ketones with Na/Li in liquid NH_3/EtOH leads to the formation of alcohol.

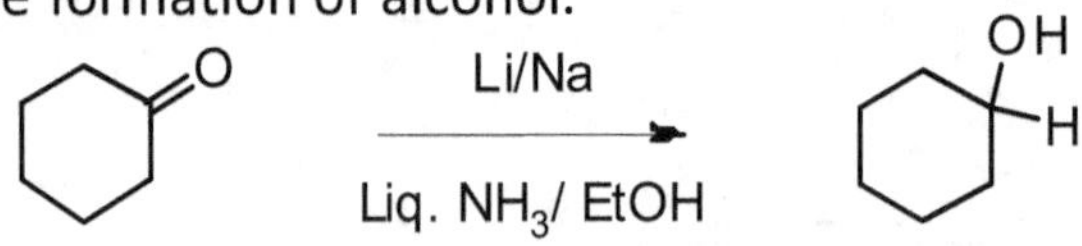

The α,β-unsaturated ketones are cleanly reduced to saturated ketone or saturated alcohols and nature of the product depends upon the reaction condition. If one equivalent of proton donor as NH_3 is used the enolate ion can be exploited for further alkylation.

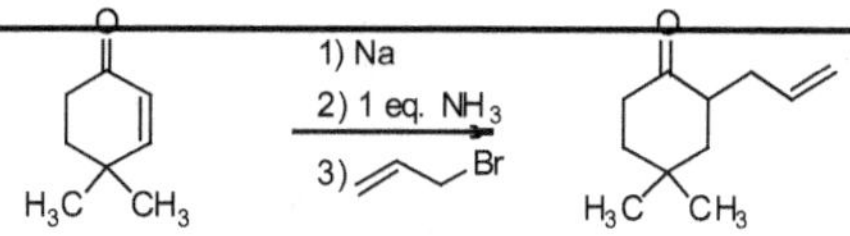

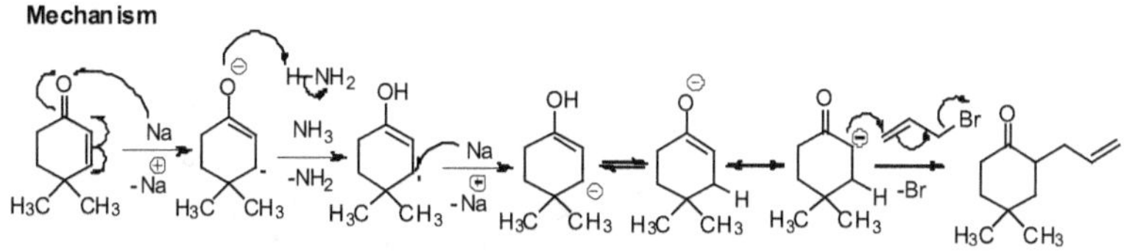

Mechanism

When some reactions are carried out in the presence of one equivalent of proton donor as solvent EtOH.

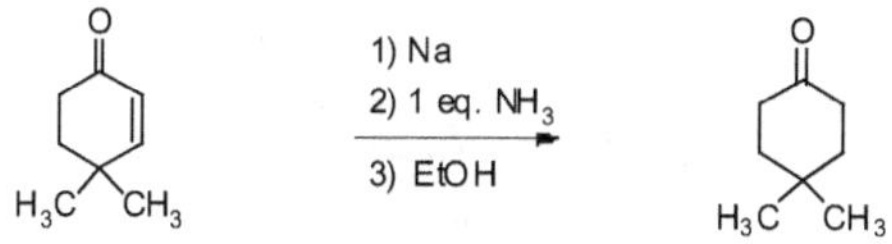

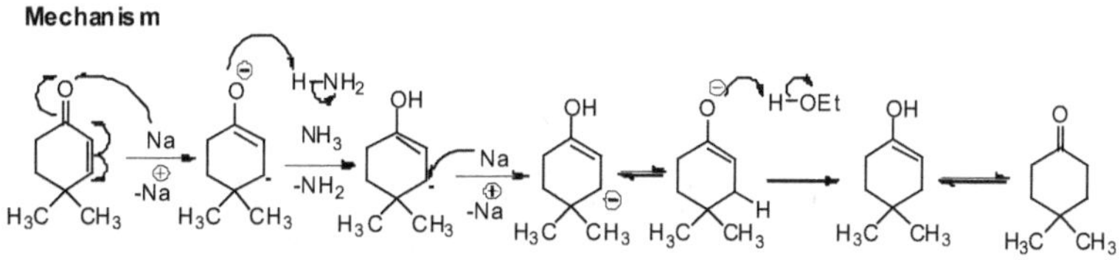

Mechanism

Other examples

1)

2)

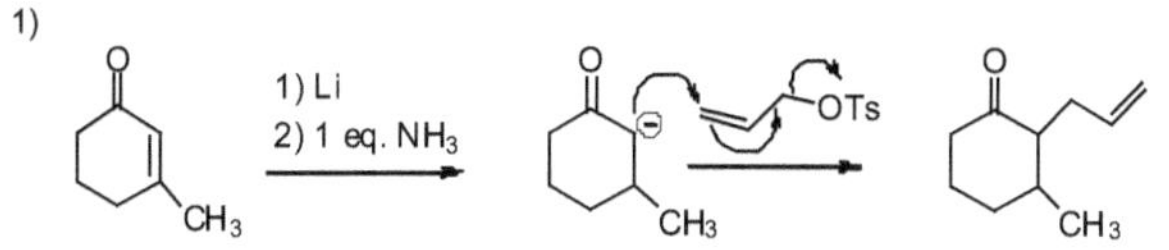

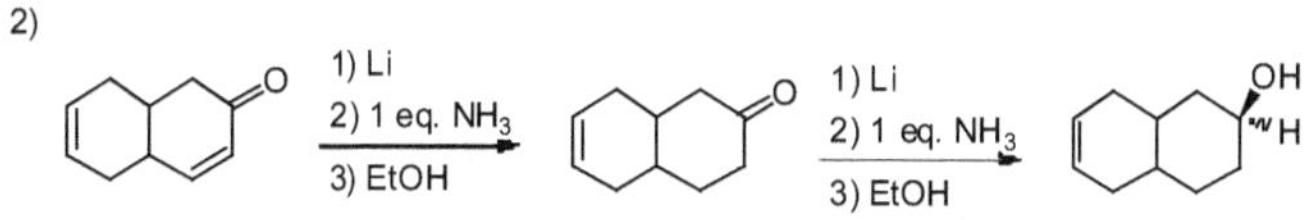

Reduction of α-substituted ketones

If ketones have leaving group such as -X, -OH, -OAc, -SPh and -OTs then these groups can be removed by hydrogen with $Na/NH_3/t$-BuOH.

e.g.

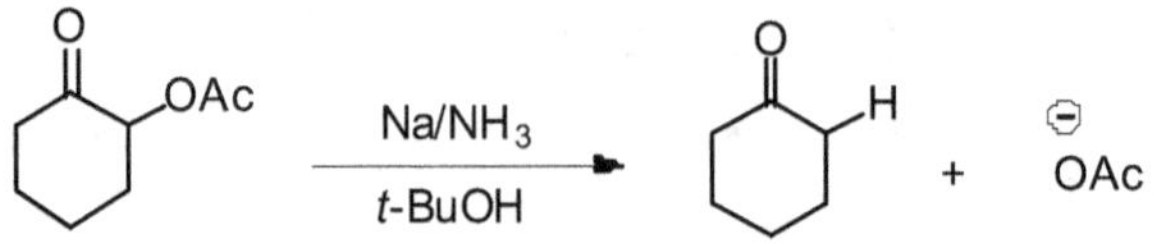
OAc
Na/NH3
t-BuOH
H
+
OAc

Mechanism

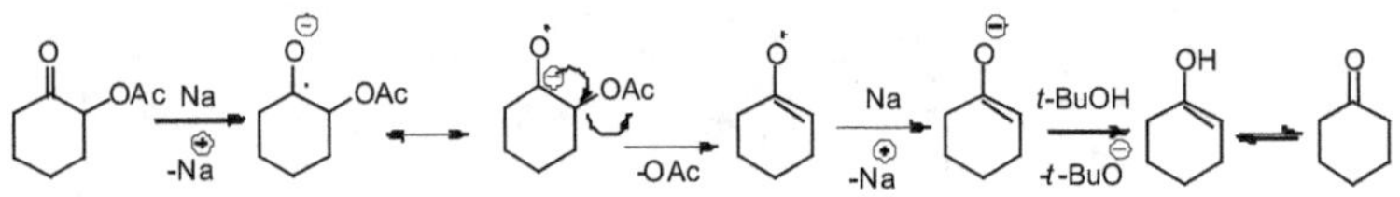
OAc Na
-Na
OAc
OAc
-OAc
Na
-Na
t-BuOH
t-BuO
OH

Other examples

1)

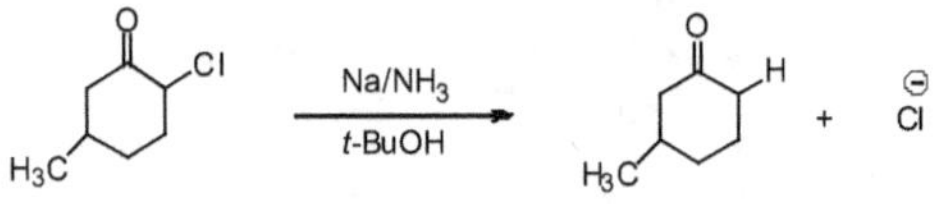
Cl
H3C
Na/NH3
t-BuOH
H
H3C
+
Cl

2)

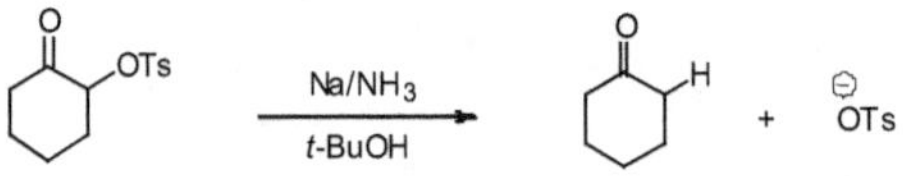
OTs
Na/NH3
t-BuOH
H
+
OTs

3)

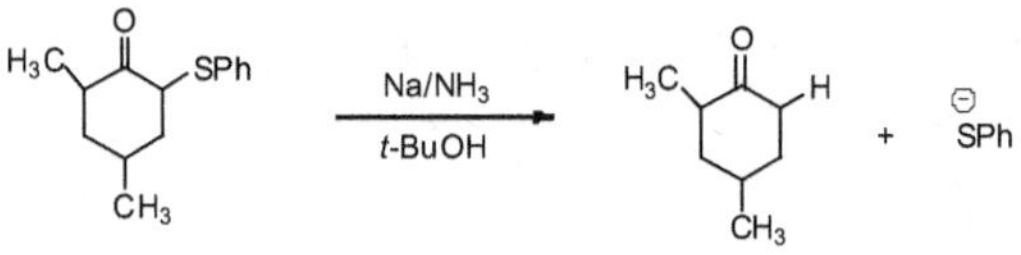
H3C
SPh
CH3
Na/NH3
t-BuOH
H3C
H
CH3
+
SPh

4)

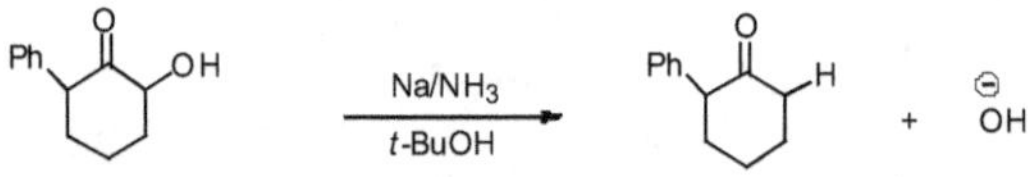
Ph
OH
Na/NH3
t-BuOH
Ph
H
+
OH

Birch Reduction

Reduction of aromatic ring into 1,4-dihydro derivative in presence of alkali metals such as Na or Li in liquid NH_3 and ethanol is known as Birch reduction. This reagent is powerful enough to reduce benzene ring with different substituent but specific enough to add only two hydrogen atoms.

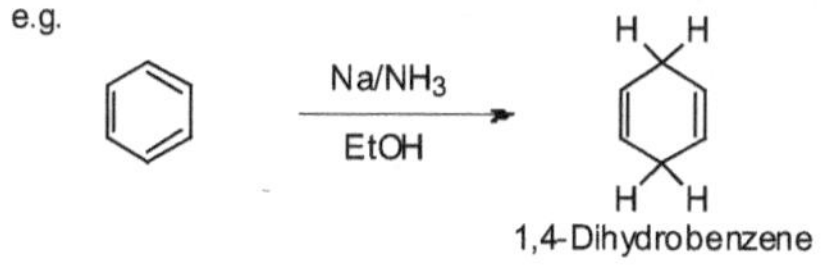

e.g.

$$\text{Benzene} \xrightarrow[\text{EtOH}]{\text{Na/NH}_3} \text{1,4-Dihydrobenzene}$$

1,4-Dihydrobenzene

Mechanism

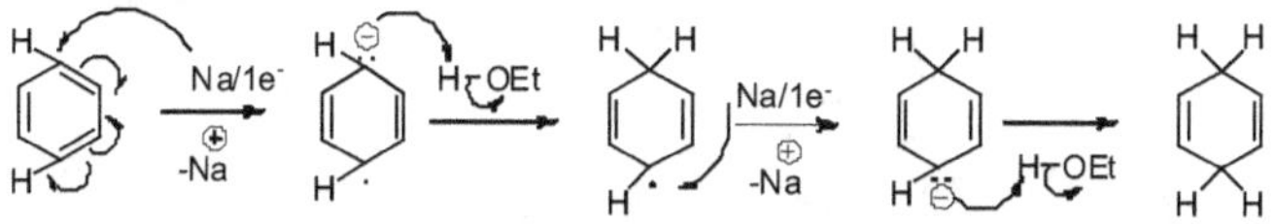

The two double bonds in the reduced compounds are not in onjugation with each other which appears little odd at first and the mechanism of the reduction involves conjugate addition i.e. 1,4-addition. The reaction occurs by two successive electron transfer and protonation steps. Birch reduction is useful for the reduction of wide variety of aromatic compounds varying in their degree of substitution and the nature of substituents. The relative rate and the regioselectivity are affected by the type of group present on the ring.

Electron withdrawing group as substituent

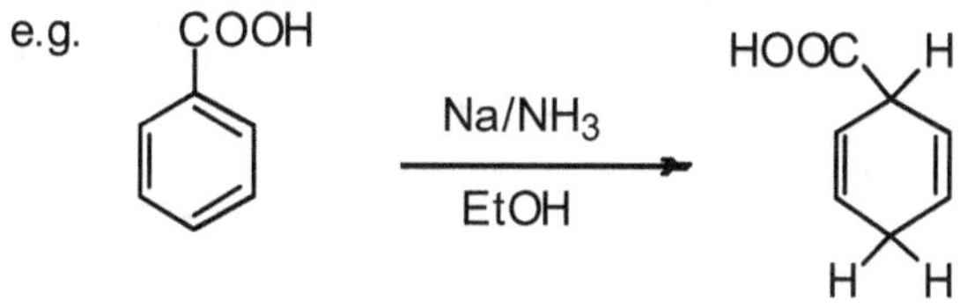

e.g.

$$\text{C}_6\text{H}_5\text{COOH} \xrightarrow[\text{EtOH}]{\text{Na/NH}_3}$$

Mechanism

Radical anion

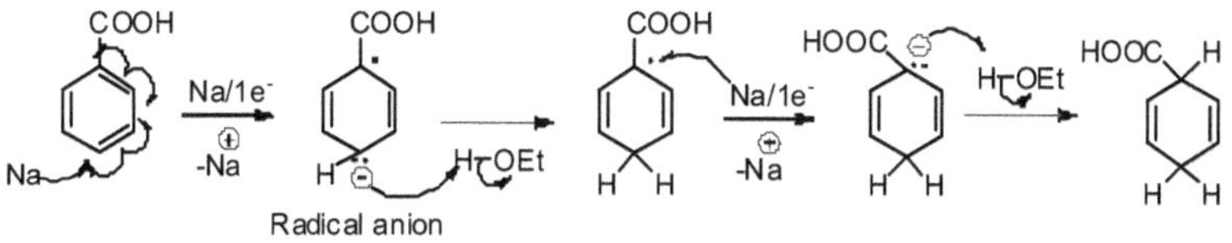

From these examples it states the general principal that the electron withdrawing group promotes *ipso-para* reduction and the product is 1-substituted 1,4-

dihydrobenzene. Whereas electron donating group promotes *ortho-meta* reduction and the product is 1-substituted 2,5-dihydrobenzene.

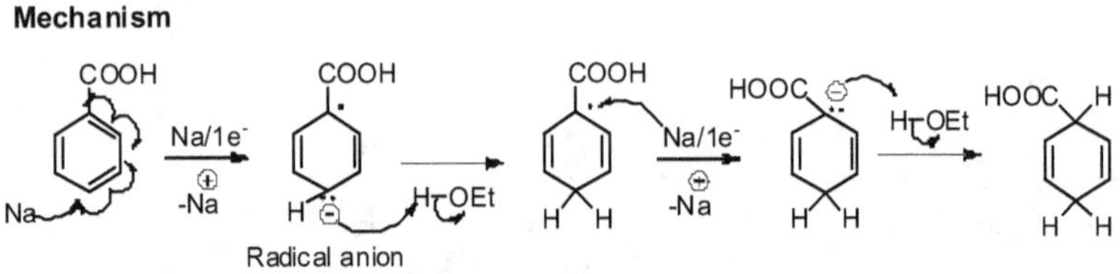

Mechanism

Radical anion

From the mechanism radical anion must protonate preferentially of C4 as it leave behind a radical that is stabilised by conjugation with carbonyl group and furthermore addition of another electron forms a stable anion adjacent to carbonyl group as an enolate which protonate to have final product as shown above mechanism. When excess of ammonia with electrophile as allyl bromide is added to the reaction solution the anion formed on second electron addition can be trap to have 1-alkylation product as shown below example.

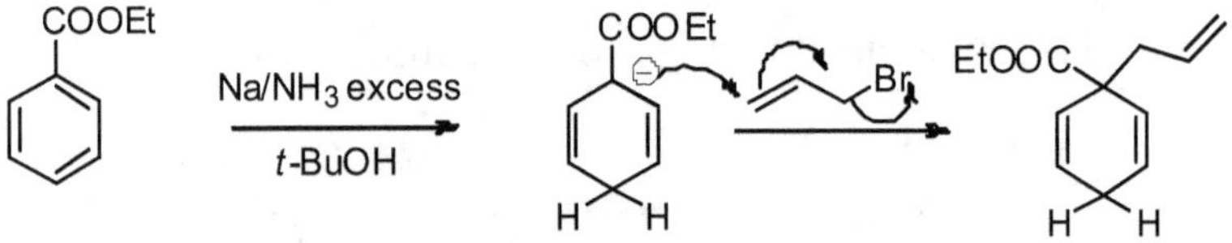

Electron donating group as substituent.

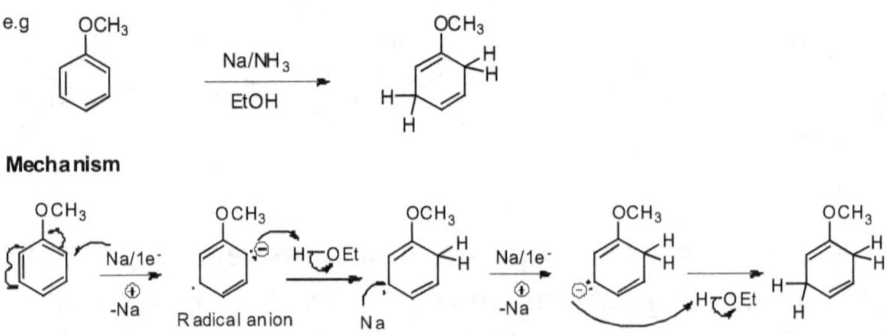

Mechanism

Radical anion

From the mechanism radical anion must protonate preferentially at C2 carbon because it can not be C1 to as negative charge is less stable adjacent to oxygen or Nitrogen atom. Furthermore addition of another electron at C5 to have final product after the protonation as shown in the above mechanism. Polysubstituted aromatic rings can easily reduced with the preference to the nature of substituents.

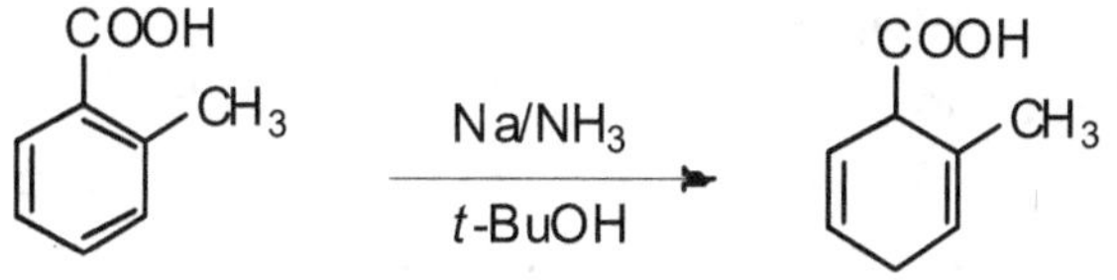

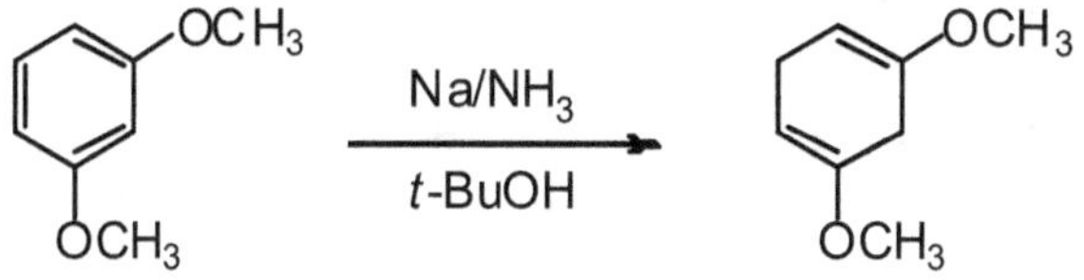

Birch reduction is very useful method for the preparation of ketones from aromatic compounds having methoxy group or tertiary amino group.

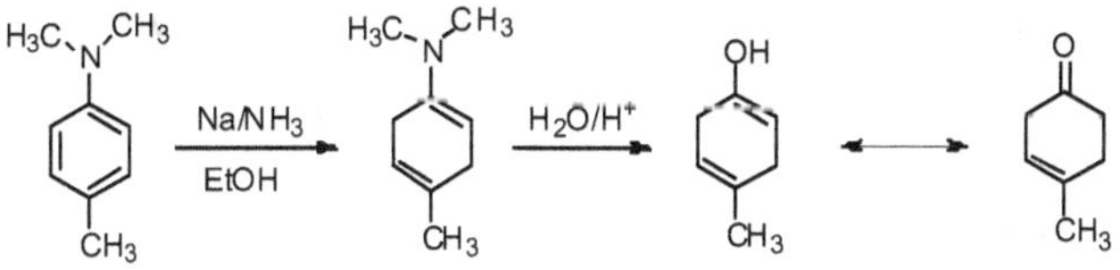

Five member heterocyclic aromatic compounds can also be partially reduced with Li/Na in liquid NH_3. But this reduction can only be possible if position-2 is substituted with carbonyl group as ester because this group stabilized the radical anion.

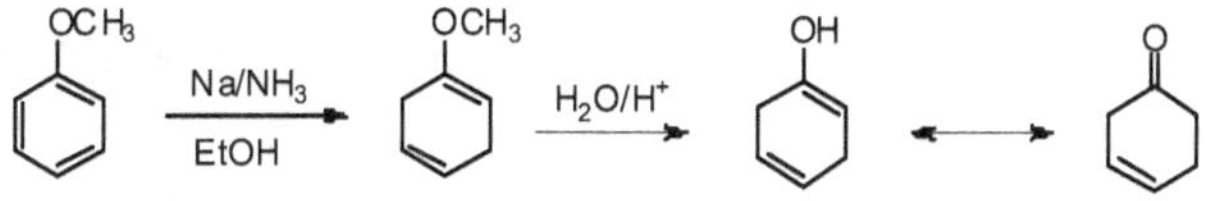

1)

$$\text{(furan-COOEt)} \xrightarrow[t\text{-BuOH}]{\text{Na/NH}_3} \text{(dihydrofuran-COOEt)}$$

2)

$$\text{(pyrrole-COOEt, N-COOEt)} \xrightarrow[t\text{-BuOH}]{\text{Na/NH}_3} \text{(dihydropyrrole-COOEt, N-COOEt)}$$

Reduction of Alkynes

Reduction of alkynes with Na/Li in liquid NH_3 and alcohol as EtOH or t-BuOH lead to the formation of stereospecifically only one product as *trans*-alkene via *anti*-addition. This reaction conditions do not reduced isolated double bond hence it stop selectively at alkene stage.

e.g.

$$R-\!\!\equiv\!\!-R \xrightarrow[\text{liq. NH}_3/\text{EtOH}]{\text{Li/Na}} \substack{R \\ \diagup \\ H}C\!\!=\!\!C\substack{H \\ \diagdown \\ R}$$

trans alkene

$$H_3C-\!\!\equiv\!\!-CH_3 \xrightarrow[\text{liq. NH}_3/\text{EtOH}]{\text{Li/Na}} \substack{H_3C \\ \diagup \\ H}C\!\!=\!\!C\substack{H \\ \diagdown \\ CH_3}$$

The mechanism involves one electron transfer into an antibonding π-orbital of the alkynes which results a radical anion and subsequently protonation by alcohol. The radical again takes electron from the Na to have anion which further protonate but anti to the first proton added results into the *trans*-alkene.

Mechanism

Examples of Birch reduction

1)

H_3C–C≡C–CH_3 chain $\xrightarrow[\text{EtOH}]{\text{Na/NH}_3}$ (trans alkene product)

2)

H_3C–C≡C–CH_3 $\xrightarrow[\text{EtOH}]{\text{Na/NH}_3}$ (trans alkene product)

3)

Ph–C≡C–CH_3 $\xrightarrow[\text{EtOH}]{\text{Na/NH}_3}$ (trans alkene product)

Problem with Solutions

Predict the products in the following reactions.

1)

EtOOC–(cyclohexanol with OH) $\xrightarrow[\text{NalO}_4]{\text{RuO}_4}$ EtOOC–(cyclohexanone with O)

2)

(naphthalene) $\xrightarrow{\text{Ni/H}_2}$ (decalin)

Trans Decalin

3)

(aryl structure with H_3C, CH_3, OH) $\xrightarrow[\text{Ether}]{\text{DDQ, C}_6\text{H}_6}$ (chromane with H_3C, CH_3, CH_3)

4)

(CH_3, O, COOEt decalone) $\xrightarrow[\text{(CH}_3\text{CO)}_2\text{O}]{\text{Zn}}$ (CH_3, H_2C, COOEt)   Clemmensen reduction

5)

(2-methylcyclohexanone) $\xrightarrow{\text{CH}_3\text{CO OOH}}$ (lactone with CH_3)   Baeyer Villiger Oxidation

6)

H–(CHO chain)–COOCH$_3$ $\xrightarrow[\text{KOH}]{\text{NH}_2\text{-NH}_2}$ H_3C–(chain)–COOCH$_3$

Wolff-Kishner reduction

7)

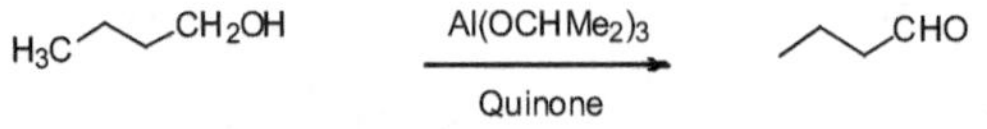

H_3C—CH$_2$OH $\xrightarrow[\text{Quinone}]{\text{Al(OCHMe}_2)_3}$ —CHO

Oppenauer Oxidation

8)

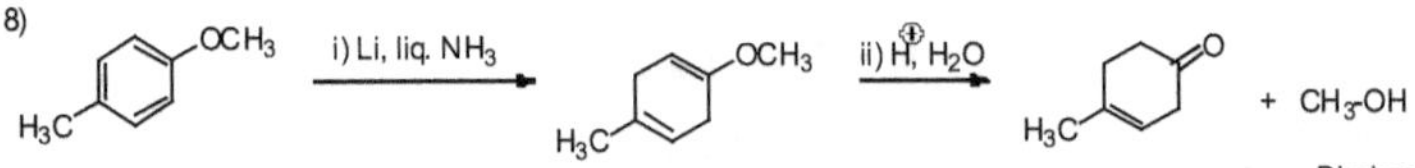

(p-methyl anisole) $\xrightarrow{\text{i) Li, liq. NH}_3}$ (dihydro product) $\xrightarrow{\text{ii) H}^{\oplus}, H_2O}$ (4-methylcyclohex-3-enone) + CH_3-OH

Birch reduction

9)

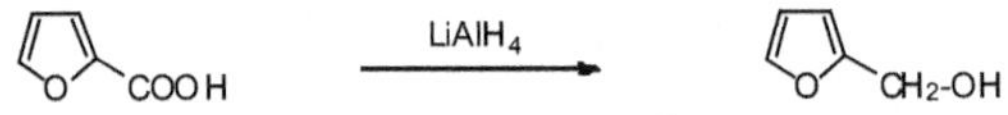

(furan)—COOH $\xrightarrow{\text{LiAlH}_4}$ (furan)—CH$_2$-OH

Hydride reduction

10)

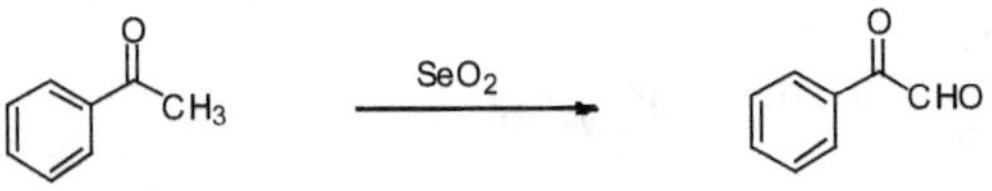

(acetophenone) $\xrightarrow{\text{SeO}_2}$ (phenylglyoxal) CHO

Selenium Oxidation

11)

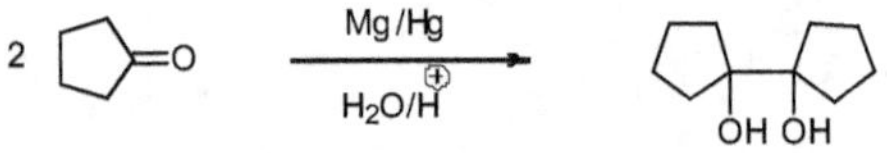

2 (cyclopentanone) $\xrightarrow[\text{H}_2\text{O/H}^{\oplus}]{\text{Mg/Hg}}$ (bicyclopentyl diol) OH OH

Reductive coupling

12)

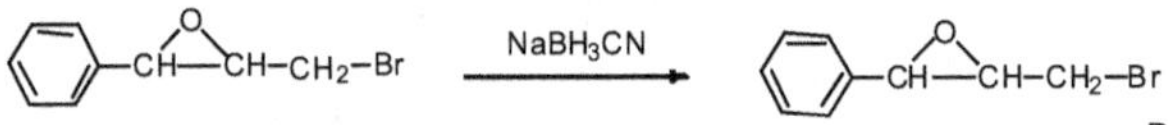

(phenyl epoxide)CH—CH–CH$_2$—Br $\xrightarrow{\text{NaBH}_3\text{CN}}$ (phenyl epoxide)CH–CH–CH$_2$—Br

Reduction of halide

13)

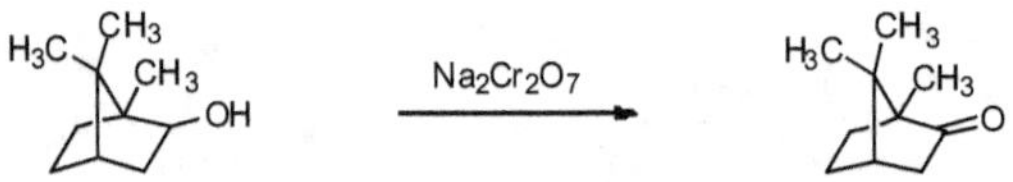

(camphol) $\xrightarrow{\text{Na}_2\text{Cr}_2\text{O}_7}$ (camphor)

13)

(camphol) $\xrightarrow{\text{Na}_2\text{Cr}_2\text{O}_7}$ (camphor)

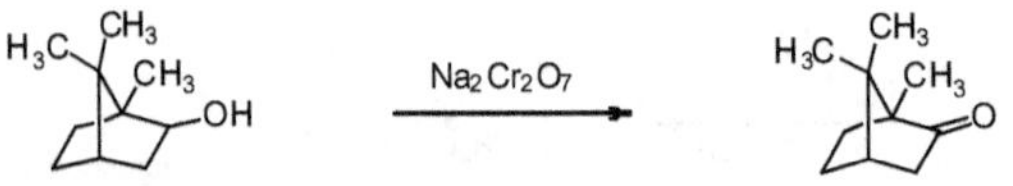

Chromium based oxidation

14)

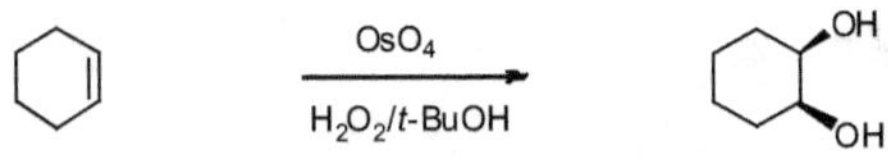

(cyclohexene) $\xrightarrow[\text{H}_2\text{O}_2/t\text{-BuOH}]{\text{OsO}_4}$ (cyclohexane-1,2-diol) OH OH

15)

CH$_2$-OH | CH$_2$-OH $\xrightarrow{\text{HIO}_4}$ 2 H-CHO

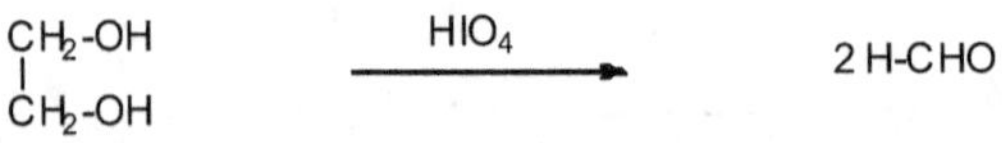

16)

CH_3-CHO $\xrightarrow{SeO_2}$

CHO
CHO

17)

$CH_3-CH_2-CH_2-OH$ $\xrightarrow[H_2SO_4]{KMnO_4}$ CH_3-CH_2-COOH

18)

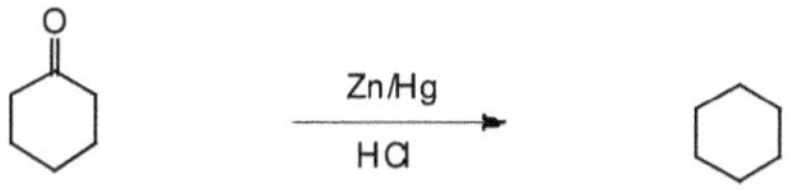

$\xrightarrow[HCl]{Zn/Hg}$

Clemmensen reduction

19)

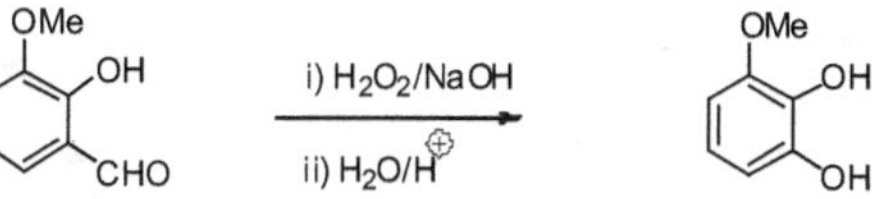

$\xrightarrow[ii)\ H_2O/H^{\oplus}]{i)\ H_2O_2/NaOH}$

Dakin reaction

20)

$CH_3-\overset{O}{\underset{}{C}}-\overset{O}{\underset{}{C}}-CH_3$ $\xrightarrow{mCPBA}$ $CH_3-\overset{}{\underset{O}{C}}-O-\overset{}{\underset{O}{C}}-CH_3$

21)

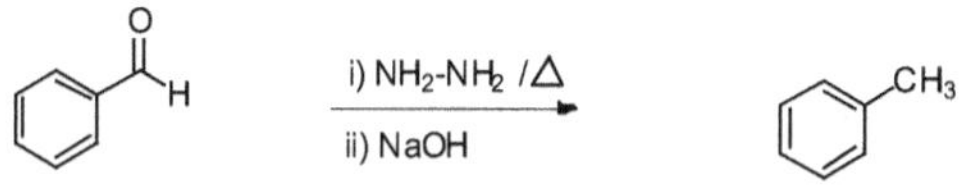

$\xrightarrow[ii)\ NaOH]{i)\ NH_2-NH_2\ /\triangle}$

Wolff-Kishner reduction

22)

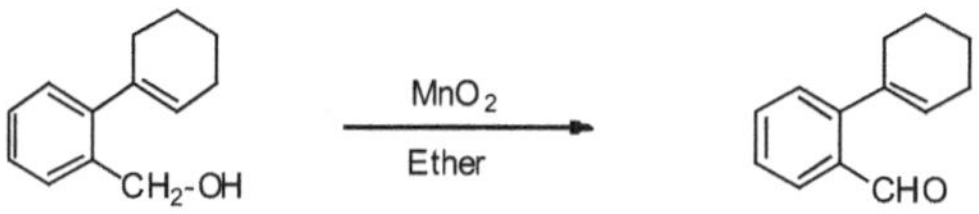

$\xrightarrow[Ether]{MnO_2}$

Oxidation

23)

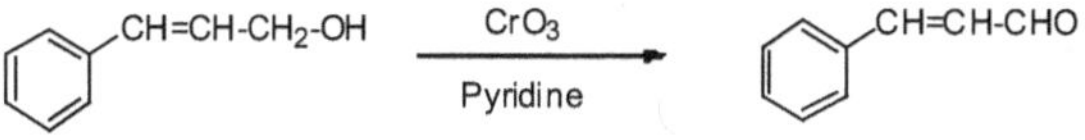

$\xrightarrow[Pyridine]{CrO_3}$

Collin oxidation

24)

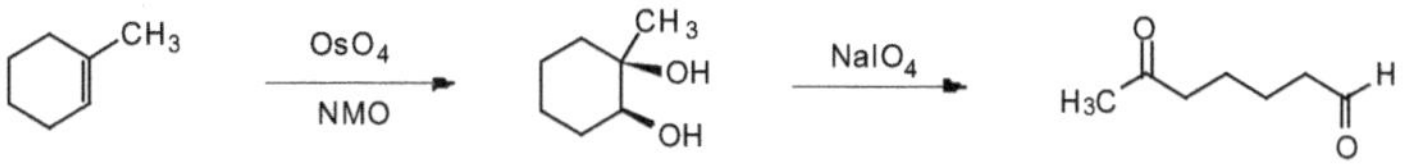

$\xrightarrow[NMO]{OsO_4}$ $\xrightarrow{NaIO_4}$

25)

$\xrightarrow{mCPBA}$

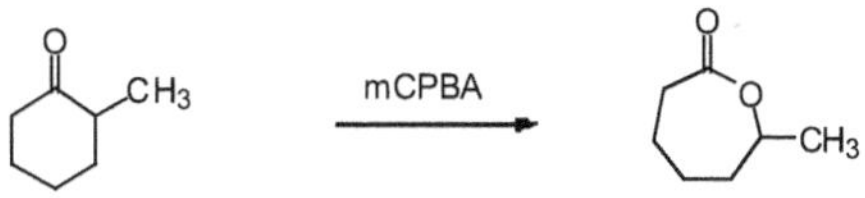

31) $C_4H_9-C\equiv C-CH(OH)-CH_3 \xrightarrow[\text{Jones Reagent}]{(O)} C_4H_9-C\equiv C-C(=O)-CH_3$ Jones Oxidation

32)

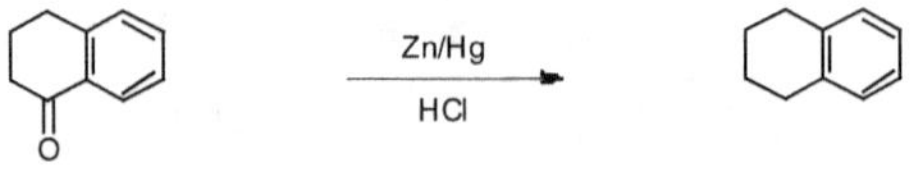

Zn/Hg
HCl

Clemmensen reduction

33)

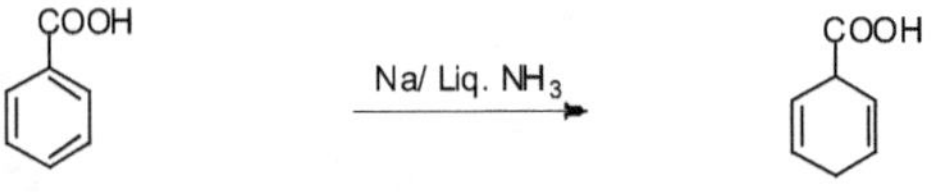

COOH
Na/ Liq. NH3
COOH

Birch reduction

34)

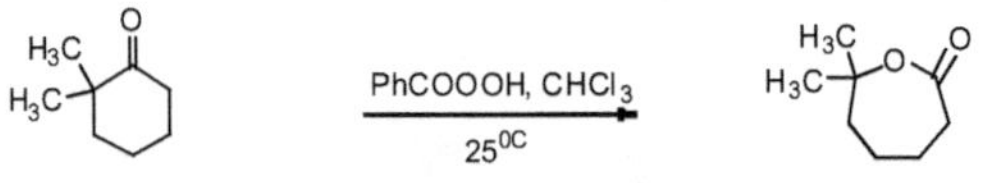

H3C
H3C
O
PhCOOOH, CHCl3
25⁰C
H3C
H3C
O
O

Baeyer Villiger oxidation

35)

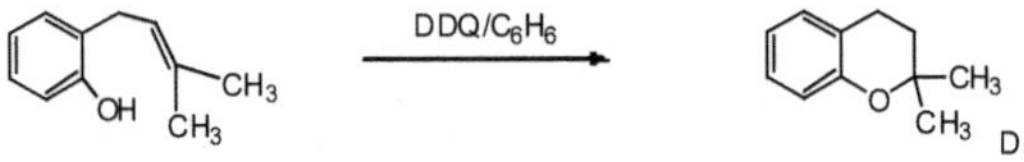

OH
CH3
CH3
DDQ/C6H6
O
CH3
CH3

DDQ oxidative cyclization

36)

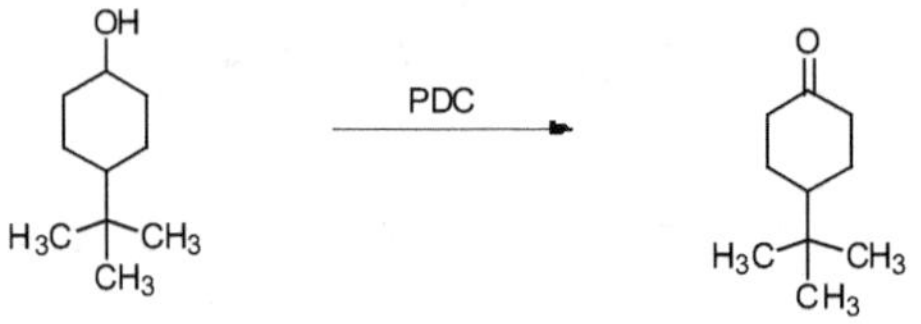

OH
H3C
CH3
CH3
PDC
O
H3C
CH3
CH3

37)

O
H3C
OH
CH3
HIO4
H2SO4
CH3-COOH

38)

H3C
9
CH2
OsO4/NaIO4
Dioxane/H2O
H3C
9
O
H
+
O
H
H

39)

RuO4/NaIO4
COOH

40)

OH
COOEt
RuO4/NaIO4
O
COOEt

41)

O
OsO4
OH
HO
O

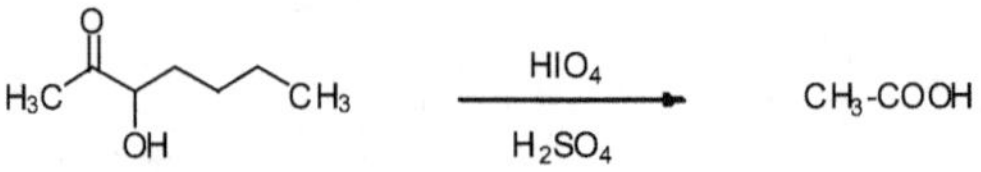

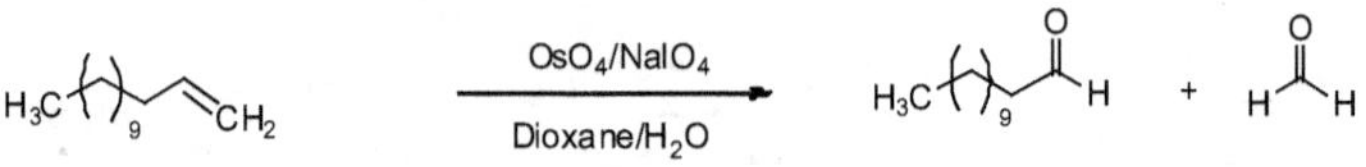

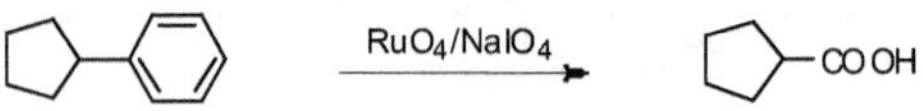

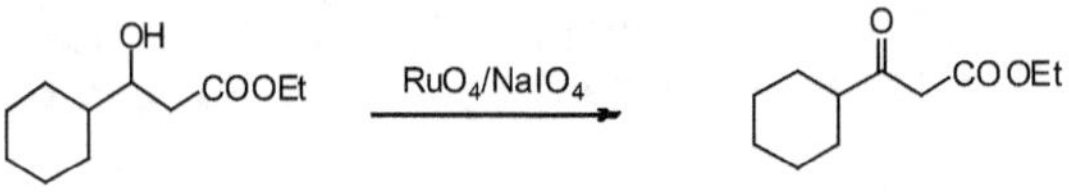

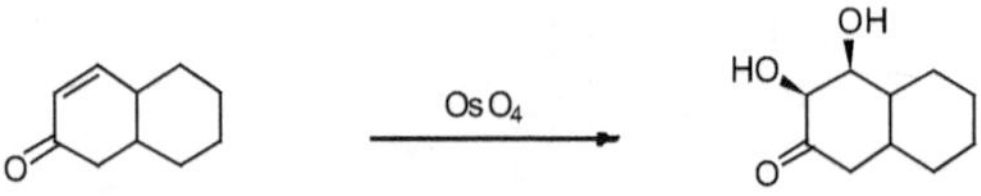

43)

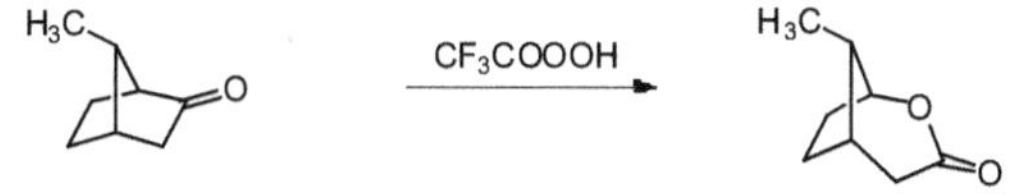

CF_3COOOH →

44)

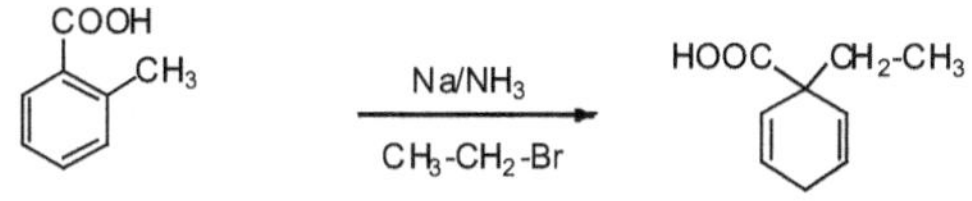

$\xrightarrow[CH_3\text{-}CH_2\text{-}Br]{Na/NH_3}$

45)

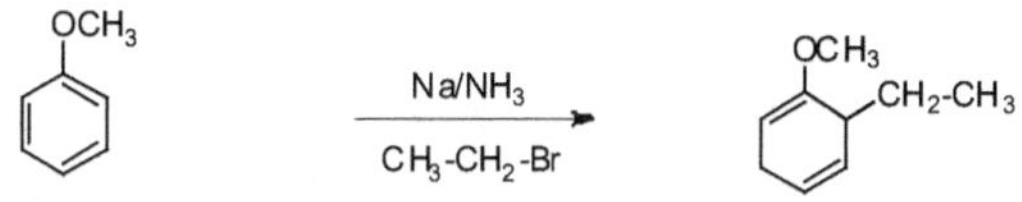

$\xrightarrow[CH_3\text{-}CH_2\text{-}Br]{Na/NH_3}$

46)

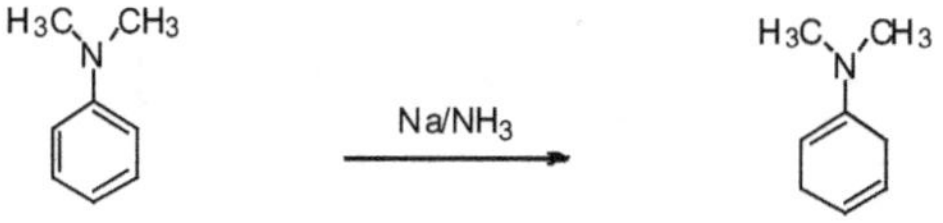

$\xrightarrow{Na/NH_3}$

47)

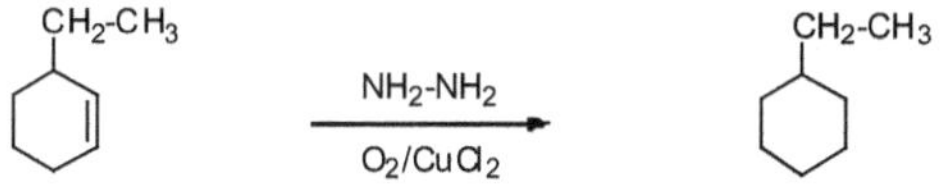

$\xrightarrow[O_2/CuCl_2]{NH_2\text{-}NH_2}$

48)

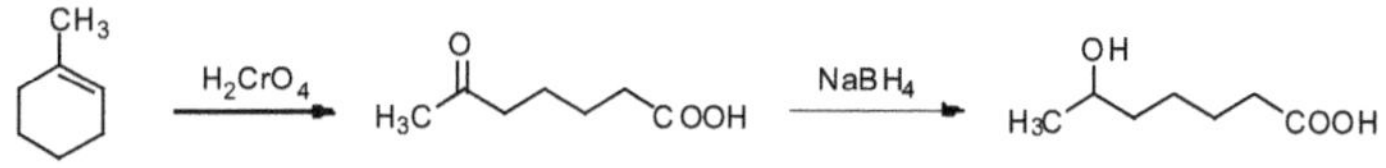

$\xrightarrow{H_2CrO_4}$ $\xrightarrow{NaBH_4}$

49)

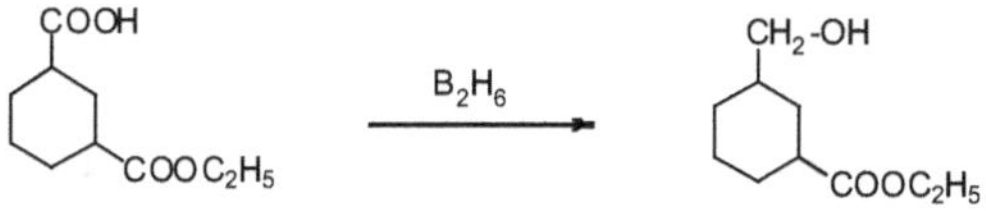

$\xrightarrow{B_2H_6}$

50)

$\xrightarrow{Na/NH_3}$

☐   ☐   ☐

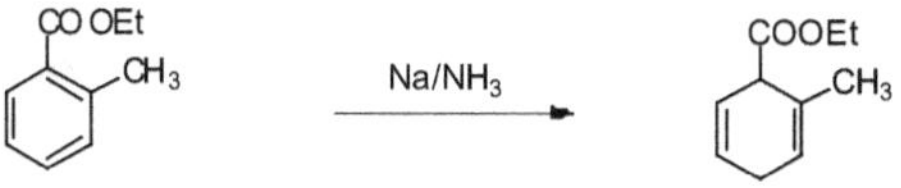

10
Unidades

La Breve Historia del

Holocausto

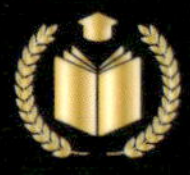

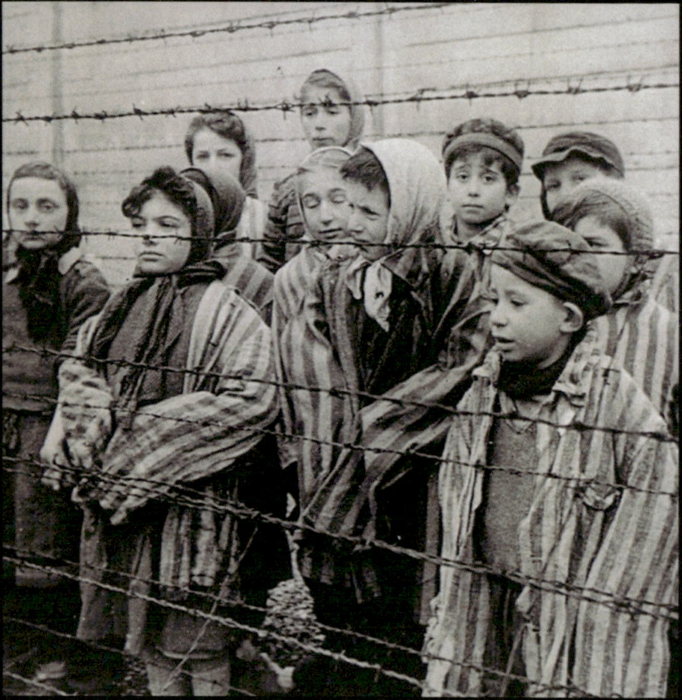

Academy Archives

La Breve Historia del Holocausto

El auge del antisemitismo en la Alemania nazi, Auschwitz y el genocidio de Hitler contra el pueblo judío impulsado por el fascismo

(1941-1945)

Descargo de responsabilidad

1